POKER WARS

MURDER, MAYHEM, AND THE BLOODY HISTORY THAT LED TO THE WORLD SERIES OF POKER

Philip Guitar and Jim Martyka

CROOKED LANE

NEW YORK

Books should be disposed of and recycled according to local requirements. All paper materials used are FSC compliant.

Published in the United States by Crooked Lane Books, an imprint of The Quick Brown Fox & Company LLC.

Crooked Lane Books and its logo are trademarks of The Quick Brown Fox & Company LLC.

Library of Congress Catalog-in-Publication data available upon request.

ISBN (hardcover): 979-8-89242-647-3
ISBN (paperback): 979-8-89242-648-0
ISBN (ebook): 979-8-89242-649-7

Cover design by Emily Mahar
Printed in the United States.

www.crookedlanebooks.com

Crooked Lane Books
34 West 27th St., 10th Floor
New York, NY 10001

First Edition: August 2026

The authorized representative in the EU for product safety and compliance is eucomply OÜPärnu mnt 139b-14, 11317 Tallinn, Estonia, hello@eucompliancepartner.com, +33757690241

10 9 8 7 6 5 4 3 2 1

CONTENTS

THE FLOP

BET

THE TURN

BET/RAISE

THE RIVER

ALL IN

THE WIN

CHARACTER LIST

THE ANTIHEROES

Benny Binion—"The Cowboy"—An illiterate horse trader from the prairies of Pilot Point, Texas, who rises to become a cutthroat businessman and *THE* boss gambler of Dallas, heading up the powerful Southland Syndicate, and eventually becoming the driving force behind the World Series of Poker.

Herbert Noble—"The Cat"—An ambitious and savvy man who rose from the slums of West Dallas to become a force in the Texas underbelly, earning the nickname "The Aristocratic Gambler" and becoming both a rival for Benny Binion and a determined survivalist.

THE MENTORS

Warren Diamond—A brilliant risk-taker and kingpin in the Dallas policy numbers racket, working out of the notorious St. George Hotel; the man who gives Benny his start and his influence.

Sam Murray—A rough-and-tumble adrenaline junkie who rises up to take control of all South Dallas gambling, also providing mentorship and opening the door for Herbert Noble.

Mr. Wade—Proprietor of the Otter's Club private poker club in Dallas who recognizes the talent of a young Johnny Moss and teaches him the game.

THE CRIMINALS

Arnold Rothstein—Infamous and brilliant crime boss and racketeer, known mostly for rigging the 1919 World Series, and a friend of Titanic Thompson.

Al Capone—"Scarface." "Public Enemy Number One." Legendary gangster who weaves his way in and out of the lives of many characters in our story.

Paul Roland Jones—A midlevel associate from the Chicago Syndicate who comes to Dallas to try and influence local politicians and crime bosses to lay stakes for the Mob.

Raymond Laudermilk—A tough guy from the streets of Dallas who works his way up in Benny Binion's operation, becoming his right-hand man . . . for a time.

Ivy Miller—A street-smart, cold-blooded killer and an associate of Benny Binion.

Bob Minyard—A low-level petty criminal who rises up the ranks in Benny's outfit, earning trust through violence.

Lois Green—Thief, bodyguard, sharpshooter, and a nemesis of Herbert Noble who would later lead The Forty Thieves gang.

Johnny Grisaffi—Homicidal maniac known as "Brazil" and an associate of Benny Binion.

Jack Darby—A young and inexperienced hired gun in Dallas trying to make his way in Benny's orbit.

Eddie Gillihand—An incompetent gambler and even worse thief who squares off with Noble.

Sonny Lefors—An untrustworthy thief who readily flips loyalties between crime bosses at the first threat of violence.

R.D. Mathews—A lethal enforcer and trusted bodyguard of Benny Binion.

Harold Shimley—A disgraced and despised gambler who somehow finds himself trying to negotiate peace between two deadly rivals.

Franklin Strong—A member of The Forty Thieves gang who encounters Noble on more than one occasion.

Leroy Gross—Another member of The Forty Thieves with a score to settle with The Cat.

Jack Todd—Known as "Gentleman Jack," a strategic racketeer who also has a dangerously violent side.

Blackie—An immoral, degenerate gambler who dresses like a pimp and loves to cheat, leaving an early impression on a young Johnny Moss.

THE LAW

Smoot Schmid—A seasoned sheriff, once known for helping track down Bonnie and Clyde, who is as willing to turn a blind eye to any Dallas gangland violence as he is to share a cup of coffee with his "friend" Benny Binion.

Steve Guthrie—A young former army sergeant who defies the odds to win the Dallas County sheriff election in an upset, reshaping the landscape of the Dallas gambling scene.

Bill Decker—A Dallas police captain with close ties to Benny Binion.

George Butler—A lieutenant with the Dallas Police Department and a friend of Herbert Noble, who, more than once, has to rein in The Cat.

Estes Kefauver—A US senator from Tennessee who launches the Subcommittee on Organized Crime and sends gangsters of all shapes and sizes scrambling.

Henry Wade—Dallas district attorney who has a hard-nosed appreciation for law and order, and a desire to get The Cowboy behind bars.

THE PROMOTERS

Vegas Vic—A cool and confident manager and promoter who helps build up both Reno and Las Vegas into entertainment capitals.

Tom Moore—Vic's protégé who comes up with a grand idea to attract business to a struggling casino through connections with the Texas Circuit.

THE PLAYERS

Nick Dandolos—"The Greek"—A gambling legend, an enigmatic personality, and the forefather of the traveling gambler, who spends most of his life jumping from city to city building fortunes and losing them only to build them up again, and earning notoriety everywhere he goes; a true "action" man.

Titanic Thompson—Another of the first true professional players, and also a master manipulator and prop bet artist that tours the country, building his bankroll and garnering the fame and acclaim that comes with it.

Johnny Moss—"The Grand Old Man of Poker"—A nine-time WSOP winner (including the first two) who takes part in a legendary event that lays the groundwork for the ultimate poker tournament.

Doyle Brunson—"The Texas Dolly"—The expert card player and legend of the Texas Circuit who becomes the first face of the WSOP with his warm, Southern charm, his devil-may-care play, and his willingness to be an ambassador for the sport.

Amarillo Slim—One of Doyle's early playing partners on the Circuit who is always looking for action, be it poker, pool, or anywhere he thinks he can find an advantage.

Sailor Roberts—Another of Doyle's early playing partners, and a master poker player . . . when he isn't busy chasing skirts on the Circuit.

Corky McCorquodale—The elder statesman of the Texas Circuit and the man credited with helping spread the game of Texas Hold 'Em to Vegas and beyond.

Crandall Addington—A self-made rich oilman and member of the Texas Circuit who is both patient and deadly at the table.

Treetop Straus—A six-foot-six lanky Texan, intimidating in size and a world-class bluffer . . . and someone who often finds clever ways out of paying his debts.

Bob Hooks—A backwoods gambler who grew up poor and saw poker as his one chance to change his fortune.

Doc Ramsey—A traveling partner of Hooks despite a sizable age gap, and an expert card player with the heart of a philanthropist.

Cowboy Wolford—Cheerful and charismatic poker player on the Circuit who gets you laughing while draining your chip stack; also a mainstay on the pro rodeo tour.

PHILIP GUITAR INTRODUCTION

Saturday night in my hometown of Abilene, Texas. I am seven years old, and I am spending time at one of my favorite places—my grandparents' house. A stately brick two-story home nestled on the corner of a quiet street, with massive pecan trees guarding the front yard. My grandfather, Earl Guitar Sr., a wiry, spirited individual, mixes a gin and tonic while simultaneously pouring a ginger ale for me. With drinks in hands, both of us check in on my grandmother, Anita Guitar, a silver-haired, saintly woman who is preparing supper in the kitchen. The sweet aroma from the stove engulfs my nostrils. She hugs me and proceeds to tell us both to please step away from the kitchen, the food will be ready soon.

The sun is setting on a cold wintery evening in West Texas. My grandfather loads kindling into the stone fireplace, and I help place the mesquite wood, which came from our ranch, in the rack. Da, my grandfather, loves to tell me stories about his friends. Such as the man who ran a Mississippi prison and would send truckloads of kindling to him free of charge. He lights the fire.

POOF!

The fire roars to life, the orange flames are dancing.

Da and I take our seats in the large, overstuffed chairs facing the TV. Their favorite program is starting. *The Lawrence Welk Show.* He hollers at my grandmother to come take a look. He loves to tell me about how he met Lawrence Welk. My great-grandfather, John Guitar Sr., was partners with Conrad Hilton on hotels in Dallas, Waco, San Angelo, Plainview, Cisco, and Abilene. It was during the Depression that my grandfather was a rancher and hotel

manager of the Hilton Hotel in downtown Abilene. A tired and hungry band leader entered his office looking for help. He said his name was Lawrence Welk and he had a five-piece band with him. Earl said Welk and his band could stay at the hotel and play in the ballroom for their room and board. Welk agreed, and the rest is history.

A few years later in Los Angeles, I was backstage with my grandparents. I had no idea what we were doing or who we were there to see. A few minutes later, Lawrence Welk is on stage, behind the mic, saying hello to thunderous applause. He calls my grandfather out on stage and says, "This is the man who helped give me my start. Earl Guitar." My grandfather proceeded to lead the band. I was starstruck!

Back to the living room in Abilene, Texas. We soak up the show. My grandmother calls us to eat. A succulent combination of quail, mashed potatoes, and green beans. Besides being an explosion on the taste buds, the next best thing was these were quail my grandfather and I shot on our ranch east of Abilene with his bird dogs. Both sets of my grandparents were magnificent cooks. Being at their homes and eating with them was always a treasured event.

Once my belly is full from the savory meal of Southern comfort, it's time to move on to the next phase of the night's entertainment:

POKER.

Earl puts on some of his favorite Lawrence Welk albums. This is great and all, but I kind of wish we could listen to my Kiss albums. Nonetheless, I guess you can never have too much Lawrence Welk in your life. My grandparents and I settle around the card table near the stone fireplace with its crackling flames in the background. On the wall behind the divan is an oil painting of a snowy blue setting on a ranch with a wooden barn. It reminds me of this night. Chilly outside with the possibility of snow (please Lord, let it snow), but the atmosphere inside the house is warm and cozy.

We divvy up the poker chips and shuffle the cards. The game is Dealer's Choice (Seven-Card Stud, Five-Card Stud, Five-Card Draw). Little did I know how nostalgic these memories of playing poker with them would someday become. My grandparents were kind and loving; they had an inner strength that I attribute to living through the Great Depression and two world wars. They spent time with me and enjoyed playing a variety of games. This is where my love of games originates. Not so much from the games themselves—nor the wins or the losses—but the toasty, fuzzy euphoria of time spent with loved ones. No agenda, no conditions, just quality moments.

Before I know it, the cards are in the air. I wish I could freeze this moment in history. It's like the old beer commercial said, "It doesn't get any better than this."

I have always loved poker. I have always loved outlaws. I have always loved Texas history.

Perhaps it's the idea that Texas history and outlaws have some intertwined commonalities. Texas history is fiercely fascinating. The early Texans were rugged, defiant, independent, and believed in their own sovereignty. Texas attitude is in general to not look for handouts from the federal government. We have many resources to survive on our own down here. People like Stephen F. Austin, Sam Houston, and Davy Crockett were all fighters. They fought for justice and independence. Outlaws have a similar train of thought. They strive for independence and living an authentic life under their own code. They inevitably go overboard with their egocentric plans and turn public sentiment against them. I admired the intrigue of the rogue desperado living life on the edge.

I played cards through college and moved to Las Vegas in 1998. I was playing \$2–\$4 Limit Hold 'Em at the Mirage. I met a guy outside the poker room who was making a living playing \$10–\$20 Limit Hold 'Em. We became friends and started to meet and discuss poker. I could tell he knew what he was talking about. This was

before there were hardly any poker training videos or books. Before long I was showing up to our coffee sessions with a notebook and pen in hand. He was happy to impart his wisdom to me. It was like a college poker class. He would give me written tests and ask me how I would play with certain hands in certain situations. I eventually passed the tests and was ready to move on to becoming a true, bona fide grinder! The Bellagio had just opened, and now all the regulars at the Mirage were playing in the Bellagio poker room. This is where Bobby's Room (from the late great Bobby Baldwin) originated. Doyle Brunson and his cadre of high-stakes cash game masters would play there daily. I became a regular at the Bellagio (not Bobby's Room), moving up the ranks of the limit poker world.

As time progressed, I found myself drifting away from Hold 'Em (two-card poker) and toward mix games (Stud, Omaha, Omaha Hi/Low, Pot Limit Omaha Eight or Better, etc.), but it all started with my buddy and our study sessions. He got me thinking about poker in a different way. I sure appreciate his time and consideration. Unfortunately, I lost contact with him as he moved to Thailand to play online.

I have always been an avid reader and writer. I am fascinated with the history of Las Vegas. I had read about the WSOP, but I knew there was more to this story than had been revealed. So I dove in and started analyzing the history of the key players. I did research on each gambling persona, a complete backstory. I found an astonishing connection of dots to circumstances and events. One that I had never seen before.

Until now.

I first wrote about this sordid tale in a series of magazine articles in the *Fort Worth Business Press*. I shared this data with my then editor and now cowriter Jim Martyka, who acted like I had just dropped a bombshell on him. He couldn't believe this story was true and that he hadn't heard about it. I showed him all my notes and research material. I think we both knew we had something special here.

There's no doubt that I was destined to write this book.

This is my tribute to the poker/gambling pioneers. The men and the women who went through insurmountable odds, traveled an incredulous journey, and brought the world the greatest sporting event in history: the World Series of Poker.

—Philip Guitar, 2025

JIM MARTYKA INTRODUCTION

There are always signature moments.

An extraordinary accomplishment from a dynamic individual, a company that launches a product that revolutionizes an industry, the tidal wave of a historic social or political movement, a sudden surge or trending fad that takes the world by storm, or a monumental event that redefines a culture and becomes a mecca for folks of different backgrounds who share a common interest or desire.

The history of poker, more specifically, the World Series of Poker, is no different.

If there is one shared characteristic among professional poker gamblers, it's a drive for *more.* There is an aching, a yearning, to get more, be more, win more. To win it *all.* To be the absolute best and then find someone or something else to beat. There is always the next hand, the next bet, the next move, the next game, the next tournament, the next rival, the next prize, the next moment to fill the void and cement their legacy. So when poker started to become *the* pastime of the modern-day outlaw, perhaps it was only natural for it to grow in size and stakes.

Those moments weren't always about the game itself.

The first signature moments, the opening hand if you will, that led to the beginnings and inevitable rise of the World Series of Poker go back even further, into a dark and sordid past not considered fitting of a beloved sporting institution and yet extremely appropriate for the nature of that sport. And these moments ain't pretty.

They're tense, dirty, raw, and violent. They involve lying, cheating, bullying, and killing. They involve outlaws with nothing to lose

and everything to gain, career criminals—whether they were caught or not—connected to some of the most notorious characters in American history. They are ambitious men who grew their bankrolls, reputations, and the gambling trade by any means necessary. Once they all started to interact with each other, becoming a part of each other's narrative, they created signature moments that not only defined their personal legacies, but those of cities like Dallas and eventually Las Vegas, and what would eventually become the multibillion-dollar poker industry as a whole.

It's those moments of poker's lesser known yet fascinating past and the outlaws involved, as well as their individual and collective stories, that led to the true beginnings of the WSOP that we're exploring and connecting in this book.

I've been working in book publishing for over twenty years, in both fiction and nonfiction, including working as a writer, editor, and consultant on a number of sports books. I've been an amateur poker player even longer. Emphasis on *amateur*. The king of the "nickel, dime, quarter" house game with friends, I, too, became addicted to watching the World Series of Poker when it took off on TV with its big pots and bigger personalities, made for the celebrity spotlight. I had no problem breaking down each player's strategies . . . from the comfort of my couch, never getting the mettle required to drop the cash and register to play in the big game, content to grab twenty dollars or so off my friends and family.

Then I met Philip Guitar. A mutual friend connected me and Philip as he was looking for some help with a series of articles he was working on for the *Fort Worth Business Press* on the true history of the World Series of Poker. In our initial chat, what he told me changed my entire perception of the WSOP. With each story, my jaw dropped a little farther. As someone who (pardon the pun) went all-in when the event got televised and started to grow in popularity, I read and learned as much as I could about where it all

came from. What Philip was telling me never came up. Anywhere. Ever. And only one question kept swirling around in my mind:

Why the hell isn't anyone talking about this?!

It wasn't just me. In his playing days, Philip would hear fellow gamblers talking about bits and pieces of this wild history, but never the whole story. The more he learned, and the more he realized that this history was starting to get lost or possibly ignored by the very people who now benefited from the chaos and sacrifices of those early days, the more he realized the story needed to be told.

While the series turned out well, there were limits to publishing in a magazine. And "no. limit" is always more fun for a gambler. Now is the time for the *full* story to be told. It's a story of ambition. It is brutal and dangerous, as most stories involving big money often are. It's a story of Texas, where poker, *American* poker, came from, from its dusty backroads to its dirty card rooms. It's a story with incredible personalities, each with their own tales of desperation, and how they all connected to each other . . . for better or for worse. It's a story of celebrity, influence, scandal, and timing. It traces the rise of the tourney to its actual beginnings, the personalities who inspired it and the trouble they caused, paving the road with cash, opportunity, and sometimes, death. It's the story behind the World Series of Poker.

Over the next several chapters, we'll introduce the sequence of events that connected to each other and led to the first-ever World Series of Poker, told mainly through the stories of the game's most iconic personalities, some more familiar and some just now getting their moment in the spotlight. From Titanic to The Cowboy to The Cat to The Texas Dolly and more, it's through these larger-than-life legends and a combination of exhilarating events, deadly voyages, and chance circumstances that we'll show you what the *real* World Series of Poker is all about.

So let's get to it. It's time to "Shuffle up and deal."

—Jim Martyka, 2025

SHUFFLE UP AND DEAL

The most famous phrase in poker.

PROLOGUE
THE OLD MAN

Badeep . . . Badeep . . . Badeep . . .

The sounds of heart rate monitors, breathing respirators, and mechanical defibrillators vibrate with piercing urgency. A frail, elderly, wrinkled man in a gown lies in a hospital room bed. His face is hidden but the tight, tensioned skin and the scars on his weathered hands tell us this man has lived a life of adventure, a life of peril.

A faded Silver Belly Stetson cowboy hat rests on a bed post. The greyish white tone of the long-worn hat might allude this man is a "good guy," a hero who has ridden into town to save the day a time or two. It might also confer that he is a law-abiding citizen or perhaps even an officer of the law. Any who assume that would be incorrect. Although, there is a city that revers him, a city that embraces the darker parts of man.

A muted rerun of Gunsmoke *plays on the television.*

A miniature decorated Christmas tree brightens up the room on a table near the window. Today is Christmas and soon it will be 1990. The old man has seen a lot in his eighty-five years and he wonders what the next decade and century will bring, especially when it comes to what he built.

Outside, amidst the rare overcast sky, a view of the Las Vegas Strip looms in the west. Alladin, Dunes, The Frontier . . . these geriatric towers kiss the clouds. He might be able to sneak a peek at them if he wants, perhaps even his palace, but it's no good. They're a distant memory of what they once were, just as he is. The infant Mirage mega-resort kicks fireballs to the sky. It is perhaps a signaling, a premonition of a new era. The dismantling of the old guard and the emergence of a fresh envoy.

Badeep . . . Badeep . . . Badeep . . .

The heart rate accelerates. The man jerks awake, panting, gasping for air. Realizing that he only has a finite number of breaths left. He scans his room briefly, a struggle to even move his once piercing eyes. He thinks of someone else who spent a lot of time in a hospital room just like this, a man he put here many, many times, a man that would not just go away. If he could laugh, the old man would, amused by the irony and still proud that he won, he lasted.

But nothing lasts forever.

Not even old outlaws.

The man, a legend that was known for most of his life as The Cowboy drifts back into unconsciousness. As he does, his weary mind is overcome with flashbacks of a life of ambition, passion, and adventure. A life of violence and constant danger.

His mind drifts to El Paso, when he was a teen. A shadowy silhouette of a lean, rugged, young cowboy riding a solid built sorrel horse sloshes knee-deep through the murky waters of the Rio Grande River. He leads a team of two pack mules as their backs sway from the overloaded contraband concealed by a canvas tarp on their withers. The cowboy looks back as he crosses onto dry land. Texas. Two Mexican banditos wave a pleasant goodbye. He waves back.

Inside a wooden barn, hidden contraband is uncovered. Whiskey! The bottles are stacked on shelves. He hears a click. The hammer cocked on a six shooter. A gun blast. A drifter at the door frame crumples to the ground. The cowboy is on the other end of a smoking revolver. It wouldn't be the last time.

He then drifts to a time in his late twenties. It is pitch dark. He sits atop wooden apple box crates in a derelict backyard across from a frightened but dangerous man. All he can see are the whites of his wide eyes and the occasional flash of gold in his teeth. A lighthearted conversation is taking place. It is a game of patience. Suddenly, the cowboy figure rocks back in one fluid motion. He swings upward, gripping a pistol.

BLAM BLAM!

The black male across from him is thrown with the force of a mule kick backwards onto the ground. Two bullet holes leeched from his chest. His eye lids closed, mouth open, while blood congeals around those gold teeth.

In the hospital bed, the elderly man bristles uncomfortably with angst.

He drifts to 1936. A bustling afternoon on a crowded east Dallas city street. People converge in all directions. A new Pontiac is parked in front of a liquor store. From the backseat a forty-year-old dapper gangster in a striped-suit barks orders to his driver. The shadowy cowboy figure emerges from a sedan idling across the street. Along with him is a stout, rough-and-tumble character with hands of steel. They race toward the Pontiac.

The gangster caught up in his litany of instructions to the driver fails to see the two vicious men approaching. The cowboy reaches through the open window and places a strangle hold vice grip around the gangster's throat. His accomplice manhandles the driver with a pistol to his cheeks.

BLAM BLAM!

The blood-soaked remnants of the gangster are splattered across the back windshield.

The withered cowboy can still hear the gunshots and the visions rattle his old bones and pump his heart rate once again. The machines beep faster. The flashbacks come quicker, this time of people and faces, those that impacted him most.

He sees old movie and newspapers images of gambling legends, the same ones he saw as a boy that inspired him and an old neighborhood friend who would later become a partner in his legacy. He can these two clear as day, one named after a famous ship, he thinks, and the other a foreigner who epitomized class, something the old man never understood.

He remembers wild nights at a fancy Dallas gambling room, and a mentor who looks at him proudly, until his face disappears in a flash of

bright light. He sees a woman, who he is pretty sure is his wife, and kids. He thinks of happiness and love and—

Then he sees a cat in a suit.

The old man twists in his hospital bed. He wants this man to go away. The machines cry out. He visualizes gunshot blast after gunshot blast and the cat-like figure takes each and every one and just stands there staring at him in his fancy getup.

Why won't he go away?!

He coughs, violently, and his mind clears . . . mercifully.

He drifts again and he's in his Cadillac darting across the bleak desolate desert in darkness. In the backseat, the shadowy cowboy figure surveys the landscape. In the front seat sit two amped up, beefy bodyguards alongside their two tommy guns pointed at the floorboard. The Cadillac high beams freeze on a sign that reads "YOU'RE NOW LEAVING TEXAS."

He sees an affluent neighborhood with traditional ranch style homes and massive pecan trees lining the street. The sweet aroma of turkey and dressing coming from open windows. Football team flags hang on front porches and on manicured lawns. A middle-aged, delicate woman in a conservative dress opens the door of a Mercury parked in front of her home. She twists the keys in the ignition switch.

BOOOOOOM!!

The car erupts into an inferno of charred metal.

The old man feels a sting with this vision. His heart races.

He sees a car coming down a driveway, the heat and humidity sucking the life out of the air. A hand reaches out of the driver's side window and grabs the mailbox. There is a slight pause and then the hand pulls the door down.

BOOOOOOM!!

For reasons his fading mind can't comprehend, this vision brings him peace. For a moment. Back in the hospital bed, the cowboy jolts sideways. He is clearly disturbed and wrestling with his mental trauma. He slips back into a bewildered sleep. The flashes are starting to fade and they

are becoming more and more confusing, rapid firing like his old six-shooter.

It won't be long now.

There is a government hearing, with an irate Senator shouting into his desk microphone.

More shooting.

A judge cracks his gavel among gasps from the onlookers.

More explosions.

The echoing clang of a prison door slamming and the freezing cold of a lonely cell.

Blood, screams, death . . .

. . . and poker.

Why poker?

The old cowboy stops his shifting and lays still, letting his mind focus for its last moments on the card game, HIS card game. He sees a casino floor filled with people playing, a glass wall of money, tables full of familiar faces he can't quite recognize now, cards being dealt, chip stacks moving, and more and more people watching the action.

Dozens. Then hundreds. Then thousands. Then millions. It won't stop. The crowd keeps growing.

Back in the hospital room, the elderly cowboy grapples with more palpitations. His hospital gown has become moist with perspiration. His body is finally failing. The beeps are faster and shorter. Excited nurses rush into the room in a frenzy and they are surprised to see a smile on his face.

As the flashbacks float away, the cowboy hears a question. "Was it worth it?" Whoever it is asking doesn't matter a lick. The answer is quite clear.

You bet your ass.

THE BUY-IN

A predetermined amount of chips that must be bought by a player to become involved in a game of poker.

CHAPTER 1
THE GAME

$438 Million.

That's how much the World Series of Poker paid out in prize money in 2024. And that's nothing compared to what it brought in.

The World Series of Poker ranks alongside Coca-Cola, McDonald's, and Apple as one of the most iconic and lucrative brands in the world. Comparatively, it's also the most thrilling.

Even the casual observer who doesn't play poker is mesmerized by the theatrics of the televised face-offs, the antics of the sometimes charismatic, sometimes polarizing players, their unique sponsor-adorned wardrobes with dark sunglasses hiding any tells, and the gargantuan multicolored chip stacks that change hands with deadly quickness. All backdropped by stacks of cash that could feed a third-world country.

The World Series of Poker (WSOP) holds the renowned distinction as one of the only sports where literally anyone off the street can become a legend overnight. A tournament with a complex past, a series of events involving intense eclectic characters interwoven with bombastic criminals that needed to fall in place, in the exact order, for it to grow into what it is today. Unlike other major sports, there isn't one person or one moment to point back to or to celebrate as the birthplace of this one. Reflective of the game itself, the backstory of poker and the meteoric rise in popularity of its signature tournament is rich in true-crime history.

But there is a timeline, a thrilling and chaotic sequence of events involving these major players who all came together at the right time and place (mainly Dallas) and loved, fought, killed, and mostly gambled as they all looked to make their name and their money . . . *their destiny*. Without these men and women, the events they triggered, and the shitstorms that followed, there would be no WSOP.

Gambling, and even card playing, has a long history, dating back well before it found its way to Big D, the heart of North Texas. A little context would do us well as we venture forth into that storm, showing how the groundwork was laid long ago, waiting for these heavy hitters to make their bets . . .

Fate of the Cards

Playing cards themselves can be traced back first to Korean divinatory arrows used to determine everything from fates to daily responsibilities of the common man. These would eventually be turned into cards and would soon feature suits (eight at the time), laying the foundation for cards to eventually be used for gaming purposes. Playing cards came from China, more specifically from the Tang dynasty, dating as far back as the ninth century. Funny enough, one of the earliest documented occurrences of card playing in the world involved two gamblers—Yan Sengzhu and Zheng Pig-Dog—being caught and arrested for gambling in 1294. Card playing spread through Asia and eventually found its way into Egypt, where cards became more decorative and more reflective of the modern deck with fifty-two cards and four suits (polo sticks, coins, swords, and cups).

As all things do, cards eventually continued to spread, making their way to Europe sometime in the 1300s, at first within royalty and later, commoners. The earliest record of card playing in Europe is an official ban on cards issued in the city of Berne, Switzerland, in 1367, though the date is somewhat debated. But what is known is that card

playing soon spread to European hotspots like Barcelona, Florence, Paris, Germanic cities, and more, exploding throughout the continent from 1377 on, sometimes changing in appearance (mainly in the suits) and uses. Over the next few centuries, card playing would spread throughout the continent and beyond, with advances in printing, trade, and the ever-present human need for distraction.

And vice.

As for poker itself, most say its origin comes from a tenth-century Chinese domino game. Skeptics disagree and point to its real origin as the sixteenth-century Persian game known as *As Nas*. The most familiar ancestor to poker is a game that went by various names in Europe from the seventeenth century on. In Spain, it was *primo*. In France, it was *poque*. In Germany, it was *pochen*. In England, they featured a different game called *brag*, which had some similarities. Whatever the name, the game involved cards, betting, and bluffing, the cornerstones of modern-day poker.

Poker Finds America

These European games were eventually brought to the United States in the late eighteenth century to ports in New Orleans and the surrounding areas by French merchants. When the United States absorbed the territory with the Louisiana Purchase in 1803, poker's spread was inevitable.

As with most things, the game of poque got "American-ized" with changes in rules, cards dealt, betting, etc. and then quickly made its way up the Mississippi, spreading east and west throughout the new nation, mainly through waterway trading. The Civil War helped poker's expansion as bored soldiers on both sides picked up the game for entertainment. Not long after, it found its new home in those settling in the Wild West seeking land and fortune. With each stop, the game would be tweaked, adding new varieties (Straight,

Stud, Draw), new winning hands (straights, flushes, full houses) and ways to win (lowball, split pots, community pools). Poker became the American game, played by outlaws, farmers, bootleggers, soldiers, business leaders, and even politicians, including most of our nation's presidents. This new American game soon spread itself back overseas.

Numerous variations of the game have evolved, but the most popular is Texas Hold 'Em, a variation of Seven-Card Stud with a community pool. The game was originally called *Hold Me Darling*, then *Hold Me*, then *Hold 'Em*. When Texas decided to take credit for its origins, regional players changed it to its most commonly used name. However, that history is a bit shaky and muddled. There is simply no record of its origins, even though the game itself is supposedly not that old. Some say it made its debut at the turn of the twentieth century. In fact, in 2007, the town of Robstown, Texas, declared itself as the birthplace of the game and was supported by the Texas legislature, though nobody knows why or how the town can prove it.

Some historians suggest the game was played in Texas and surrounding states by traveling gamblers throughout the 1930s. Others say it was birthed in the sixties with a quick debut in Texas before hitting the streets of Vegas. The earliest record of it is in *Time* magazine in 1968 in an article titled "Hold Me: A Wild New Poker Game and How to Tame It." But that sheds little light on its true origins.

Beyond Robstown, other cities like Waco, Corpus Christi, Castle Hills, Fort Wort, Dallas, and more have all laid claims to being the game's birthplace. Many folks have no problem remembering when Texas Hold 'Em was introduced to them, but the underlying history of the game, that's where most become baffled. They know little beyond the game play itself. Perhaps that's a testament to the addictive nature and the thrilling attributes of the game. Who has time for history lessons when there are cards to be dealt and money to be won? What can be agreed upon is that it is a Texas game and undoubtedly a Texas story. *Hail to the Lone Star State!*

The *Real* History Begins . . .

The origin of the World Series of Poker isn't just about someone somewhere dreaming up a tournament featuring the top gamblers in the game competing to see who was the best and most worthy to win a shitload of cash and prestige. Sure, that happened, but there were so many other things that needed to happen before it got to that point. It's in *that* sequence of events where one will find the true story.

That story is reflective of the game itself. It's a story with incredibly colorful, slick, and dangerous men, all with tremendous egos, itchy trigger fingers, and a willingness to do whatever it takes to win, straying as far outside the law as necessary. It's a story of their rivalries with each other that would turn into bloodbaths, metaphorically at the tables and in reality on the streets and in the saloons and clubs of Texas.

It's a story of high stakes, of the desperation of people with steely nerves coming from the deepest pockets of poverty, the upper echelons of wealth, all with the burning tenacity to make a name for themselves. It's a story of risk and conflict all built around the need to outmaneuver each other and sometimes the game itself. It's a story of men with composure . . . who could lose control at the flip of a switch. It's a story of lying, cheating, and extreme violence as some seek to gulp down the elixir of power, while other members' stories are rooted in honor, courage, and unwavering loyalty. A band of characters who supported one another through crippling hardships, devastation, and pinnacles of prosperity.

More than anything, it's a story of chasing the big prize and how winning it is everything, perhaps even life and death. Benny Binion knew it. Herbert Noble knew it. The players you see on TV playing today know it. If you play poker, you know it too.

THE ANTE

A forced bet required of two players before the hand begins.
Set as a small blind and doubled for big blind.

CHAPTER 2
THE GREEK

"The next best thing to playing and winning is playing and losing."

One would be hard-pressed to meet a true gambler who didn't adapt those words as a personal creed or motto. For most poker players, it's all about the *game.* It's all about the risk, the action, the pulsating rapid-fire blast of adrenaline, the sweat, tears, hours that turn from dusk to dawn and back again, mental fatigue, endurance, adversity, running hot, running cold, watching and patiently waiting for the right moments to strike, and then doing so with no mercy and no fear of repercussions. For a true gambler, all that matters is action.

Action, action, action.

The next hand, the next card, the next bet, that's all that matters. Don't be fooled—it's not about the money. These are brilliant men and women, crafty and determined enough to find an opportunity and exploit it for their gain. These folks could succeed in any endeavor they wanted with their lives. They chose poker for a reason. They chose it not for the pay, but for the play.

There is no one who both embraced and epitomized that mantra more than the man who said it himself, perhaps the game's most intriguing figure: Nick "The Greek" Dandolos. The only difference is that when it comes to the money in the playing career of The Greek, we're talking about half a billion dollars.

As in $500,000,000.

That's how much Dandolos estimated he won and lost over the course of his life. Anybody who knew The Greek consistently saw him rise and fall over the course of his playing career. We're not talking the waves of hot and cold streaks that all players find themselves riding. We're talking going from Vanderbilt-type money—old-world opulence with the sleekest automobiles, glistening jewels, and custom-tailored silk smoking jackets—to playing for nickels and dimes on the bread-and-beans circuit.

Again and again.

No poker player wants to lose. Ever. But if it came down to losing or not playing at all, Dandolos wouldn't have hesitated in giving up everything. That's what made him one of the original poker forefathers and one of two high-profile gamblers that first laid the groundwork. Without men like The Greek, there would be no such thing as professional poker.

The Mystery of The Greek

To this day, The Greek is still an enigmatic personality, even to those who knew him best. A conundrum of a man who walked between the raindrops. The story of twentieth-century poker on US soil starts with him. He is the elder statesman in a group that brought the legend of the ramblin', gamblin' man to the masses, and his influence was felt most in those who idolized him, young boys who would grow up to be powerful men in the world of poker and make it the spectacle it is today.

Not much is known about where he came from, and more importantly, where his money came from. Especially when he was just getting started. There's a legendary story that circulates around poker circles that involved Dandolos losing about half a million dollars in a single poker game. When it came time to pay, he went to

his hotel room and grabbed the cash out of a chest he had with him. Witnesses say that chest wasn't even locked!

Like most poker legends, a mythology surrounds The Greek. He sought to excel at the highest levels, no matter what endeavor he undertook, but he loathed the recognition or celebrity sensationalism that came with it, viewing that only as a distraction or worse.

"In my profession, fame is usually followed by a jail sentence," he once said.

That said, fame was a hand he couldn't fold. Because of his roller-coaster career, his passion for marathon poker matches and notorious gun molls, as well as the stories that preceded him, Nick Dandolos was at one point the most infamous poker player in America. His exploits are directly responsible for growing the sport he so loved.

He was generally quiet, not offering much—literally playing his cards close to his chest. When he did talk, he was known to have a biting wit, a sharp tongue, and a quick temper that contradicted his typically calm demeanor and his reputation as the "Gentleman of Gambling." Or he was reciting poetry verses or quotes from great philosophers. Unlike many of his contemporaries, he was an educated thinking man, a sophisticated and romantic intellectual who believed in exercising his mind and the power of reading as a means of reducing stress. He also believed in giving back: It's been reported that his charitable contributions escalated north of $20 million during his lifetime. Some speculate that figure was a mere starting point. The Greek filled the coffers and asked for nothing in return.

He believed in dignity, grace, and respectability; his manners would have a butler blushing. Not exactly characteristics that defined professional poker players of the time, or even of today. Whether winning or losing, his appearance and threads were of the

utmost importance. His thick black hair was always neatly combed. His face smoothly shaven, fingernails meticulously manicured, an eccentric nature of extreme cleanliness followed him. One could find him at the tables in a blazer and bow tie with his custom gold cufflinks, sitting straight and upright, making only the slightest movements with his cards and chips, or tipping the ash off a Cuban cigar. The Greek was not a man of nervous fidgeting; he was statuesque.

A Lifetime of Wealth

Unlike most of our poker heroes, Dandolos came into his profession with a heavy bankroll, starting out as a big-stack bully before he even knew how to play the game. He was born Nikolaos Andreas Dandolos on April 27, 1883 in Rethymno, Crete, to a wealthy family that committed their time and resources to doting on their son. His father worked in luxury commodities, selling carpets, silks, linens, and other textiles. His grandfather, who took a particular interest in the prospects of his young grandson, was a highly successful shipbuilder who amassed a fortune in his lifetime.

His family preached the importance of education, an early life lesson that would stick with The Greek all his life and often work to his advantage in the thinking man's card game. As a youth, he lived for a period with a wealthy godfather in Turkey to attend the acclaimed Baxter School. Over the course of his childhood, he learned (and became proficient in) English, French, Spanish, Turkish, Italian, and Yiddish, on top of his home language. In his teens, he studied philosophy and poetry at the Greek Evangelical College, which he would memorize and recite throughout his life, earning him the nickname "The Aristotle of the Don't Pass Line."

When he turned eighteen in 1901, his grandfather financed a move to America for the young intellectual, giving him a weekly

allowance of $150 (equaling over $5,500 in today's money). The idea was for young Nikolaos to see the booming industry in America while becoming educated in the world of business before eventually returning home to expand one of the family's many prosperous enterprises.

That didn't happen.

America—The Land of Adventure and Opportunity

Dandolos landed in Chicago, a fast-paced, madcap city with tremendous opportunities for a young foreigner looking for adventure and with money to burn. It was in Chicago that he fell in love. First with a girl (though that would be short-lived) and then with gambling (that would be forever).

Perhaps surprisingly, The Greek didn't stay in Chicago long, opting to pull up stakes and head to Montreal, where he discovered the thrill of horse racing and the profits that can come from doing one's research and playing the odds. Or befriending a jockey.

Dandolos had killer instincts as a thoroughbred handicapper, keen calculations for picking the ponies. However, his friendship with Phil Musgrave, one of Canada's leading jockeys, certainly didn't hurt. In his first year of racehorse wagering, Dandolos made over half a million dollars. He claimed it was because he could understand the odds better than the common man and that Musgrave would help him identify trends and tricks of both riders and horses. Others would claim it was because the two were working together to cheat the system, perhaps even rigging races. To avoid controversy (and potential legal issues), their partnership dissolved and they parted ways, sending The Greek back to America, where he decided to pursue his luck at the tables.

Faro and craps were among The Greek's favorites, but soon poker became his one true love. Packed tables or heads up, quick

games or marathon matches, thousands on the line or a bet for bet's sake, it didn't matter. If there was poker to be played, The Greek would be there. He traveled all over the country, playing against the best. The educated man dedicated himself to not just learning but mastering each and every variant of the game, spending entire weeks playing day and night and dropping hundreds until he felt comfortable with it, knowing without a doubt that money would eventually once again be back in his money clip.

Such dedication, and one might say obsession, attracted an audience and soon casinos and poker rooms would see an influx of spectators to watch the kid who would become master ply his trade with elegance and violence against his opponents. Whether it was New York, New Orleans, Chicago, or Las Vegas, The Greek brought a crowd with him, and he outlasted all of them.

Marathon Man

Beyond his reputation as the classiest of poker players, if there was one thing Dandolos was most known for in his poker career, it was his endurance. He was (and posthumously still is) the master of the marathon match. The Greek didn't sleep. He couldn't, not when there was poker to be played. He once said he averaged just a couple hours a night and could easily go days without any sleep. At one such session in Vegas, a tired dealer was fading at the table, hoping to wrap up the game and catch some shut-eye. Dandolos told him, "Death is a sound sleep undisturbed by foolish dreams" before demanding he deal the next hand.

Over the years he would play in some of the most legendary matches in professional poker history, one of which is at least partially responsible for the creation of the World Series of Poker, but we'll get to that later. These matches were epic in both their purses and their sheer length and duration, some of them days, weeks, and months long.

The long game suited The Greek and his playing style. He called the game "the art of civilized bushwhacking" and he played it accordingly, the gentleman often turning to guerrilla warfare in his approach, showing both endless patience and stamina with an assassin's instinct. A "fearless" attitude when it came to betting, throttled not by the results but instead by the heart-pounding action exemplified.

"I play for the risk, not for the money," he said. "A trout fisherman fishes for sport, not for meat. This attitude creates mystery in the mind of the opposition. Nobody wants to put a mystery out of action. They want to see how it comes out."

Like other great gamblers, The Greek played people more than he played the cards. Dandolos knew the odds better than any of his opponents, which fueled him with unwavering confidence. He also didn't pay any attention to what he called ridiculous notions like superstitions or good luck charms when it came to the game. There was no *feel* involved in the mechanics of card playing, just facts and strategies proven by time, practice, and intelligence. He liked to use his opponents' flaws against them, first building up their confidence about those flaws and then using them to rip his opponents to shreds.

When that didn't work, he leaned on his reputation. The Greek knew he could intimidate most players simply by sitting at the table with them. Not physically, of course, as there was nothing inherently threatening about his calm demeanor or polite and respectful mannerisms. It was just his reputation itself and how he would look at them with dagger eyes, a slight tilt of the head, and a faint wry smile. Or it would be the in-game and often in-hand chitchat, the gentleman praising his opponent's play or crying foul of his own luck or an exasperated and overly dramatic call or raise just to keep the game moving.

The Greek was also a master of the bluff.

His cavalier attitude toward money gave him a tremendous advantage against his opponents. It's hard to lose when you truly

feel you have nothing to lose. Dandolos thrived on mammoth bets, wagering extemporaneous sums that weeded out gutless players. The Greek had a firm understanding of the word *acceptance*. He genuinely accepted the ups and downs, twists and turns of this thing called life. He unapologetically admitted it wasn't unusual for him to win or lose over $100,000 a day, about $3.5 million in today's money. He once won over a million in a two-day stretch playing poker. He also once lost almost $2 million in a dice tournament.

If there's one twenty-four-hour stretch that perhaps best defined the bouncing ball career of Dandolos, it happened in Vegas on New Year's Eve. Playing poker in the early evening, he just couldn't catch any cards. And bluffing, after all, will still only get you so far. He could never develop a rhythm at the table and the cool, calm professional even let his feathers get slightly ruffled, eventually calling it quits just before midnight, some $300,000 in the hole.

As the clock struck midnight, The Greek tossed out his wishes for the new year: "I hope the change of the year will change my luck as well."

The next morning he was back at the tables, refreshed and invigorated, ready to get back to work. By the early afternoon, he had won over $1.2 million . . . which he lost playing roulette and betting the horses later that day. Only to find himself back at the poker tables that night.

One Must Play an Honest Game

While The Greek could handle winning and losing, one thing he did *not* tolerate was a cheat. The Greek would be damned if anyone even conceived of the slightest notion of putting the screws to him! Which is exactly what he perceived Ray Ryan had done.

Ryan was an oilman from Wisconsin with a big personality and a knack for making good business investments, especially in Midwestern

oil fields. He was loud and flashy and attracted the attention of celebrities and mobsters alike over the course of his adult life. In 1949, he was also an aspiring poker player who was making his mark in the profession. He eventually caught the eye of The Greek.

The two played in a weeklong game of Five-Card Stud Lowball poolside at the Flamingo Resort in Vegas along with some other pros. The Greek was losing to the wannabe. Losing big time!

After six days, Dandolos claimed to be out $550,000, though reports varied. Feeling like a whipped pup and not wanting any more abuse, The Greek called it quits, perplexed at how this amateur had gotten the best of him playing the honest man's poker game. Not one to dwell, The Greek moved on, looking for the next game and the next opportunity to rebuild his reputation and his bankroll.

It wasn't until years later that the rumors started.

Dandolos heard that Ryan had a man perched on the roof of an adjacent building with a spyglass, sneaking glimpses of The Greek's hole cards while simultaneously relaying this information to Ryan through a buzzer underneath his pants that was synched up via a shortwave radio. Of course, that had to be it. There was no way Ryan could beat him straight up. With that came a small sense of relief that The Greek wasn't losing his touch.

When that feeling subsided, Dandolos exploded with rage. Instead of a knee-jerk reaction and a solo confrontation with Ryan, Nick sought out a friend. That friend was Marshall Caifano, nefarious mobster and member of the Chicago Outfit, just one of many dangerous personalities that orbited in The Greek's circle. Caifano was short in stature (around five feet tall) but tall in sheer brawn. He lugged around a chip on his shoulder the size of a manhole cover. He was a vicious enforcer that took extraordinary pleasure in extracting pain, always eager for a good shakedown.

In April 1963, Caifano threatened Ryan, telling him he wanted $60,000 a year with an additional sum to pay to Dandolos for the

disrespectful cheating episode. Ryan at first refused, despite being roughed up by Caifano and his goons in a hotel room in Vegas. When they showed up again a month later, Ryan sprinted from his room into the lobby, yelling behind him, "Shoot me in the back! That's how you do business!" Afraid for his life, Ryan went to the feds, who were looking for a way to nail Caifano. Extortion would work just fine.

Dandolos ended up testifying at the trial and when asked what he did for a living, he claimed he was retired. When the prosecuting attorney asked if he was retired from gambling, he only coyly answered, "That description might fit it." Dandolos also distanced himself from the mobster, saying that he and Ryan had made an agreement and that Ryan was paying him back over $100,000 to avoid the reputation as a cheat.

Caifano ended up serving ten years in prison. Dandolos moved on. So did Ryan, until Caifano got out of jail.

On October 18, 1977, Ryan came out of a health club in Evansville, Indiana, having just finished a workout. As he started the ignition of his Lincoln Mark V coupe, within milliseconds the bomb was detonated and the car was eviscerated, sending shrapnel flying in all directions and killing Ryan instantly.

His murder was never solved.

The Company You Keep

Caifano was small potatoes compared with another underworld persona involved in Dandolos's life. Frank Costello, a.k.a. "The Prime Minister of Crime," was the boss of the Luciano crime family in New York (which would later be known as the Genovese crime family). They don't get any more powerful than Costello. Never one to shy from danger or a challenge, The Greek had no fears about taking money off the notorious gangster, or the consequences.

The Greek, Costello, and Farouk I, the king of Egypt, were deep into a hotly contested card game. Nick took control of the poker table and wiped out the Mafia don's chip stack while the king watched the show. The Greek decided it was time to depart with his winnings. When Dandolos started gathering his chips and cash, Costello called him a coward. Without missing a beat, The Greek handed a deck of cards to Farouk and asked him to shuffle. He challenged Costello to a high-card draw for $500,000. The stoic Costello froze for a second, perhaps stunned at the balls The Greek had on him. Then he lit a cigar, put on his coat, and exited without saying a word.

The Greek later hit up Chicago, taking hard-earned dough from commoners with the blessing of Al Capone, with Scarface taking a percentage of the action for allowing Dandolos the privilege of playing for massive stakes in his city. With the mobsters came the Rat Pack, as they went hand in hand in Vegas and the other casino cities of the time. Dean Martin, Frank Sinatra, and some of their colleagues welcomed The Greek into their inner circle. Even renowned escape artist Harry Houdini formed a bond with Dandolos, one magic man respecting another.

Perhaps one of the most unusual of The Greek's celebrity companionships was history's favorite physicist, Albert Einstein. It was a story Dandolos enjoyed sharing with friends and colleagues, adding to the romanticism of this truly compelling gambling man. In 1940, Dandolos received a call from a friend at the US State Department saying there was a prominent figure looking for the grand tour of Sin City, and who better than The Greek, a man who seemingly owned Vegas, to be the guide. Other times, Dandolos remarked the acclaimed physicist was looking to join a game in New York. Regardless, when Dandolos found out his charge was Einstein, he told his colleagues they should call him "Little Al from Princeton."

As much as his celebrity was a part of his incredible story, nothing topped the dramatic shifts in his hot and cold streaks. The Greek

declared he had been wealthy and busted seventy-three times in his life, leading to yet another of his best quotes: "The exhilaration of this form of economic existence is beyond my power to describe."

Toward the end of his life, most of that money was gone; the multimillionaire now found himself playing for pocket change, to which he always quipped, "Hey, it's action, isn't it?" Even when his health started to decline, he refused to give up playing, sometime even having doctors and nurses at the table with him to treat him as needed. When he could afford it.

Nick "The Greek" Dandolos passed on Christmas Day, 1966. When he died, he left literally no physical possessions behind. Some of his wealthier friends chipped in for an elaborate gold casket fitting of the man who once defied poker convention and stylized the idea of the snazzy professional. His funeral was attended by gamblers coast to coast, as well as mobsters and celebrities. Sinatra cried.

The Greek was not just a legend; he became a gambling god icon in a sport built on huge personalities, influencing the egos and laying the groundwork for the mayhem and chaos that was on the horizon. However, he didn't do it alone. The Greek would play second fiddle to only one man. Some would argue Nick's "partner" had the most magnanimous influence of any risk-taking warrior. With every ante in a game of Hold 'Em, there are two blinds. If The Greek was the small blind, the big blind was tossed on the table right after him.

CHAPTER 3
TITANIC

"I can do it."

The kid had giant brass balls; he had to give him that. The nineteen-year-old didn't look like much, with his long, lanky frame and his ragged yet boyish appearance. In fact, he looked like what he was in desperate need of was a sandwich, heavy on the bread, to put some meat on the bones. What he did have was a swashbuckling swagger. The confidence emanated from his aura and the pride that came with hustling much bigger men out of their hard-earned money.

Which he had been doing all week shooting pool.

One of the unlucky victims included Snow Clark, the proprietor of the pool hall in Joplin, Missouri. The kid and Clark had just finished a round a pool for $500, what some men were lucky to make in a year in 1912. Snow Clark was unbeatable . . . until the kid torched him. The loss momentarily paralyzed Clark like an uppercut to the chin. Dually stung and surprised, Snow prepared to pay the boy with a contemptuous warning that it might be best for him to hit the trail, for his own good.

Maybe Clark was right, but the kid had his sights set on loftier goals. He had noticed a sign on the window of Clark's pool hall proclaiming "$200 to Any Man Who Jumps Over My New Pool Table." The new table was Clark's pride and joy, and lengthier than most at nine feet long and four and a half feet wide. Now this rabble-rouser was bragging that the jump, and earning two hundred more greenbacks off Clark, was inevitable.

The spectators of the match, men who had all been drained by the kid over the past week, doubled over with howling cackles. They were dazzled by his eight-ball mastery, but this was a feat of sky-high improbable odds. The kid furrowed his brow and hustled out the door, and Clark watched and waited with bated breath.

Ten minutes later, just as life in the pool hall found a resemblance of normalcy, the kid returned dragging two withered, raggedy mattresses with him.

What the hell is this now? Clark thought.

Before he could ask the question aloud, the kid placed one mattress on each side of the table. As everyone gathered in confusion, the kid backed outside with the front door deliberately left open, he crouched down, and took a moment for a deep breath, focusing on the table inside the pool hall. Later, in his own words, in an article for *Sports Illustrated*, the kid, who was then an old man and an icon in the world of professional gambling, would say that what they didn't know was that he could "jump farther than a herd of bullfrogs in those days."

He bolted forward in a dead sprint, like a jackrabbit with his ass on fire. Using one mattress as a springboard, he propelled himself toward the ceiling, sailing airborne over the entire pool table below, then stuck the landing perfectly on the opposite-side mattress. Gymnastics judges would have given three perfect tens. Once again, the kid had done the impossible.

After Clark paid him his money, now $700, one of the bystanders innocently asked Clark, "What's that kid's name?"

"I don't know," Clark replied with a chuckle. "But it should be Titanic because he sinks everybody."

The Making of a Legend

Alvin Clarence Thomas became Titanic Thompson the same year the infamous luxury boat hit an iceberg and sank, killing 1,500. He liked the name. He liked the meaning behind it even more.

In a profession built on infamy, grit, and deception, a game that celebrates the outlaw while it prides itself as an honest game, Titanic Thompson is *the* legend among legends. Along with The Greek, Titanic and his voracious exploits blazed a trail that would fill his pockets, build his legacy, and awe and terrify those that dared to play, well, *anything* against him. Most importantly, they would inspire and pave the way for some young boys who would themselves grow up to be the celebrated godfathers of professional poker.

Thomas would be the first to admit that as excellent as he was at poker, playing cards wasn't even one of his favorite pastimes to make money. For Titanic, it was all about the cash. The man had endless talents: golf, billiards, dice, horseshoes, target shooting, and of course, poker. So talented, in fact, that people he came across often wondered if he was a wizard. They were mesmerized by his skills. As all would soon learn, prop bets were his specialty, his true calling, and in that regard, yes, he was Merlin.

Iconic golfer Sam Snead once called him "the greatest hustler ever."

Poker legend Doyle Brunson called him "the archetype of the poker-playing golf hustler."

Famed cue man Minnesota Fats called him "the greatest action man of all time."

Perhaps the greatest quote ever about Titanic came from an old columnist named Damon Runyon who wrote a story about a father warning his son about the big city. "Son, no matter how far you travel, or how smart you get, always remember this: Someday, somewhere, a guy is going to come to you and show you a nice brand new deck of cards on which the seal is never broken, and this guy is going to offer to bet you that the jack of spades will jump out of this deck and squirt cider in your ear. But, son, do not bet him, for as soon as you do, you are going to get an ear full of cider."

Runyon was talking about Titanic Thompson. Despite his reputation, Titanic was not a con artist. Not that he was above it, but it's

too simple of a label. He was a gambler who was an artist at manipulating odds, objects, and people. He was a mastermind at making sure the game, any game, and its outcome would be in his favor. He had timing, skill, patience, dedication, endurance, and a need for constant action. And he won millions. In other words, he was the perfect gambling man.

Titanic had a looming trauma to conquer and a fire in his belly, both of which stayed with him his entire life. He trusted no one, always assuming others were also ideological schemers looking to get over on him. He was anxious, unable to rest, and many claimed he was often irritable, even when life was rolling in his direction. Not terribly surprising, considering his very first experience in the world was parental abandonment, followed by the need for rapid retribution. This inner pain would set him on a trajectory to quell the unrest that flooded his mind. The journey he embarked on to find answers for these burning desires would eventually lead him to a portfolio of masterful accomplishments.

Chasing the Vanishing Man

Titanic was born on November 30, 1893, in Monett, Missouri, to Sarah Thomas and her deadbeat husband Lee. In fact, at the time of Alvin's arrival, Lee was in a local saloon playing cards. When told his wife had given birth to his first son, Lee took another swig of his "hollerin' whiskey" and shuffled the cards, calling for bets. He didn't go home till the next day, and when he staggered in drunk, exhausted, and broke from another night of losing, he wasn't thrilled to see the baby at her breast. Not long after, on a chilly Midwest morning, Lee packed up his few belongings, took the last of the family money, and skipped town without saying goodbye.

Sarah called it a blessing, but Alvin grew resentful as his father's leaving gnawed at him. Sarah remarried, this time to a pig farmer,

and moved the family to Arkansas, close to the Ozarks. They lived in a cramped three-room log cabin—Alvin, his mother, his stepfather, and his stepfather's four other kids.

Everything, including bathing, was a shared, uncomfortable experience. In the country, there was nothing but work and financial hardship. His stepfather was a Baptist who brought religion into their family, but he wasn't above a little gambling himself, teaching Alvin how to play cards and throw dice. And shoot firearms.

The boy who would become Titanic acquired knowledge at a lightning pace. He was blessed with a brilliant mind and bear trap instincts. He became adept at learning the percentages of card playing and how to read both hands and people. He visualized at an early age how these skills would deliver what he desired most besides retribution . . . cold hard cash.

When the restless boy turned sixteen, unsatisfied with his life on the farm, he ventured out. It was time to make his mark.

"I was strong as a wild razorback hog," he would later say. "There was no place for me out in the country. It was time to see what the world held for a boy of my talents."

Sarah knew she couldn't restrain him, so she let him go, asking only that he promise not to drink or smoke, a promise he kept his entire life. That vow, and the clear head that came with it, would serve him well.

Especially as he tried to track down the man who didn't want him: his father.

Titanic started his solo adventures barefoot with nothing more than a dollar in his pocket as he made his way across Missouri, Arkansas, and surrounding states as a door-to-door map salesman, followed by a stint in a Wild West traveling medical show. Thomas utilized his accuracy as a trick-shooting Doc Holliday-like character actor. His big gimmick was to throw a silver dollar into the air and shoot a hole through it to awed audiences who had no idea he was palming the coin he showed them and tossing one that already

had a hole in it. After the day's work, he and the other drifters would play cards, and that's where Alvin ignited his skills and his bankroll.

At each stop, Thomas would search every saloon and gambling hall, hounding locals about a pitiful drunkard by the name of Lee Thomas and every time, he had just missed him. Lee's chair was still warm. Alvin never gave up, forging on, knowing that his pappy would soon be within arm's reach. What Thomas did not comprehend at the time was that at each new stop, at each new card table, he was becoming an accomplished card player. The veil was lifted one night in 1911 in a smoky, rambunctious room in Oil City, Louisiana.

Alvin found his mark. There he was. Finally!

Lee was drinking and gambling and "terrible at both," according to Titanic. Dad was dressed to the nines in a three-piece suit with a satin vest, with a large chip stack and cash in front of him as he dealt cards around the table. His son had over a thousand dollars in his pocket when he sat down to play Stud at twenty-five dollars a hand. Alvin didn't reveal himself but instead worked diligently, draining his old man (close to $1,600) and his humility. During the early morning hours, Lee couldn't handle any more. He brazenly shot up from his chair and yelled, demanding to know the youngster's name.

"I'm Alvin Thomas," he said. "And I'm your son."

Wasting no time, Alvin slid all the chips back to his father, content for the one and only time in his life with just the victory itself and not the spoils that came with it. Lee took a moment and then laughed, embracing his boy and declaring, "My own boy cleaned me out!"

Suckers and Sharps

The father and son duo played cards together as partners for a few days, while Titanic stayed with Lee in a shoddy hotel room. They

didn't talk much about the past or even why Lee left, focusing instead on the money they could make together.

The reunion was short-lived, though. Less than a week after finding a sliver of peace at tracking down the man who helped bring him into the world, it was déjà vu all over again. Lee abandoned Alvin once again, stealing his son's winnings one night and sneaking out without so much as a goodbye. It was one of just a handful of times somebody would get the best of Thomas. The kid decided right then and there that in a world of suckers and sharps, he would be the best sharp that ever was.

Within a year, Alvin Thomas had morphed into Titanic Thompson. The news of the legendary escapade at Snow Clark's pool hall had circulated around the country. Thompson spent the rest of his life roaming, drifting, never staying in one place for too long. Never staying with one person, or one trade, one trick, one mark . . . always getting out at just the right time. He was a lifelong vagabond, always searching for the next opportunity, never settling down nor containing the constant wildfire within that burned for action.

He also exemplified patience in his quest, a skill most hustlers tend to lack. Composure became a hallmark of Titanic's trade. He spent hours upon hours studying, training, practicing the tools he'd need to succeed in this profession. He dealt thousands of hands of poker and shot thousands of dice rolls by himself, just to learn the percentages; he was a gambling statistician before there were any stats. Titanic was not only exceptionally talented, but also undeniably disciplined at doing whatever was needed to be the best.

Titanic was drafted in early 1918 as the United States became more embroiled in World War I. He saw no action, nor would he ever leave the States during his months of service. Proud to serve, with an exceptional understanding and practice of what was required in the military, Titanic was quickly promoted to the rank of sergeant and found himself in charge of training younger draftees. At

night, Titanic would continue their education, teaching his soldiers a variety of poker games. Later, he would use his expertise, coupled with his men's newfound enthusiasm for cards—and novice level of play—to plunder and deplete the poor souls' pay. He was charming, while also gifted at making naive players believe he was setting them apart from the field . . . and then using those newfound skills against them to line his own pockets.

Titanic achieved this objective to the tune of $50,000 by the time he was discharged at the end of the war.

With the proceeds, Titanic bought his grateful mother a quaint home back in Monett. Sarah didn't ask too many questions. She didn't need to know where the money came from. She was optimistic about the idea of being near her remaining family in Missouri.

The windfall also gave Titanic the cushion he needed to make burgeoning bets while taking healthier-sized risks. Whenever he won, no matter the amount, he needed the next opportunity to be heart-pumping, more exhilarating, and most importantly, more satisfying.

Ramblin' Man

As Titanic traversed through Black Gold Country, he embraced and made sure he lived up to his moniker. He'd work a town, find the suckers, build his bankroll, rile up the locals, and hit the road, cruising out in his rare and pricey nickel-plated Pierce Arrow. With each stop, his reputation grew as the backwoods, barefoot kid turned sophisticated, stylish hustler. The name Titanic was soon whispered and often later yelled by those who came across his path in the southern part of the United States.

Especially those he left behind, most notably the women . . . and there were *plenty* of women. As Titanic drifted into a town, he would quickly take on a lover or two. Attractive to most women, he would use his charm to woo and his cash to stimulate, offering adventures

to their often sullen lives. As his celebrity grew, many women would come out of the woodwork with tales of passion with the legend. He even had affairs with actresses Myrna Loy and Jean Harlow.

Titanic also married five different times in his life. In most cases, he would marry young, hang around for a short stay, get restless (especially if they got pregnant), and take off, leaving his wife behind, just like his daddy did. The only difference was that Titanic would often leave them a little nest egg, perhaps doing so to calm those voices in his head who compared him to Lee. The first was Nora, a chambermaid in Joplin, Missouri, when Titanic was in his early twenties, a marriage that lasted less than six months. Later there was JoAnne, who was fifteen years old, a minor he married to avoid trouble with the law. Soon after was Maxine, a sixteen-year-old who by all accounts won over Titanic with her stunning looks. Later in his life, there was Jeannette, another minor he married when he was sixty-two and left after learning she was pregnant. He would return to Jeannette, however, and live with her and their son until his final days, despite their divorce.

All his marriages ended in divorce except Alice, his second wife, who Titanic met when she tried to pick his pocket in Pittsburgh. Alice accepted and even celebrated Titanic's cravings, demons, and lifestyle. They even traveled together briefly, hitting towns and bleeding them dry. Or she would simply let him go on his own, vowing she wouldn't try to change him. It's curious to think if she would have been the one to stick for Titanic, as they were together for years before she was tragically struck by a car and killed crossing the street not far from where they met in her home city.

Shoot and Survive

Death was a prevalent part of Titanic's life story. To go along with his five wives, he also racked up five killings. Shockingly—or

perhaps *not* with his nature and luck—he never served any time in prison for any of them.

The first happened in 1910 when Titanic was still a teenager. He had won a boat off a friend named Joe Green tossing dice. Titanic brought his then girlfriend aboard the *Rambler* for a leisurely outing down a river in Mark Tree, Arkansas, along with Green, who Titanic allowed to still work on board. One of Green's cronies accused Titanic of cheating and a struggle between the men ensued, resulting in Titanic being thrown overboard. A humiliated and drenched Titanic swam back to the boat and, like a pirate in the night, he scaled back up onto the deck with no one taking notice.

The sanctimonious Green was in the midst of threatening Titanic's girlfriend with a dagger. The situation was headed for disaster. Titanic swooped in and swiftly grabbed a hammer and bludgeoned the oppressor into oblivion, eventually heaving him overboard, where his lifeless body turned up floating a few days later. The sheriff, who was also judge, jury, and executioner of the small town, told Titanic he could avoid a murder charge if he would hightail his ass out of town. Oh, and one last thing: "Be sure to leave the deed to the boat with me."

The second and third murders occurred after Titanic's notorious reputation had spread from coast to coast. By this point, he had hired a bodyguard, which was the norm among hotshot gamblers who carried loads of money. Titanic and his bodyguard got into a craps game in St. Louis at a hole in the wall called Dalton's. After taking close to $40,000 of the proprietor's money over a couple weeks, Titanic and his bodyguard became alerted to some irregularities.

As they attempted to leave one night, two armed and masked marauders were lying in wait outside to rob them. The gunmen had been signaled by Dalton on the gambler's departure. Titanic was lightning quick on the draw. Being an expert marksman, his shots

got off first, leaving both bandits dead in their boots. A cornered Dalton sobbed like an infant, pleading for his life.

Titanic's bodyguard urged him to leave, but Titanic insisted on waiting for the authorities. When questioned, he told them the Luger that he used to kill the men wasn't licensed. "But I carry a lot of money, and I'm going to kill any hijacker who's out to rob me," he said. "That's pure self-defense."

The police agreed, especially because the two hoodlums Titanic had killed were wanted for armed robbery and murder, including the killing of a baby. They not only let Titanic leave the scene, but they sent him off with a thank-you and a permit to carry.

Amazingly, Titanic's fourth murder went down in similar fashion. Titanic and another bodyguard were in a high-stakes Five-Card Stud game in St. Joseph, Oklahoma, when two hijackers came in blasting with both barrels. Titanic and the bodyguard ducked for cover behind an overturned card table and began returning gunfire, each hitting and killing a would-be robber. Again, they informed the police and *again*, Titanic was told that the man he shot was a wanted killer and he was sent on his way as a hero.

The fifth and final murder came after a round of golf in Texas with nosebleed stakes, in which Titanic once again came out on top. Later that evening, while he was settling in with two young sisters (one of whom would eventually become one of his wives), he heard a commotion outside. When he went out to investigate, a masked man accosted him with a gun. The ill-fated attacker was no match for the surly Titanic, who emptied four shots into his chest. Titanic jerked off the mask to reveal that his attacker was his young caddy from earlier in the day, eager to get a piece of what he saw Titanic rake in on the links. As he lay there bleeding from the mouth, he called out, "Help, Mr. Thompson, I think you killed me." The young man lived long enough to confess to police that he had tried to rob Titanic, so once again, Mr. Thompson was free to go.

Titanic would later say that he didn't feel much about the murders, nor did he feel any real anger at those who tried to rob him, whether they fired on him or not. He showed sympathy after murder number four, sending condolence letters to the wives of the victims, claiming it was nothing personal, simply part of the lifestyle. The bottom line: Nothing was going to get between Titanic and his money.

The Prop Master Hustles

Money was a key motivating factor for most of Titanic's life. Perhaps it was his upbringing where money was always tight, or lessons he learned from his time pursuing his father. Or perhaps it was simply the early tastes of success leading a skilled and ambitious young man to squeeze the orange of life and drink its nectar.

Titanic's ability to hustle and outmaneuver people was his greatest asset. Or as he liked to call them, *prop bets*.

It started when he was fourteen. Titanic spent quality time at the pond near where he lived with his spaniel dog Carlos. He trained Carlos to fetch rocks that he threw into the water. One day he noticed a local there who had some impressive fishing gear. He bet the man his dog would fetch a rock he threw into the water. The suspicious man told him to mark it so they would know it was the same rock, which Titanic did. Sure enough, once he tossed it, Carlos jumped in, dove under the water, and came back with a marked rock, earning his owner a new rod and reel. What the bewildered man didn't know is that Titanic had covered the bottom of the pond with marked rocks.

To cover all of Titanic's props and their mechanisms for success would take literal volumes, but no story of the mythical figure would be complete without some of his best. They all read like Southern gothic mythology, folk tales shared with a bottle of whiskey around

a fire, or stories youngsters tell to one-up each other in the exuberance of youth. The one difference is that these are all *true*:

*He would bet people he could throw a walnut over a building, even one as high as five stories. When someone would take that bet, he would even let them pick the nut . . . before coolly pocketing it and replacing it with the one he carried that was filled with lead. He would do the same with other objects, including fruit, and in one such case, a pumpkin he had filled with steel shot.

*He'd bet he could hail a taxi in less than a minute during standstill traffic. He'd whistle and that cab would pull over for him . . . driven, of course, by a hired accomplice.

*He once bet he could find a hairpin over twenty consecutive blocks in New York. He did, of course, because they had all been planted by him.

*He made a bet on a drive back into Omaha with a colleague once. After they passed a sign saying it was still ten miles to the city, Titanic bet they would make it there in less than ten minutes. His poor friend took the bet, not knowing Titanic had uprooted and moved the sign five miles closer that morning.

*In a club in Ohio, he bet a group of men that the club was so infested with rats, he could go downstairs and shoot one at any time. They took the bet, warning him that the body need still be warm to prove it wasn't a plant. Earlier in the evening, Titanic had trapped a rat under a barrel, leaving it as easy prey.

*He bet he could drive a golf ball five hundred yards in a time when pros couldn't even hit three hundred. He waited until winter, then assembled the group of bettors by a frozen lake. He casually placed a golf ball on a tee, swung with ease, sending the ball skyward. The ball crested, landed and glided down onto the sheet of ice, rolling, rolling, rolling . . . out of sight.

*Perhaps his most clever was betting a boxer he couldn't knock Titanic down even if they stood on the same newspaper page. After the boxer took the bet, Titanic unfolded the standard-size page and

strategically laid it perfectly centered in a doorway. He quickly picked his spot to stand on the page and then invited the boxer to take the other half directly across from him. Once the boxer was in place, Titanic briefly stepped off the page and shut the door between them, before stepping back on the page. While they both stood on the single piece of newspaper, the heavy wood door made even the slightest tap from the boxer impossible!

Not all his prop wagers came from setups. Many of them required the discipline and commitment to practice he possessed. Titanic could throw playing cards with such precision that he could fill a hat with all fifty-two cards from across the room. Anybody would take that bet, and then marvel at his expertise, no matter the distance. He could also throw a sewing pin into a ceiling and make it stick, another near-impossible feat that he made look easy. He figured out how to literally throw keys into keyholes, landing them perfectly. He mastered checkers, horseshoes, and tossing dice. There was seemingly nothing Titanic couldn't do, especially if money was on the line. No matter the mark.

Even if it was *Al Capone*.

Titanic had been introduced to the cheek bustin' goombah by none other than Nick "The Greek." There are several accounts of how these two titans of the felt met in Chicago—some say it was on a train, some a shooting range, and some say at the poker table. Titanic and The Greek were both instantly impressed with each other. They were brothers in a nonsymbiotic way. They developed a playing style between the two of them. This collaboration ballooned into one of the most lucrative times their careers, as they raked in thousands on a nightly basis.

Titanic favored "The Greek." On the contrary, he didn't like Scarface.

Capone's obnoxious vulgarity set the soft-spoken, strait-laced Titanic seething mad. Capone ran Chicago and gamblers needed his blessing to operate, but that's as far as it went with Thompson. Titanic had won more than $100,000 in the games Capone set up

(after taking his 25 percent), but he wasn't finished. He wouldn't be satisfied or ready to leave Chicago until he had the opportunity to hustle that nasty-talking Capone, and then maybe even wash his mouth out with soap.

Titanic decided on his famous throwing trick. As they strolled passed a fruit stand near Capone's car, Thompson nonchalantly swiped a lemon and bet Scarface he could toss it over a five-story hotel across the street.

"You got a bet," the mobster grumbled as he looked at the hotel. "But wait a second."

Al was no sucker. He chose his own lemon from the stand and squeezed it dry, leaving any advantage Thompson might have had dripping on the sidewalk. As he tossed him the fleshy lump of dead fruit, he told Titanic, "Fling this one."

This butchered Titanic's plan. Earlier, he had planted a lemon filled with buckshot with the vendor of the fruit stand, promising a small cut from the wager. Now he had to toss his perfectly weighted piece of fruit to the side and take a shot with the soft-squeezed lemon. Luckily, Titanic had nerves of steel, incredible physical talent, and eternal positive outcomes that seemed blessed by the Good Lord himself. With a shrug of the shoulders, a wind up, and a grunt, Titanic sent the lemon flying. As it sailed over the building, Capone just shook his head and laughed.

Setting Up the "Crime of the Century"

Titanic never shied away from pressing his luck . . . from a challenge or from danger. He said he always believed that no matter what, he would win. This attitude eventually caught up with him. The one gamble he could never master was horse racing, and it cost him millions over his lifetime. No worries. Whatever Titanic lost at the track, he would recuperate at the dice or poker tables.

Titanic used a combination of analyzing percentages, reading people, and maneuvering angles to excel at poker. A math wizard, he memorized odds and percentages through his diligent and dedicated practice dealing hands and writing down the outcomes in a notebook. He spent hours at a table methodically examining players, digging deep behind the mask, the facial facade, and searching for body language tells or any valuable info he could record in his mind to dissect a person's psychological playbook. Titanic claimed he was never scared to try and take advantage of anyone, or to get in over his head.

Which is exactly what unfolded with Arnold Rothstein.

Titanic not only helped orchestrate a poker game that would lead to the "Crime of the Century," but most people involved allege that he helped rig it.

Arnold Rothstein was an infamous crime boss and racketeer, most notably responsible for rigging the 1919 World Series, which became known as the Black Sox Scandal. His notoriety, as well as his power, continued to grow in New York as "The Brain," as he was often called, showed himself to be an omnipotent vice lord. Titanic met him in the spring of 1928, turning on his Southern charisma and asserting his way into Rothstein's inner circle. A curious man, Rothstein took to Titanic after being hustled by him, with Titanic gracious enough to explain his methods. There weren't many people out there who could teach "The Brain" much of anything; his intellect reigned superior over the common thug. Titanic was no common thug.

However, as with Capone, the respect was one-sided. Titanic didn't appreciate Rothstein's smugness; his pompous demeanor soured Titanic's stomach. As a result, Titanic wanted Rothstein to take a hit, a double whammy to his ego and his bankroll.

Rothstein was an iconoclastic wagering whale who was eager to collect when he won and slippery to collect from when he lost, often issuing paper IOUs. That hesitancy would perpetually seal his fate. Titanic arranged a Seven-Card Stud game through George "Hump"

McManus, a leg breaker and connected Irishman with a constant smirk and a glint in his eye that alerted everyone that he was not quite right upstairs. One Saturday night in September, as Rothstein, his crew, the writer Damon Runyon, and Titanic sat around Lindy's Deli nursing drinks (soda water for Titanic and milk for Rothstein), the man friends referred to as A.R. got a phone call. The game was on.

"Arnold, let's go play some cards," Titanic said as he slapped his back.

A.R. had one condition: Titanic had to be his partner. Titanic had predicted this would be the case, and he gladly accepted. To help with his plan, Titanic enlisted a fellow gambler from LA named Nathan Raymond. The players congregated into an upstairs apartment close to Midtown for this highly anticipated, high-stakes poker event.

Soon, the cards were in the air. Raymond rolled in, apologizing for being late and explaining it was because he had just won $8,000 shooting dice. Rothstein's ears perked up. He immediately propositioned a high-card wager for the cash, just as Titanic expected. Not afraid to cover his friend's losses, Titanic shot Raymond a quick nod and agreed to play with A.R. Raymond won. Throughout the night, Titanic would pull the other players aside and tell them to take any high-card bets A.R. made. Soon, the floodgates to Rothstein's losses were turned wide open. Titanic gave him a chunk of his winnings and informed Rothstein that he needed to end the partnership because the high-card gambling was too damn risky. Little did A.R. know, Titanic was disguising his true intentions, by turning the tables to play against him and siphoning away his cash.

The marathon session went on for more than thirty hours with Rothstein's betting climbing to unfathomable heights of desperation as each hour ticked away, offering thousands of dollars on side bets and even the turn of the next card being played. As the session concluded in the wee hours of Sunday night, A.R. once again bet

Raymond on a high card, this time for a whopping $40,000! When the agitated Rothstein lost by cutting a deuce, he got up, grabbed his hat, and calmy but forcefully exclaimed, "I think I've been playing with a pack of crooks." While Titanic could barely conceal his grin, A.R. barreled out of the room in a huff, leaving a mountain of handwritten IOUs piled on the table that Hump reminded him would need to be paid in full.

All told, Arnold Rothstein had lost over half a million dollars, and the majority was to his partner, the illustrious and unsinkable Titanic.

Weeks went by and the gamblers were all eager—and in some cases desperate—to collect their winnings. Rothstein's defiance grew, circulating the news that he had been cheated and now refused to pay. His closest confidants replied with the advice that this was a bad look for him. A man of his stature that controlled bookmakers across the United States was now welching on a card game. Not a good look at all! After constant badgering, mainly from the trifling Hump, A.R. gave in . . . to a point. He needed a little breathing room until after the upcoming US presidential election, where he was confident he was going to earn a massive payday on his wager on the man called Hoover. His horse was soon to come in.

Hump had Rothstein meet him at the Park Central Hotel to discuss the matter. Once inside, Arnold was surrounded by an inebriated McManus and three hired enforcers, who all showed that they had been drinking. When A.R. demanded more time, the belligerent McManus declined. Rothstein rose to leave, and all four of the mugs whipped out revolvers. Calling their bluff, A.R. walked toward the door. He was instantly blasted full of lead.

Just after eleven PM, Arnold Rothstein stumbled from the hotel and collapsed in the street. Two police officers found him bleeding from the groin. He was rushed to the hospital and died the next day, never revealing to police who fired the fatal shot.

Because McManus had left his coat behind at the scene of the crime, he was eventually arraigned and brought to trial on murder charges in what was then the most widely covered homicide case in US history. When prosecutors learned about the infamous poker marathon, Titanic was called to testify. The district attorney believed that McManus had shot Rothstein because he had lost $50,000 to him during the game. This was a revelation since Hump was the only man at the table Rothstein had beaten that night. On the stand, Titanic was evasive, claiming he couldn't remember things well, but he did know that Hump was a stand-up guy and a good loser who would never resort to such drastic measures. Following a strict code, all the players from that night toed the line and McManus was eventually acquitted due to lack of evidence. The Crime of the Century would go unsolved.

One of the most memorable exchanges from the trial came from Titanic's testimony. When a prosecutor asked him what he did for a living, Titanic replied, "I run a café."

"You have other means of income, do you not?"

Titanic smiled and said, "I play a little golf for money."

Greenbacks on the Greens

That was perhaps the understatement of the century as, by all accounts, even by professionals, Titanic Thompson is one of the greatest golfers to have ever lived. Most who knew him said golf was his best game, and one he used to bring home boatloads of money.

Titanic didn't discover the game until he was in his thirties. His blessed physical gifts and almost robotic hand-eye coordination made the game easy for him. Once he figured out that he could make money on the links, he studied and practiced like a madman. From the time he discovered the game until well into his golden

years, Titanic played multiple times a week, often taking country club members to school.

He could beat lifetime players straight up, but his true talent was that he could golf . . . both right- and left-handed!

Titanic would use this attribute to proposition golfers that he could beat them right-handed and then go double or nothing he could do it left-handed. An eager golfer would take the bet not knowing that Titanic was naturally left-handed. They didn't have a chance.

Titanic's golf game was as legendary as the man himself, as were the prop bets he would make within the rounds. Ever the clever oddsmaker, Titanic would control how much he beat someone by, keeping it to just a stroke or two and giving them false hope that they could whip him on the next round. They never did. Over the years, the question was asked a thousand times: Why didn't he ever go pro?

"I couldn't afford the cut in pay," he'd say.

During his time, top professional golfers were lucky to make $30,000 a year. Titanic could make that in a week. Sometimes a day.

His time on the course was also spent with Hall of Fame pros, legends themselves who marveled at Titanic's game. He played with Byron Nelson, Sam Snead, and Ben Hogan, to name a few. Some say he taught them some of his techniques. Others say they simply played together as partners or against each other as rivals. All said they were awed by him.

"He's the best shotmaker I ever saw," Hogan said.

Titanic also had an eye for talent. In his later years, he set up a match in El Paso, Texas, between a young Lee Trevino and up-and-coming pro Raymond Floyd. Titanic recognized that Trevino had talent, but he was more interested in the players at Trevino's club, who all thought he could beat anyone. Titanic backed Floyd and a group of Texas millionaires backed Trevino . . . who won on the first day. And the second day. Titanic's sure thing, Floyd, who had

won a PGA Open earlier that year, was pushing him to financial ruin. Not to be deterred, Titanic set up one final day of golf, this time for $20,000 he didn't have. Lucky for him, Floyd eagled the final hole and Trevino's putt came up an inch short, giving the PGA pro the win and Titanic a sigh of relief.

The Legend Lives On

Unfortunately, Titanic's hustle would dim later in life, though not from lack of effort. He was a prop man right to the very end. It's just that his fame and notoriety had people wary of playing anything against him. Plus, his age had slowed his abilities, and his marks could occasionally recognize what he was doing. He had reconnected with his oldest son Tommy (one of three he had with three different women) and they played poker together toward the end, but Titanic no longer had the game to intimidate or even to win straight up. He would get caught cheating, even by friends and colleagues who would sometimes let him get away with it, not wanting to hurt the old man they respected so much.

Titanic would quietly pass in a nursing home near Dallas in 1974, but his legend would live on. In terms of his contribution to the beginning of the World Series of Poker, Titanic Thompson did more than even he could imagine.

It was the legend of Titanic Thompson and Nick "The Greek" and their mythical lives that would inspire future players over the years, including two young boys, one of whom would go on to become the founder of the future world-renowned card-playing championship. Before that would happen, though, there would come a lot of chaos as egos who were inspired by these glorified outlaws clashed, leaving destruction and death in their wake.

HOLE CARDS

Two facedown cards that make up a player's starting hand.

CHAPTER 4
THE COWBOY

Intuition. One of man's greatest gifts. Like the healthy fear of a rattlesnake, intuition has been saving lives since the dawn of time. To some, intuition brings the discovery of potential treasure, and others definite treason. Psychologists claim it is hardwired in us; it's at the heart of our fight-or-flight syndrome. Intuition is how we survive . . . as long as we listen to it.

Perhaps intuition was whispering into one man's ear on that hot and humid evening in October 1931. *He* certainly would tell you that was the case. Intuition spoke loudly to him in those younger days and well beyond.

And Benny Binion always listened to what it had to say.

A hazy, dim-lit glow of a single bulb splashed barely a volt of illumination on the two male shadow silhouette figures sitting on box crates in a South Dallas backyard. A breeze crept in like a thief in the night, adding to the eerie gloom that satiated the energy in the night air. Somebody here was headed down the wrong direction of a one-way street with no indication that an eighteen-wheeler loaded with dynamite was barreling toward them with its lights off.

Frank Bolding, a middle-aged Black bootlegger, was probably wondering if he would be receiving a trick or a treat from the young upstart Binion, who had called him in for a meeting at one of his safe houses. Benny had booze on his mind. Specifically, a load of booze that had recently been stolen from him. The conversation was cordial as both men rocked back and forth on their boxes. Benny let

Frank do most of the talking, trying to get a read, waiting for Frank to reveal something, to show Benny he knew a little something about looted liquor. He was also biding his time as he waited for his trusted intuition to start its seductive whispering.

Eventually, it did.

Without hesitation, quick as a rattlesnake attack, Binion fell back on his box, drew one of the two .45 automatics he carried with him (along with a .38 revolver), and fired. Binion was a sharpshooter and nailed Frank right in the neck, ensuring there would be no chance of survival. A stream of blood gurgled from the throat of the stunned Bolding, who still had a look of both pure surprise and disappointed acceptance on his face, as he lay in the grass grasping for air. Benny cautiously walked over to what would soon be Bolding's corpse and stood over him, the muzzle still smoking. As Bolding took his final breaths, Benny proceeded to lecture Frank on the attributes of life, making sure his final words would be what the thief would take with him to hell.

Benny's crew inside the house filed outside and crowded around Bolding's trembling body, watching its final spasms with indifference. No ambulances were called, but eventually, the authorities did arrive on the scene. Benny had his story straight, one that he would share, and then change often, later.

"Me and him was sitting down on two boxes . . . he was a bad bastard. So he done something I didn't like and we was talking about it, and he jumped up right quick with a knife in his hand. Then he'd cut the shit out of me, but I was a little smarter than that. I just fell backward off of the box and shot the sumbitch right there."

Benny had no choice. It was kill or be killed. It's a shame that Bolding was not as connected with his own intuition.

The local police hauled in Binion. He didn't spend a night in jail but did plead guilty to the murder. Frank might have enjoyed hearing this. Still, there was little proof to counter Benny's story. Certainly, none of his men were going to offer up anything different.

Plus, the cops knew Frank was a despicable dude, one less on the street. So, for his guilty plea, Benny received a two-year suspended sentence, which enabled him to walk as a free man. Later on, Benny would tell his son a slightly different version of the story. Frank, who nobody denied was a brutal slobber-knocker with a history of stabbings, jumped up a little too aggressively for Benny's liking. Benny didn't wait to see what he would do next, and shot. Frank did have a concealed knife, though it was never pulled. Benny never gave him the chance.

With his quick-draw shooting skills, Benny earned the nickname "The Cowboy," a name he loved and embraced over the course of his life, no matter the venture. Local vice lords were taking notice. The young doughy-faced hoodlum not only carried firepower, but he was an expert marksman who wasn't afraid to show his skills. He was the type of a shooter that could blow off a gnat's ass blindfolded. And he had the temper of a fella who just got bit by one.

The Man, the Myth, The Cowboy

"He was either the gentlest bad guy or the baddest good guy you'd ever seen." This is how four-time poker world champ and longtime friend "Amarillo Slim" Preston described Benny Binion. The decision on which he would be if you crossed his path often came down to that fabled intuition.

There is no denying that Lester Ben Binion is a monumental mover and shaker in the history of gambling. One could argue he is *the* most important figure in poker's history. That's why there is a monument, a bronze statue of Benny riding one of his favorite horses, in the entrance of the South Point Hotel/Casino. Whether he is the great savior of Sin City or not, Benny is at least in solid company with Rafael Rivera, the first White man to find the Las Vegas Valley.

Benny's statue epitomizes everything Benny was from childhood until his last breath—a cowboy. *The* Cowboy. No one exemplified this lifestyle more than Binion. He was a true lover of the Western way of life: horses, cattle, ranches, rodeos, cowboys, cowgirls, and yes, even gunslingers. He also embraced the cowboy values of independence, fairness, taking risks, and finding an edge. Benny was a throwback to the type of cowboy who wore a black hat more times than he wore the white, and he always carried a pistol. Always. Cinema loves the antihero, be it the Joker, Tony Soprano, Walter White, and before them, J.R. Ewing. Benny was a precursor to them all. He was a combination of Don Corleone mixed with John Wayne. He was a hero all right—just depends on what side of the coin you want take a gander, and when.

On one side, there was generosity. Thousands of road-weary, broken-down rodeo riders owe Benny a debt of eternal gratitude. He never refused their hand in need. He did as much for pro rodeo as anybody in the business. From the contestants to stock contractors and everyone in between, Benny was there for them all. His generosity helped build the city of Las Vegas and put it on the map as the world championship rodeo destination. He would later give a lot to the city in terms of professional gambling. He was also a family man, and relatives and friends alike say that he could be kind and compassionate.

Could be, not *was*.

On the other side of the coin, Benny Binion was brutal and merciless. Debtors who owed Benny money, competitors that proved to be a speedbump for any of his numerous enterprises, criminals, gamblers, and business leaders alike that he felt disrespected him . . . well, these folks, they got Benny's violent brand of justice, and it usually didn't end well for them. In his eyes, Benny was fair about doling out his extreme punishment. He was not the kind to take things personally. He listened to excuses and pleas with an open mind, and he was willing to give second chances. At least

that's what he told himself. Rivals, and even some friends and colleagues, told a different tale, just not anywhere Benny could hear them.

But Benny had ears everywhere. His reach went well beyond whatever city he found himself in and included cowboys, criminals, cops, judges, politicians, entertainers, and many an outlaw. They all saw the light and dark sides of Benny Binion, depending upon which way the wind was blowing.

More than anything, Benny Binion was a true pioneer. He was an eager and aggressive industry leader who always looked for his opportunities. He was an ever-forward man who liked to share a personal motto to any who listened: "Never holler whoa or look back in a bad place."

So what does Benny Binion have to do with this story? Everything. This iconic gambling pioneer scorched the trail from Texas to Nevada. He is the man at the center that put all the pieces together. While The Greek and Titanic inspired, Benny did the doing. Without Benny there is *definitely* no World Series of Poker. There would be a giant hole in the heart of the Glitter Gulch.

The Cowboy puts our story, poker's story, in motion.

A Humble Beginning

Benny was born to Alma Willie and Lonnie Lee Binion in 1904 on the dusty prairie of Grayson County, Pilot Point, Texas, a town that endured harsh storms, destructive fires, business closures, and ebbing population through most of his childhood.

The Binions came from the country, simple living. They didn't thrive but survived on the most modest of means, living in a beat-up shack that was too hot in the summer and too cold in the winter. As cramped as it was, the Binions sometimes took in boarders for extra cash, which often went to booze before food. Benny's

father was a heavy-drinking horse trader, and the family lived a hardscrabble life. It was tough times at the turn of the century in North Texas.

As a youngster, Benny was initially held back from attending school due to breathing difficulties. Even as he recuperated and got better, Benny received no formal education. His father didn't believe in the pen and paper. He believed in the bridle and the saddle. He pulled Benny out of school early in his life and forced him to work the horses. Life outdoors proved to help Benny's health, but as a result, Benny wouldn't learn to read for many years to come. In fact, he would be in his fifties when Benny finally learned how to read, and only out of boredom during a stint in federal prison.

Benny learned the art of promotion by the time his feet could barely reach the stirrups. After being jerked out of school by his father in second grade, the two traveled horseback with a band of horses from one auction to another. In the early 1900s, the Industrial Revolution was just starting to take hold in America. Most farmers didn't own a tractor yet; modern mechanization was still considered a wonder experiment in the making. Horses and mules provided the engine for all labor on farms and ranches. These animals were traded, bought, and sold at auctions in the rural towns known as *Trade Days*. Benny and his father would travel to these Trade Days, where they would buy and sell horse prospects. Benny learned from the old-timers how to "mouth" a mule and how to spot "snides," a horse with respiratory problems. These issues could be covered up or masked for a short period of time with tonics and medications to keep the heaves at a minimum.

More importantly, Benny learned about cheating and how not to be cheated himself. He could size up a pony within minutes or hide major defects from one he was trying to peddle. One such trick of the trade included getting a horse on a high point and a potential buyer on a lower point of ground to deflect attention from problematic areas.

This all added up to dollars and cents. Benny was no bossman (yet), but he was certainly a "hoss man."

These Trade Days were also where Benny got into gambling, which would give him everything he needed to fill his pockets and build his legacy.

In the camp, gamblers would run a craps game. These games were on the fringes, away from the crowds, masked in the brush. Players would roll dice on blankets against tree trunks. Benny wandered into one of these games and was gifted with a special opportunity. A rough-and-tumble gambler who knew him proposed that the kid secretly lure cowboys back to the game. Preferably ones with cash. For each player Binion brought to the game, he would receive a few silver coins.

It was his first foray into "steering" customers. Benny's eye grew saucer-wide, and he seized the opportunity. Even as a youth, Benny was both charismatic and a good talker. He knew how to get anyone's attention and make people laugh, and then buy what he was selling. Benny had no problem steering unsuspecting horsemen to the dice game. He learned firsthand that promoting equaled easy money. As he watched the games unfold under the canopy of mesquite and oak trees, he also picked up on the players' tendencies, their tricks, their skills. He compiled these attributes neatly in the back corners of his mind.

By twelve years old, Benny was becoming the main man in the Binion household. He was a grown-up and presented himself as one. He knew the race to riches was not going to come from hustling horses or from the tips he was collecting wrangling dice tossers. His family needed more money. Young Benny started spending some time in the big city, where his time as a youth built his character, taking on any kind of odd job for a couple of coins. He spent those days listening to the stories of the celebrity gamblers, players like Titanic and The Greek. He spent them dreaming, watching,

learning, and working his ass off to earn a couple bucks and build his reputation.

Putting in the Work

In 1922, Benny headed for one of the great smuggling viper pits in America: El Paso. Even for someone who could handle himself like Benny, it was a bold choice. Benny had cousins there and wanted to start venturing out more on his own. He was eighteen and wanted to put his talents to work. The place was crawling with outlaws and Mexican bandits. It was a deathtrap and violence oozed out of its every pore. Still, like all places he went, Benny thrived. He was a young pistol in the area, and his inner outlaw began bubbling to the surface.

With Prohibition in effect, the country was "dry." Benny, like other prospecting businessmen, felt Americans deserved a drink, if they so chose. FBI records reveal that in 1924 Binion embarked in the moonshine trade, though it was probably even earlier than that. He moved contraband across the Rio Grande. Most of the whiskey and other goods were hauled across the river by pack mules and wagons. But you still had to know where to peddle it. Benny proved crafty in finding such places, including at a parking lot for a club. Benny knew they were hocking hooch out of a booth in the lot, so he would introduce himself to would-be buyers when they first arrived, tell them he would lead them to the spot, and take them to his own stock.

El Paso is also where he first "put in work," getting his hands dirty on the other end of a revolver. Not limiting himself to just bootlegging, Benny also committed several armed robberies, crimes he would never acknowledge even later in life, but rather deny with a wry smile. The Texas Rangers were swarming the area, but had little effect in the lawless region.

Benny *was* arrested several times, including twice on bootlegging charges. On one such occasion, he pulled the wool over the jailer's eyes and was able to get a duplicate skeleton cell key made. He proceeded not only to take back his own confiscated alcohol but also every other bottle of hootch in the evidence room.

Benny and the Big Man

After a short time out West, Benny decided to move back to familiar ground. He hightailed it back to Dallas. But now he was no longer a kid with holes in his britches scrounging for nickels and dimes. Now he was dressed to the nines with fancy dancing shoes and a derby hat. He had cash, but even more importantly, he had experience and knowledge of how the world of vice worked, and he was ready to make his mark.

By 1928, Benny progressed from bootlegging into the more lucrative numbers game. A numbers operation is like the lottery back in a time (like the 1920s) when there was no state lottery. Customers would pick numbers and buy them from various runners all over town. The winning numbers were generally selected from the outcome of a particular horse race that day.

As his numbers game began to grow and attract customers, Benny went to the big man in Dallas to ask for his blessing over his small numbers racket. Benny knew the score, and he was still too fresh to not pay his dues and operate without the blessing of the boss himself, Warren Diamond. Little did Benny know that he wasn't just playing the game properly, he was also about to find himself a father figure who would shape his approach to all his business ventures moving forward, a man whose advice Benny would carry with him to his dying days, and as such, forever shape how gambling operated in Dallas, Vegas, and beyond.

Warren was an incredibly intelligent, ambitious, and generous man who knew people, especially what got their adrenaline going. While he spent most of his young life on the straight and narrow, building a career in medicine, he quickly discovered that being a pharmacist wasn't near as alluring as being a big-time gambling boss. Quitting his profession, Diamond set up a dice game on a dirt lot behind the pharmacy on Camp Street near downtown Dallas. Making rookie operating mistakes, he was soon busted by the authorities. He received two years in the state penitentiary.

But instead of giving up a life of crime before it really got started, Warren came out with a fresh game plan. He learned from his mistakes. This time around would be different. He set up shop not in a vacant dirt lot, but in the most prestigious hotel in Dallas, the St. George. Diamond brought in business partners, muscle, spies, and couriers to conduct payoffs and grease the wheels of local law enforcement. Warren Diamond learned how to play the game, grew from it, and became a big fish in the pond of the Dallas underworld.

Never Turn Down a Bet

As he watched the young kid's operation grow, Diamond was intrigued by Binion's tenacity. He gave his blessing along with the kind notation that Benny would now be required to pay him a 25 percent cut of his revenue. Benny took the offer, knowing this wasn't a negotiation.

He also soon realized he both liked and admired Mr. Diamond, who was seemingly always willing to share support and a word of advice for the young upstart. Benny became a regular, hanging around the St. George, and Diamond took him under his wing. He saw a promising young talent amid his ranks. He schooled Benny in the art of the gambling business. Benny soaked up the wisdom, including Warren's most benevolent lesson:

NEVER TURN DOWN A BET.

It didn't matter how big, Diamond's dice games were always uncapped, no-limit. This was exactly the opposite of how other operators took wagers: They were stringent on their limits. Diamond's strict adherence to this policy is best encapsulated in a story that soon became the stuff of legend in Dallas, its lesson still rippling in backroom games in cities across the country and casinos in Vegas, Reno, Atlantic City, and everywhere millions are made off ambition and risk.

One evening an eager and successful businessman came into the St. George, filled with a little liquid courage. He threw an envelope stuffed with cash on the "pass line" and looked Diamond, who was on the floor, dead in the eye.

"Diamond! I'm going to make you look!" he declared as the workers and other gamblers looked on in stunned silence, waiting to see how Diamond would respond. There was no telling exactly how much money was stuffed in that envelope, but that it was bulging enough.

Cool and calm, Diamond simply replied, "Pass him the dice."

The man caught a point, but then missed it as the crowd around him gasped. The man turned and left without saying another word. Diamond opened the envelope and counted out $172,000. He put the money in his pocket and walked away from the table, telling everyone to get back to what they were doing. Benny was working that day. He was in the lobby, so he didn't see it firsthand, but he instantly heard about it and it stuck with him.

Never turn down a bet. Never limit a bet. Eventually, the house will win.

Benny on the Rise

Benny's policy racket continued to catch fire. Like a flame engulfing a field of dead broomweeds, he invaded the Dallas ghettos with his number runners. He would tell his men that this was where the real money was to be made. "These people are wishing and hoping on a

prayer, and we're just the people to give it to 'em," he said. They weren't in the numbers business; they were in the dream-making business. For some spare change (which wasn't really spare then), a person living in poverty could take a chance, and at least for a few hours that day, could dream that their magical numbers might just hit.

By the late 1920s, something shifted in the relationship between Benny and Diamond and things began to sour. Nobody really knows for certain what happened and Benny, in his later years, only ever spoke glowingly of his then deceased mentor. They saw less and less of each other and as Benny's business grew, he became less concerned about paying his respects and tribute to Diamond. He stopped hanging out at the St. George and started taking more risks in territories he would never have dared step foot in before. Diamond was aging and becoming more exhausted by the constant pressure of leading Dallas's premiere gambling organization. Benny, on the other hand, was just getting ramped up, and vice, and the opportunities to make serious money that it brings, waits for no man.

With his success operating the poor man's sweepstakes, Benny was infused with a new bravado and confidence. He made a move by opening his own craps game in the Southland Hotel just west of the Adolphus in the center of the action downtown. The Southland was owned at the time by Galveston mob boss Sam Maceo. Diamond didn't give his approval on Binion's move. But he was too wise to challenge his protégé at this point, so he stepped aside. Benny, being cold and calculating, saw the opening and took the incentive. Benny's entire gang moved into the Southland Hotel and became known as "The Southland Group."

A Diamond Fades

By just twenty-four years of age, Benny had blossomed from a toddler trading horses to an enterprising young boss involved in the bootleg and policy rackets, enjoying the energetic fruits of his labor.

Meanwhile, his old mentor was questioning life. Diamond, at age fifty-five, was in no mood for a midlife crisis. The man had it all—the cake, the icing, and the cherry on top. That's what makes the events on August 10, 1932 even more devastating.

Warren came home to his palace overlooking Turtle Creek around midday. His congenial wife greeted him at the front door. He said nothing to her as he passed, head down, and marched in a trance up the stairs. A bathroom door slammed shut. The next thing his wife heard was . . .

BLAM!

The echoes of gunfire reverberated throughout the mansion walls. Mrs. Diamond raced upstairs. She flew past the master bedroom into the bathroom. A nightmare of unfathomable proportions, her beloved husband lay on the cold tile floor in a pool of his own blood and brain matter. A revolver, still hot, was next to the body. Shrieks of terror rang out as she collapsed to the floor in tormenting pain.

What leads a man of this stature to commit such a heinous act? What pushes him to this point? What could make a king give up everything in such a desperate and violent way?

The answer is quite simply the cruelty of life, which often doesn't distinguish between good and evil, young and old, rich or poor.

Warren had gone to his doctor's office earlier that year for a prostate examination. The doctor had a hard time finding the right words but eventually they came out: Diamond had prostate cancer and it was terminal. From that time on, Diamond spent less time on his operations and more trying to find treatments in various hospitals and retreats. Despite his best efforts, he saw the writing on the wall. He had a granite mausoleum with a bronze, brass, and Italian marble interior constructed for himself. A tomb built for an emperor. He knew something was coming, he could feel it in his bones. He had grown tired of the racket, of the business, of life itself. His diagnosis was just confirmation of what he already knew.

It was time to pass the dice.

On the morning of August 10, Diamond found himself writhing in pain in St. Paul's Sanitarium in downtown Dallas. Again. Enough was enough. He forced himself to get up, get dressed, and get a cab. Warren Diamond wanted to die at home.

Death affects people in different ways. Benny was heartbroken. The kingpin, the father figure, the mentor, had abruptly decided he no longer wanted to live in this cruel world. The sadness was real, and it hurt. It was dejection like he had never experienced. The emotions became complicated, and grieving turned to aspiration. Benny exclaimed, "I don't miss nothing after I leave it," and he looked to the future.

Deep down, he understood there was no better way he could pay tribute to Warren Diamond.

A Cowboy Becomes a King

Benny continued to prove himself in the Big D underworld. With that came money, influence, and power, which he took advantage of with local authorities and politicians, who soon found themselves in the kid's pockets, which were lined with cash and benefits. Those connections kept Benny free and clear of the law. The open, no-limit games kept the gamblers in a frenzy, and the sweet-talking and cash-flowing kept the authorities satisfied. Keeping the competition in their place would require another set of tools from the toolbox.

In the dark and dirty world of gambling and vice, a player's rise to power attracts all manner of danger and demons who are looking for their own moment to strike and ascend the throne. The king must constantly watch his back, often forced to send a message to remind those underneath and on the periphery who is still in charge.

No one learned that lesson more than Ben Frieden.

At forty-six, Frieden appeared to be a model citizen. A transplant from California, he was married with a teenage son, Ben Jr., and had a nice home. He worked in the produce business, but soon got bored and went looking for ways to make a little extra dough. As such, he found the numbers game and decided he could run one better than he could play. So far, no problem, a person is entitled to find a little extra excitement in life and even be a little entrepreneurial in how he does so. But in the world of vice, there are rules to follow. The most important is not to step on the toes of the big hombres. If you do, and you're lucky enough to get a warning, you'd best adhere to it.

Frieden had started making a few moves on Benny's territory, and he had been warned. A man emerged from the shadows one night in early 1936 as Frieden was getting into his car and shot him in the hand. The man was suspected to work for Benny. Still, here Friedman was, six months later, sitting in his Pontiac outside the Pride of Dallas café. He was in a Black neighborhood that fell under Benny's kingdom. A young Black man leaned in and handed him a paper bag full of money and policy slips.

The problem for Frieden was that Benny and one of his most cold-blooded muscle men, Harlis "Buddy" Malone, had been out checking business in the neighborhood and witnessed the whole thing.

Upon seeing the exchange, Benny yelled out a "Goddammit!" and both he and Malone jumped out of Benny's Cadillac. They both pulled out their guns: Malone, a .45 pistol and for Benny, his trusted .38. As they approached, they saw a smiling Frieden in the back seat, pocketing the money and talking to his chauffer, most likely telling him where to go next. As mad as a hellhound, Benny reached in the open window and slapped Frieden, yelling, "You son of a bitch!"

Then they opened fire, both Binion and Malone shooting from opposite ends of the car, riddling Frieden with bullets and a strong

lesson he would take with him on his journey to the great beyond just moments later.

Benny and Buddy fled the scene, ironically leaving the bag with the cash and slips behind. The cops who showed up found the money, a gun that had fired one bullet on Frieden's lap, and a chauffeur who was too rattled to share any useful information. They also found Frieden's dead body.

Later that day, Benny surrendered with a high-powered attorney at his side to a police station that was well lubed with Benny's money. He showed the officers a scratch under his armpit, saying it came from Frieden's gun and that he had shot back in self-defense. With dramatic flair, he told the police, "I'm lucky to be here!" Malone turned himself in not long after. Both were indicted for murder, but within months the case was dropped for lack of evidence. Benny was never too shy in bragging about getting away with that one.

It's good to be the king.

Reporting on the killing, the papers questioned whether this was the start of an official gang war in Dallas. It wasn't. In order for that to happen, Benny, the young dreamer who was now *the* cowboy in Dallas, would need a much bigger rival, one equally ambitious and dangerous and without fear.

He would be coming soon enough.

CHAPTER 5
THE CAT

The midday sun crept overhead, already boiling for early summer. Sweat poured from the paramedic's forehead. He feverishly tested the vitals, pressed on the chest, and tried to resuscitate the breathing of the struggling male laying prone on the concrete. Blood flowed through the victim's body like a sieve and left a trail on the concrete where he had tried to crawl away from his attackers. The paramedic could tell that blood was going to leave a stain, as was the crime itself, another broad daylight murder on the streets of Dallas.

From the steps of the Dallas National Bank, a throng of onlookers circled around the emergency medical technicians with hands covering their hearts and mouths. Their eyes wallowed in dread. The paramedics motioned for the crowd to part as they wheeled the stretcher down the steps. A violent and bizarre scene had impacted and forever changed their simple lives, but little if any words were being spoken.

Blood zig-zagged its way down the steps even after the body had been removed. More dripped from the gurney. There was a lot of damn blood, more than one body should carry.

Inside the bank, a repugnant and well-known (at least by authorities) hoodlum named Ivy Miller was being cuffed by officers. He had been followed into the bank by a plainclothes police officer after the shooting. When the cop cornered him, he made no trouble. He calmly dropped his gun and said, "I'm ready. I'm not going anywhere." It was

chilling how cool he was now, just minutes after violently sending another man to his grave. The officer, who assuredly told this tale at family gatherings and social events till his own passing, made the arrest and quietly escorted Miller away through a side door.

The slaying of Sam Murray shook the Dallas underworld to its core. Everybody in that scene was aware of Murray and his control over South Dallas gambling. They also knew he had a history of violence and a penchant for stepping on the toes of other bad men. It didn't come as too much of a surprise that Murray had met his Maker full of lead.

What *was* surprising was who was missing from the scene and why . . .

The Aristocratic Gambler

The "who" was Herbert Noble, Murray's top bodyguard and an ambitious racketeer in his own right. The "why" is a bit more complicated. Short answer: greed. The longer answer would become more evident over the years as Herbert Noble became the man he was destined to be, riding a meteoric rise to power in the void left behind by Murray and setting himself into a merciless showdown with our other antihero Benny Binion that would forever change the streets of Dallas, the world of organized crime, and the profession of gambling.

No matter the game, every player needs a rival, and Herbert Noble filled that role for Benny with aplomb. Unlike many of his contemporaries, he was no Neanderthal of a gangland boss. He was smooth as porcelain, like the voice of Rudolph Valentino or Ginger Rogers gliding across the dance floor. He brought glitz and glam to the game. The man preferred Monets and Picassos hanging from his walls rather than Roy Rogers and Trigger. He dressed razor sharp in camel hair coats and imported Italian silk scarfs. Herbert carried himself with an air of autocracy, head held high, chest out, brimming

with confidence. He was known around town by his moniker, "The Aristocratic Gambler." He was in fact a *NOBLE*.

He opened the doors to one of the swankiest gambling joints in Dallas: The Airmen's Club. It was an aberration in its sophistication. Herbert took the city by storm with the club, and his forward thinking in the world of gambling was unparalleled. Others could sit back, take notes, and learn the ABCs of becoming a casino kingpin from him.

Noble's importance to this story sits at the mountaintop. He is a key spoke in the wheel of it all, a starred section in the story of crime and violence in Dallas. The problem was Herbert didn't sit alone. He sat at one end of the table while his overbearing counterpart Benny Binion sat at the other. What happens when you get two ambitious, savvy, obsessive men with no fear and a penchant for violence trying to survive and thrive in the same town?

Chaos.

It was this bloodthirsty rivalry between Benny Binion and Herbert Noble that ultimately put Dallas organized crime in the national spotlight.

The Birth of a Rival

There was nothing ritzy about Herbert's early upbringing. In 1917, his family settled on the west bank of the Trinity River known as the West Dallas slums. Born in Palo Pinto County, Texas, Herbert was nine years old when his family relocated to the west side of Dallas. He was raised in a clapboard shack with no running water or electricity. His parents weren't around, and Herbert was left to fend for himself. He did, however, have the distinction of sharing the neighborhood with the most vile and ruthless killers ever to come out of Texas, including Clyde Barrow and Bonnie Parker. In fact, some of his closest childhood pals would spend their last breaths strapped to an electric chair.

Herbert had book smarts, which led him to be an analytical-thinking young man. He made it all the way through school until he turned sixteen, which makes him one of the most educated of all our forefathers in Texas poker history. After dropping out, Noble became a truck driver for Sims Refinery. He was getting his first taste of the "oily" lifestyle. It was a precursor to his future. Nothing clean, all dirty.

After a short spell driving trucks, Herbert set out for the gold, the black gold. He ventured into the East Texas oil fields. He found himself in the same section where such legendary gushers as the Daisy Bradford blew out, showering a rain of crude on exuberant speculators below. Herbert took to the oil patch, where he worked as a roughneck on cable tool oil drilling rigs. He became a derrick man, engaging in the backbreaking and life-endangering work. He slaved from one drilling camp to another. The boom towns weren't for the faint of heart. It was a cutthroat world full of cutthroat characters who would just as soon, well, cut your damn throat as look at you.

Trying to stay alive and survive the Depression era in Texas, Herbert kept movin' and groovin'. He made a geographic change from East Texas and worked in the oil fields of West Texas. He worked the rigs while he also made it a goal to learn everything he could about all things mechanical, especially automobiles and airplanes. Noble became a respected engineer. But he wasn't getting filthy rich; he was just getting filthy. He kept breathing air, however, and that was the important thing.

Herbert always managed to keep his nose clean . . . that is until 1932, when he first ran afoul of the law. Or at least first got caught. Herbert was busted for stealing hubcaps with cars still attached: grand theft auto. The judge, unsympathetic to a man who was just doing what he had to do to make a few more bucks, threw the book at him, but luckily Herbert ducked and received only a two-year suspended sentence.

Still, the experience taught him a valuable lesson: Discretion was key. Herbert would keep a low profile and stay off all radars. He

once told a reporter, "I've done things I am not proud of," but he never elaborated. Those who dug into his past could find little, if anything at all. It wouldn't be until much later in his life, after so much death, that Noble would drop this key to self-preservation and go off the deep end. The young Herbert Noble knew well enough that if he was going to make anything of himself, especially in the type of business he was gaining an interest in, he would have to do it outside the prying eyes of the law.

It wasn't long until Herbert found himself frustrated with life in the oil patch. He had dollar signs in his eyes. He didn't want to only survive, he wanted to provide for his new family in a meaningful way. He had married his childhood sweetheart Mildred Bowers in 1930. They had a daughter, Freda. Growing up in a world consumed with poverty and surrounded by notorious outlaws, Mildred and his daughter were his bright spot in a dark world. He was burning up with ambition; a white-hot glow of aura surrounded him like a lighthouse in the fog. One thing for sure, Noble was searching for greener and cleaner pastures.

Noble Finds a Mentor

Herbert returned to Dallas with his family, moving into the posh neighborhood of Oak Cliff. It was in Dallas that he became acquainted with the city's other top gambling kingpin, the only man who could rival Benny Binion.

Sam Murray.

Sam started at the bottom of the crime pond as a minnow. Working his way up from being a pimp, bootlegger, and small-time local bookmaker, he scratched, clawed, fought, and worse to get to where he was at the top. Sam was an adrenaline junkie who craved speed, dirt bikes, and horses as his drugs of choice. He had grown to prominence with a nationally syndicated horse-wire service that posted odds,

results, and racing data from every major horse track in the country. All bookies in North Texas had to align themselves with Murray and pay to play to receive access to his service. His franchised wire service was a vital necessity for any sports bookmaker. The cash it threw off allowed Murray an entry into other gambling enterprises.

When Noble came to town, Murray was operating a casino inside the Santa Paula Hotel. Noble gained entry and was soon working as a card dealer, then a dealing supervisor, and quickly escalated to a pit boss position. Herbert was capable on many fronts. He proved himself within the organization by "putting in work," providing muscle and enforcement duties. He was a quick learner to the racket and had no delusions about his responsibilities. He was a man with brains and brawn—a dual threat.

Noble was enamored with Murray's lifestyle and his operation. Here was a man who owned several ranches and cars, had a beautiful young wife, and commanded a small army on the streets. Herbert studied his predecessor's moves and thought process, like a budding chess pro taking in secret lessons from a grandmaster. Herbert digested the game like no one else. He was learning not only when to move to the knight but most importantly *why* to move to the knight, when to make a sacrifice, and when to say "checkmate."

While Noble and Binion were similar in their roles as protégées with mentors, there was a striking difference. Binion and Diamond had a sympathetic, father/son quality to their relationship. Noble and Murray were not as emotionally bonded. Noble had proven himself as a man of respect and loyalty. He was a tough son of a gun who was an asset to any criminal syndicate. Murray allowed him into his inner sanctum because Noble was such a valuable player. The backbone of a successful operation is built and preserved with the likes of individuals like Herbert Noble. However, their relationship was built around business and not empathetic ties.

Noble saw Murray not only as a boss, mentor, and teacher but also as a ticket to a potentially grander prize. Murray saw Noble as

a rising star with a cool head on his shoulders who didn't mind getting his hands dirty. They had gone from mud to blood, and he was fine with both.

Sam felt he always needed this new power around him and brought Herbert in as his personal bodyguard. He continued to partake in his relegated duties, but now Herbert was escorting Sam to pertinent business meetings and helping keep his schedule. The symbiotic trust was building between the two men. They needed each other.

Doing Business in Dallas

Gambling, although illegal, was a well-established fixture in Dallas from the 1920s to the mid-1940s. Many of the games took place in hotels such as the St. George, Santa Paula, and the Southland, using large suites. Millions of dollars changed hands weekly whether through craps, numbers, slot machines, or policy wheels. During the Depression, Dallas tax receipts dropped precipitously. The city fathers came up with a plan: Each week, the police would raid the gambling operations and count heads. The next day the operators, or their attorneys, would go to City Hall, plead guilty, and pay a fine of $10 per head. These "fines" totaled from $150,000 to $200,000 annually, making up the shortfall. Thus began the symbiotic relationship between the city and its gamblers, who saw it as a cost of doing business.

The real threat to the high-flying gamblers was not from the law but from "hijackers." Players didn't trust banks. Consequently, they were sitting ducks, just waiting to be robbed traveling to and from games. To alleviate this, some top-of-the-line ball breakers were hired to tame the herd. This meant savage men like Jim Clyde Thomas, Tincy Eggleston, Lois Green . . .

. . . and Ivy Miller.

The vice trade in Big D was as perilous as a prick to the pecker. Hundreds of grifters, gamblers, and other unsavory types were met

with a murderous end each year. Many were only trying to survive until sunset on the day at hand. They had no aspirations or goals of living years into the future. Breathing air was a luxury. Here today, gone tomorrow.

The Mafia was primarily centered in the northeast but had families in major metropolitan cities scattered throughout the United States. During this period, the Marcello family (headed by Carlos Marcello) was based in New Orleans, and Dallas fell under this territory. However, the Dallas underworld was way too wide open to be under direct control. It was a hot commodity; a western expansion of one of the fastest-growing cities only made sense. Taking control would take some major wrangling to get the key players to fall in line. A daunting task; you would have better odds taking a ride on the *Titanic* . . . or playing *against* Titanic! But sometimes, you can get the lucky hit you need.

Or you can make your own luck.

An Orchestrated Plan

By all accounts June 14, 1940, started with plenty of promise. Sam Murray was now fifty-four and on top of the world with an ever-expanding empire. Sam considered himself untouchable, and perhaps that's why he wasn't as concerned when his right-hand man Herbert Noble informed him he wouldn't be able to accompany him while he dealt with some family matters.

Sam and his starlet wife Sue left their rural paradise that morning and drove into Dallas. He dropped Sue at Niemen Marcus for a shopping spree then cruised by himself to the Dallas National Bank. Sam parked and went into the bank to handle his business. At ten thirty AM, Sam strolled out the front doors of the bank. As he descended the front steps, he was met face-to-face with Ivy Miller,

the big-boned and well-known killer dressed in his Sunday best with a blue blazer, slacks, tie, and straw hat.

Miller offered no pleasantries to Murray and didn't leave time for Murray to offer any of his own. As soon as the local crime boss took his last step down the outdoor stairs of the bank, Miller retrieved his .38 caliber automatic pistol from his waistband. He pulled the trigger as fast as the gun would fire. Murray tried to run, but he was pelted with six shots.

BANG. BANG. BANG. BANG. BANG. BANG.

Miller emptied the chamber with four slugs into the gut, one in the back, and one in the left leg.

Jack Kilgore, a teenage street peddler selling gardenias, was hit in the left leg by a stray bullet. He was located after the melee, petrified and laying between two parked cars. He would eventually make a full recovery and receive $750 from Miller for his troubles.

Miller attempted to keep on shooting even as the gun was clearly out of ammo. Witnesses would later claim the pistol sounded like a machine gun firing. He then headed for the entrance of the bank. The crowd scattered like a covey of quail.

Murray lay bleeding on the bank steps.

When Miller was cornered by bank detectives, he said Murray had threatened him and his family. Later, his attorneys would say the dispute was over livestock. The detectives claimed it sounded like a lot of bull!

Paramedics rushed Murray to Parkland Hospital where a few hours later he would be pronounced dead, ending an era of a local legend and not surprisingly, ridding Benny Binion of a key rival.

While Murray's death was a mystery, the ten-million-dollar question on everyone's mind that day was where was his trusty bodyguard, number one shooter, and tough guy extraordinaire Herbert Noble?

The police weren't that interested in solving cases of criminals killing criminals. Hell, it made their job easier. Charges against Miller

were soon stunningly dropped for "lack of evidence." However, the murder created a ripple effect in the DFW underworld pond. Whispers and finger-pointing began to circulate. Who would orchestrate such a dastardly deed? Who could? Who had what to gain and why?

Word soon spread that Noble wasn't with Murray and that Noble was also one of, if not the only person, who knew where Murray would be that day. How did Miller know? It didn't take long for people to put two and two together, especially after the events of the months following Murray's death. It made perfect sense for Binion and Noble to work in conjunction. For the conspiracy to work, they needed to make certain that Miller could get to Murray without his top gun interfering. With Noble politely making himself unavailable that morning, he put the finger on his boss. Miller, a street-savvy killer, had plenty of notches in his belt and it was also no secret he was a Binion associate.

The pieces fell into place. The coup d'état was successful.

This hit ushered in the opportunity for new leadership. Guess who was ready to step up. Within days of the assassination, Herbert had seized control and taken over operations at Santa Paula Hotel. A few weeks later, he was seated alone at the head of the Murray organization. No one challenged or questioned his leadership. He swooped in and inserted himself as boss uncontested and unchallenged . . . and business boomed.

With Benny Binion getting his piece.

The Airmen's Club

By 1943, Herbert augmented the business by extending operations into the Majestic, Rose, and Savoy hotels. He and a fellow partner purchased the Santa Paula Hotel. A nice move, adding a layer of legitimacy to his holdings. Noble wasn't allowing any flies to congregate rent free around his head.

He kept up a fierce pace. In 1945, he opened The Airmen's Club, a destination that would soon be known as Dallas's premiere gambling club. A highfalutin, swanky nightspot with the ultimate casino experience. It was no sawdust joint; The Airmen's Club was posh with the finest amenities. Located in the heart of downtown, it became the prominent playground of the elite. A variety of casino games were available plus a private poker room that included Draw and Stud games. Notable players such as Titanic Thompson, Johnny Moss, and Nick "The Greek" all made the pilgrimage to be a part of the booming hot spot. The action was nonstop with oil tycoons, lawyers, business empresarios, and politicians coming in from all sections of the state. The spigot was turned on and the money flowed. It appeared the well would never run dry.

Herbert Noble had escalated from a midlevel operator to one of the city's most powerful racketeers. He had morphed into his alter ego; he was no longer a tool pusher on an oil rig, a roughneck in coveralls covered in grime. He was a man among men dressed in the finest linens that money could buy. Gone were the days of surviving by the river in a clapboard shack with no money or food. Now he was buying ranches and big spreads. His home base was the Diamond M (named after his adoring wife Mildred), a ranch in Denton County. If he wanted to light one of his fireplaces, he could burn some of his cash as kindling. He had plenty. He built a runway with hangars on the Diamond M and purchased several planes, following another of his passions. Herbert Noble had officially transitioned into The Aristocratic Gambler.

Meanwhile, across town, Benny Binion had an unsettling feeling in his gut.

CHECK

To bet nothing, passing action to the next player.

CHAPTER 6
THE RIVALRY

The rolling hills of East Texas were dotted with a culmination of pines and oaks. The bottomland gave way to rich black fertile soil. In the midst of this luscious paradise, a series of wooden derricks sprung up, invading the landscape in search of the crude that pooled below the surface. The East Texas oil field had come to life in the late 1920s. Men came from all walks of life to risk life and limb and make their fortune.

In one of the camps, a drilling rig sits idle. Several tents are scattered on the perimeter.

A pair of western boots clomps through the rainy puddles. The cowboy wearing the boots follows a driller toward a tent a few hundred feet behind the oil rig. The driller peels back the front flaps on the canvas tent.

"There ya go, Mr. Binion, they been playing for hours."

Benny lowers his head and enters the tent. The driller can be heard in the background. "I'm running all their asses off if they don't get back to work when the pipe arrives." Benny smirks.

A handful of roughnecks on their hands and knees are collected around one another in a tight semicircle. Money is scattered on the floor in front of them. The voracious cheer and yelling of the men signal excitement in the air. A rip-roaring dice game is in high gear! Benny knows this sound, knows this game. It reminds him of his youth, when a clever kid could make a couple extra bucks and earn himself a reputation with the wrong crowd. Benny has seen this setup a hundred times, but he finds his eyes instantly drifting to the shooter. There's something about him, something intriguing and perhaps a little unsettling.

The shooter is covered in oil, mud, and sludge. He's the filthiest of the bunch. The only clear spots on him are the whites around his eyes. No doubt, he is a grease monkey deluxe.

He shakes up the dice in both his crusty palms, blows on them, and the tent becomes deathly quiet. The dice come tumbling out of his hands onto the floor and ricochet off a cardboard box.

A four and a three. Seven. A winner.

There is an explosion of frenzied jubilation. Hollering and cheering at deafening levels within the confines of the small tent. A few losers sit back sullen with closed eyes. The scalding hot shooter scoops up wads of bills and coins on the tent floor.

Benny smiles as he takes in the action. A roughneck pats him on the shoulder and exclaims, "Damn shooter is hotter than a whore in church on Sunday."

"Is that right?"

"Hell yeah, he's hit sixteen points in a row."

Benny perks up. Sixteen? He nudges his way through the workers and sticks his hand out. "Hey there, shooter . . . Benny Binion." The befuddled shooter looks up from his cash. One mud- caked hand squeezes the bills tightly, while the other slowly rises to grasp Benny's with a firm shake.

"Herbert Noble."

There's a slight but powerful pause in that brief exchange. It's the moment that fate decides they will meet again, that they will be a part of each other's lives. For better and definitely for worse. It skips along just as quickly as it comes and the energy shifts back. The two men nod at each other and gaze for one last half second into the abyss of their pupils. Then it's back to the action. Destiny can wait . . .

This Town Ain't Big Enough

As Sam Murray was laid to rest in 1938, that brief but friendly encounter in the oil field tent a decade earlier must have seemed like a million years ago. Benny was no longer trading horses with holes

in his britches and Herbert was no longer layered in grime, floating from one oil camp to another. Both men sat atop their respected organizations. What started as curiosity and eventually became respect was now quickly turning to something else.

Unease.

Both men were scratching their heads when it came to each another. Benny wasn't certain what he had created with Herbert. Especially after the hit on Murray. While he had appreciated the help, it was apparent that Noble could never be trusted. Benny valued loyalty and Noble couldn't give him that. Meanwhile, Benny was simply not the kind of man Noble could respect . . . in any capacity. Be it appearance, manner of speaking, and most importantly, how he ran his business. Noble knew he could do it better. That he *would* do it better.

The egos swelled and when that happens with powerful men, danger follows.

Following Warren Diamond's suicide, Benny didn't wallow in despair. He came to grips with his grief and quickly refocused his energy on the business at hand. He was now the head honcho of his outfit. It was his throne, his mantle, and his crown (Stetson) to wear. Benny set up his Southland Syndicate headquarters in a suite at the Southland Hotel, the location of his highest-grossing casino operation. It was Benny's top spot and heralded as the most profitable illegal gambling establishment in Dallas.

That was until The Airmen's Club began to take off and spread its wings.

Binion controlled more than 80 percent of the policy games in Dallas County. He also controlled the horse racing wire service. The Southland Syndicate owned and operated numerous casinos that operated out of hotels across the city. The Cowboy was regarded as a gambler's gambler. He ran an honest game. Players knew they could expect the games to be fair when playing at Binion's joints. His no-limit betting set him apart from the pack. It established his bravado

and steel balls' philosophy toward casino management. A prognostic leadership quality that was progressive, especially for the 1940s.

Benny had inserted himself as the boss gambler. He immersed himself with connections to lawyers, judges, business leaders, politicians. Many were regulars at his games, as were their friends and relatives. He built relationships and fostered his role with city officials and authorities. He became a pillar of the community and pillars not only offer support, they also receive it.

There were times somebody would come around with a big swinging dick and claim they planned to cut down on the illegal operations in the city, but it was often nothing more than hot air. Everyone knew that like it or not, Benny was bringing business to the city and in turn, filling the coffers. Money was flowing in, by the millions.

While Benny ran a strict and unbreakable monopoly on the policy rackets in Dallas, he would let other gamblers set up craps games . . . if and only if he was getting 25 percent of their action. What Benny didn't respect was encroachment from competitors. That type of behavior could put a man in a pine box. Benny wanted it all. What little he didn't have seemed to point back to Herbert Noble. On top of that, Herbert was growing at an alarming rate and appeared poised to take a bigger bite out of Benny's apple.

Somebody needed to remind that son of a bitch who the actual king of the jungle was, and they needed to remind him fast.

Polar Opposites

Noble was on top of the world, living high on the hog. Anything and everything he had ever dreamed of was at his fingertips. But even as Herbert lathered in his new success, all was not exactly rosy. His world had a dark cloud that loomed on top of him, becoming more ominous every day. This cloud's name was Benny Binion. For

Noble to reach the sunny-day success he aspired to, Binion's cloud needed to be broken up.

It was clear right from the start that there would be no negotiating. The two men respected one another as much as two rhinos on a plain. Noble was the classic nemesis for a man of Binion's temperament. He was tall, suave, and debonair. A man who dressed to kill. A sophisticated leader, the well-read Renaissance man who was a lover of the arts. Binion was dumpy, paunchy, and uneducated, a proud graduate of the school of hard knocks. He was loud, crass, and didn't give a shit what people thought about him. Or anything having to do with the arts. His art was making money. Noble's was too; he just wanted to bring a little class to the craft.

Once Noble took control of Murray's operation, his and Benny's relationship was one of business and mutuality. Herbert had quickly ascended from a minnow to a tiger shark in the crime pond. But Benny was the killer whale. Noble, like the rest of the gambling fraternity, had to suck in his pride, kiss the ring, and pay the customary percentage of profits in tribute each month to Benny. This agreement was copasetic and nonnegotiable.

Despite Herbert loyally paying his 25 percent, the animosity between the two rising giants continued to bubble under the surface. Benny couldn't let it go; he didn't like the action Herbert was pulling. And the eager and ambitious Herbert started to question why he had to treat Benny like his superior, especially as his Airmen's Club became *the* place for Dallas poker.

Tensions escalated between the two rivals and their massive egos. Herbert's expansion continued to proliferate like a wildfire swallowing up a forest. He struggled with the fact that this doughy, illiterate, obnoxious ranch hand was more powerful than he was and that he had to constantly kiss his ass. He was jealous of Benny's power and political influence. He wanted what Benny had, and he thought he deserved it. The seething and scathing between The Cowboy and The Aristocratic Gambler were becoming more

evident every day. A perturbed Herbert kept his mouth shut but his eyes open for the right opportunity to present itself.

That opportunity arrived in the form of Raymond Laudermilk.

A Precursor to War

Ray was a dashing tough guy with the chiseled features of a movie star. He could have filled in as Humphrey Bogart's stunt double and never missed a beat. Laudermilk came from the mean streets of Dallas. He was no turd wrangler from the cotton fields. He was raised on the asphalt, and he knew the code of the streets. Ray worked his way up the ranks with Benny, and they were close. Binion respected Ray's tenacity to split wigs and bust heads. Laudermilk could also write a dissertation on the policy business. He knew the racket from the inside out. He had started his juvenile delinquent career as a numbers runner and eventually moved into muscle and enforcement duties.

When The Cowboy took over the reins of the Southland Syndicate, Ray came along. The enterprise was a well-oiled machine. Ray remained a trusted member of Benny's inner sanctum, a loyal lieutenant who had risen to the number three position in the organization. He oversaw all policy wheel business. To say Ray was a key player in Binion's empire is an understatement. Benny depended on him. If there was any bit of contention between them, it was that Ray would occasionally broach the subject of running his own game with Benny, who would quickly shoot it down. Benny wanted to keep tight control of things and wasn't a fan of men thinking they could do what he did. The asking bothered Benny, and the rejection bothered Ray.

Still, their relationship and the bond remained strong until Ray decided to take a trip . . . with Sue Murray.

Sue was Sam Murray's vivacious bombshell widow. She had taken a liking to Ray following her husband's death. The couple headed west to the Pacific Coast; a collusion of sun, sand, and sweaty sheets that eventually led to marriage. Sue, now Ray's wife, had some thoughts on how Ray could get his own policy operation going, even without Benny's blessing. It only takes a simple suggestion to blossom into a full-fledged idea. In this case, it was the match that was being scratched to eventually light the fuse to a powder keg.

Sue was shrewd, and she had learned much about the policy business from her late husband. She still had connections with several of Sam's cronies. It wasn't that far-fetched to think that the two of them could run a highly profitable numbers operation of their own. Ray, while in the throes of love-making madness, let this idea mull around in his mind. The more he thought about it, the more ambitious and realistic the idea became. They just needed a little capital investment to put their plan in motion.

Ray already knew from firsthand experience that their plan would not sit well with Benny. Killer whales don't prefer other predators in the waters. Speaking of, Ray and Sue knew there was another prospective suitor, and he might just have the internal fortitude.

Herbert Noble.

Herbert listened and couldn't partner fast enough with the newlyweds. While he was making a killing with his craps and casino operations, he knew the policy racket would elevate him to a new level of supremacy. One that might possibly put him on equal footing with Binion.

Ray treaded lightly when he approached his boss once again about running his own game. Benny did have a true fondness and respect for Ray. He had, after all, been as solid as granite. Once on a felony gambling case, Ray had refused to testify against Benny and he had received a hefty fine and some jail time. But this was

different. As expected, the boss wasn't happy with the latest ask. Benny tried to sugarcoat his "no" by giving Ray a raise and eventually a piece of the policy action. This was unheard of from Binion.

Ray politely turned him down.

The Cowboy was irritated. But when he found out that Ray had the financial backing of Noble, that irritation turned to rage. This was now a flat-out betrayal. Benny's top men knew his growing dislike for Noble, and his concern with his aggressive ambition. Noble wasn't shy about poking around and even dipping his toes in Benny's territories. He was pushing the line for sure. Now he had essentially taken one of Benny's top men and flipped him. This was something Benny couldn't let pass.

Somebody had to pay.

On March 19, 1943, Ray Laudermilk sat alone, idling in his car parked across the street from the Ambassador Hotel, contemplating how he could get more money to fuel his slow-starting business and what he could do to salvage his already flailing relationship with Sue. Mostly, though, he was keeping his eyes peeled for any suspicious activity. He knew all the top hitters for the Southland Syndicate, and he had heard rumblings that a price had been put on his head. He still struggled to believe it was true.

An impromptu meeting that had been called left Laudermilk frazzled. Who set up this meeting and why? All Ray knew was that he still had obligations to Benny and he had better show. He had pushed the boss enough by defying him and setting up his own game; no need to poke the bear further. Ray was thirty-six years old and had bigger plans. He just needed to get right by his boss and his wife, and then all would be back on track.

At nine PM the scraggly and scrappy Bob Minyard exited the front doors of the Ambassador Hotel. He walked directly toward Ray's parked car across the street. Laudermilk knew the unsuspecting small-time gambler who lived at the hotel and worked for Binion. He was no threat; Ray rolled the window down to speak to the

errand boy. As he looked up, before he could even get a word out, the first shot rang out.

BLAM!

Six more would follow as Bob unloaded his .45 automatic, ripping apart Ray's flesh. As soon as the final shot was fired, Bob jumped into another car that pulled alongside Ray's and sped off into the night.

Ray lay curled up dead in the passenger seat, his body riddled with bullet holes. A shattered man with shattered dreams.

Minyard soon turned himself in, saying that he and Ray had been having some issues.

"I shot him a few minutes ago."

Benny sent one of his top attorneys, and Minyard walked after paying a $10,000 bond. Despite promises from authorities to prosecute quickly, there were too many players on the "right" side of the law who were partnered with Binion and the case kept getting put off for years. All the while, Minyard moved up the ranks in Benny's operation. He had done his part.

Now he would be put in a position that would further escalate the growing tension between Binion and Noble.

The word spread of the murder like a dam had burst. The death signaled tumultuous times for the Dallas underworld. Raymond Laudermilk is a key player to this story because he put Binion and Noble one step closer on a collision course in a zero-sum game.

THE FLOP

Three cards dealt faceup by the dealer to be used in all players' hands.

CHAPTER 7
WAR PART 1

Herbert Noble did his best to digest the news. It hit like a wasp sting on the balls. The murder of Ray Laudermilk was a message sent loud and clear. A message to Noble.

Know your place.

Noble's dreams of a high-dollar policy racket went to the grave with Ray. Herbert subsequently shut the policy business down soon after the funeral. It was a safe play, the tough concession Herbert needed to make to keep the "Cowboy Don" from coming completely unhinged. Noble had a keen enough intellect to see the writing on the wall, and it was smeared in blood. No need to stoke the fire. It was time to let the embers die down.

For now.

But Herbert didn't have to be happy about it. He was fuming and had no problem sharing his frustration with anyone in earshot. Whatever respect Noble had for Binion went out the window after Laudermilk was gunned down. After a short period of laying low, Herbert refocused his energy and went back to doing what he did best: bringing in the bacon. With a newfound focus, Herbert didn't just shake the money tree, he shook the whole damn orchard. He soon realized that this was the best way to stick it to Benny and he was more than willing to poke, jab, and even thrust when needed. With each success, each dollar earned, Noble's ego grew.

When asked about this time in his gambling business life, a time when things were just about to set off, Noble remarked simply,

"I paid the man protection money. My business grew and he didn't like the competition."

It was a clear indication of his philosophy on dealing with Binion. As Noble's operation continued to swell, he felt less inclined to be a lieutenant of Binion's. Instead, he saw himself as an equal, if not the better man. He was the boss of his own borgata. The questions soon started to swirl, each one about Binion, further fueling a dangerous obsession. Why should he have to pay tribute? Why couldn't he start his policy games back up? Why should he be afraid of a lesser man who was ineffective in how he handled his business? Why should he have to bow down to this rodeo clown playing God? Many a colleague, employee, or friend who mentioned Benny to Noble would get the same response.

"Fuck him."

Still, Noble sat tight, picking here and there at Benny's territories, but not trying to rock the boat too much. When that time came, it would have to be a cautious and calculated move, one made with precision, one built on logic and not emotion.

That was the plan, anyway.

Pushing and Pressing

Benny continued to become obsessed with Noble, the only man to cross his path who he thought could actually one day be a threat. He kept a keen eye on his rise, especially his own customers who were heading across town to Noble's packed, high-action games. Right now, the dent Noble was putting in his pocketbook was still small, but if there was one rule in the Big D, it was that you didn't mess with The Cowboy's dough. What's his was his and nobody was gonna take it. Not now, not ever. Especially not someone like Herbert Noble.

"Who does his highfalutin' sumbitch think he is?"

Noble's tributes were still trickling in. Benny was concerned that Herbert might be shortchanging him on the tribute payments. Was it true or just his own paranoia? The answer is probably both. It didn't matter anyway, not to Benny. What he thought, what he said, was the truth, no questions asked, and the anxiety and angst began to eat away at him. You let one insubordination slide, the next thing you know, you have a mutiny on your hands.

Benny had a solution, one that would help alleviate his concerns and send another message to a man who seemed to not be taking The Cowboy serious enough for his liking. Benny decided to insert his own man in Noble's biggest count room.

That man was none other than Bob Minyard.

In the aftermath of the Laudermilk slaying, Bob had propelled himself from the outhouse to the penthouse. Once surviving in a simple hotel room living week to week, he was now freewheeling in luxury with cash to blow. He shot up from a low-level gambler—guarding dice games and committing petty street crimes—to a partner in one of the most profitable casinos in the city: the Majestic Hotel.

Herbert's Majestic Hotel.

Not only would Bob take on this big task for the big boss, he would be rewarded with a free percentage interest in the Majestic Hotel games. Minyard would serve as Benny's eyes and ears, keeping an accurate assessment of the accounting. That would show that slick fancy pants son of a buck. You want to try and partner up and take my money? Well, I'll shoot that down and show ya the gun. Noble would be getting a new business partner all right, whether he wanted one or not.

On January 1, 1946, Benny had one of his minions break the news that Minyard, the dirty peckerwood, would now be joining Herbert's crew at the Majestic. Bob would be supervising the hard count. Not the kind of news a man wants to wake up to on New Year's Day. Herbert sent the man packing with a message of his own for Benny.

"I can count my own damn money, and I don't need your help running my business."

A Man Has Limits

Benny retorted that it was nonnegotiable.

For his initial defiance (and because Noble's casinos were soon becoming enormous profit generators), Benny pressed even harder. If he was gonna teach a lesson, Benny wasn't a stick-and-carrot kinda guy. He was stick and bigger stick. Soon after Minyard took his post, Benny ordered a couple of his knockaround guys to visit the Majestic. The intimidating baboons delivered the message to Herbert that the cost of doing business had just gone up. He would now be required to pay a tribute of 40 percent as opposed to the customary 25. It was the best way to exact revenge on The Aristocratic Gambler and his lucrative Airmen's Club. Benny, ever the slick and wise businessman, knew exactly what he was doing. It was time for a pissing contest with that fruitcake, and he knew who had the bigger dick.

A salty Noble felt like he was being drenched in a golden shower. What type of hard-headed bastard would call for such ludicrous measures? Herbert considered his options. He contemplated his nemesis. It was detrimental to your health to cross The Cowboy. A refusal would definitely spell more trouble, and he wasn't sure he was in a position to fight. But he reluctantly backed away from every fight with Benny before, and that hick just kept throwing more at him. When was it going to end? Ever? No, Noble refused to be a whipped mule anymore.

After a few moments of intense soul-searching, Herbert responded, "Benny Binion can go to hell!"

Enough was enough. Noble had too much courage, too much backbone, and too much lead in his pencil. It was time he drew his line in the sand.

Benny's blood boiled when he received the news of Herbert's disrespectful rejection. He couldn't allow an act of brazen defiance to go unpunished. Sometimes you got to get out the belt.

Benny first doled out his punishment in the guise of the Dallas Police Department. Within a week of Noble's refusal to up the tribute, a plainclothes detective strolled inside The Airmen's Club. Noble was in the back office. He came out surrounded by his muscle to speak with one of the city's finest. It wasn't uncommon for the authorities to drop in on a regular basis to collect their fines, but this felt different.

The detective took a gander at the club, nodded his head, smiled smugly at Herbert, and boldly declared, "We have had some complaints." He caught his breath and cleared his throat, the smile growing bigger. "This club'll have to shut down immediately."

Herbert asked the logical question, "Why?"

"Because gambling is illegal," the detective responded, trying to keep from bursting at the seams with laughter.

Fear and recognition were settling in, but Noble was a proud man, someone a dirty cop wasn't going to intimidate. He puffed his chest out and began his own interrogation. He demanded to know if Binion's clubs were to adhere to the same fate. If not, there wasn't a chance in hell that Herbert would be shutting down.

Herbert stated that the detective could take that information back to their boss. Not the chief of police, but Benny Binion. The detective headed out. He had delivered the message. Noble told the casino to keep going and stay open, business as usual, but he was furious, seeing double with rage. What rock did this cock blocker crawl out from under?

The ploy to put fear in the heart of Noble didn't work. It was clear that Herbert didn't have a cowardly bone in his body. It was also clear that he wasn't going anywhere.

At least not the easy way . . .

Benny Takes His Shot

January 12, 1946, was a night that would go down as a "first" in the extraordinary life of Herbert Noble. The midnight air had a chill that under the right circumstance would freeze a witch's tit. A howling moon played cat and mouse with the drifting clouds. A ghoulish glow encircled the night sky, a glow that signifies a perilous journey ahead. Beware, the freaks come out at night!

Herbert left The Airmen's Club and proceeded to his car. Where was his goon squad this evening? The strongarms were generally attached at his hips. Herbert should have known better than anyone what happens to a boss when they travel alone.

He started the engine and the Mercury peeled away from the curb. After cruising a couple of blocks Herbert, couldn't help but notice a suspicious Cadillac in the rearview mirror. As he sped up, slowed down, and ran all the red lights, the Caddy stayed hitched.

Shit, he thought, *this was gonna be a problem.*

Wealth provides many things. For Herbert, it provided him with two homes. One, in the trendy upscale neighborhood of Oak Cliff. The second, the Diamond M, his eight-hundred-acre ranch in Denton County. Herbert was headed for Oak Cliff but with the sense of impending doom looming large in the rearview mirror, he switched direction and hightailed it toward the country. Mildred was at the Oak Cliff residence. No need to bring trouble to her.

A high-speed chase ensued. Herbert drove like his ass was on fire and his hair was catching. As he floored the Mercury, the Cadillac remained glued to his bumper. Terrified drivers on the highway dodged the two cars racing at over a hundred miles an hour. The Cadillac pulled up next to the Mercury's driver side, and Herbert finally got a glance at his pursuers, three dark silhouettes in the adjoining car who had been sent to kill him.

Herbert recognized the first face as the hot-headed sharpshooter Lois Green at the wheel. He then eyeballed the ole dirty

peckerwood, his fucking partner Bob Minyard, in the passenger seat. Before he could yell anything at Bob, Johnny Grisaffi, a veteran homicidal maniac known as "Brazil," leaned out the back window with a sawed-off shotgun.

The gun blast shattered Herbert's windshield. A second shotgun blast missed completely.

Lois and Bob then raised their guns and fired in Noble's direction, mostly missing completely.

Herbert pulled a pistol from inside his stylish vest and returned fire.

On a dirt road, a few miles from the ranch, the gun battle raged on between the two cars at breakneck speeds. Herbert drove with one hand, shooting with the other.

He soon realized he was running low on ammo. He also didn't like the three-to-one odds. He needed to get to the damned ranch, where he had a fully stocked arsenal available. Every second was precious. His life depended on it. If he could just get home . . .

Less than a mile from the ranch, Noble lost control of the car.

The Mercury, shot to hell with bullet holes, nosedived into a ditch on the side of the road. The velocity flipped the Mercury end over end. Herbert was somehow still alive but injured. He had pain shooting up both arms and down both legs. But he couldn't think about that now. There wasn't a moment to spare. The Caddy had slammed on its brakes and was already backing up.

Noble slipped away from his overturned automobile, scrambling across an open field toward a farmhouse in the distance. Bullets flew all around him. The gunshots echoed throughout the darkness.

He could feel a burning sensation in his legs. He fell to his belly. Looking down, he saw blood pouring out onto the dirt. But he knew he couldn't stop. The sounds of running and shouting let him know they were closing in. He had to pick himself up and keep moving with what little strength he had left. If he laid there any longer, he would die.

As soon as he stood back up, a piercing pain coursed through his back, another shot that pancaked him back to the ground. Crawling was his only option. He scooted along on his belly as fast as he could. He was not a praying man, but now he was pleading with the universe to not let those fuckers find him, especially crawling on his belly.

He somehow made his way through the front yard of the farmhouse. Mixed yells and gunshots continued from the angry mob hunting him, accompanied by the barking of dogs coming from inside the house and the backyard. Herbert slithered like a snake under the front porch of the farmhouse. Wounded, worn, and spewing blood, The Aristocratic Gambler's mind was racing a million miles a second. His options were all but gone. Surely this wasn't how this was going to end. His heartbeat pounded like a gorilla about to explode out of his chest as he peered through the slats under the porch. The footsteps were approaching the front yard. It wouldn't be long till they found him. There was no escape.

Suddenly, the front door swung open and Herbert could hear footsteps on the porch above him. A crazed and cross-eyed man of the land stammered out the front door, bare-chested in a robe, tobacco juice rolling out of the corners of his mouth, with his favorite hound and shotgun. He didn't take kindly to the boisterous trespassers in his front yard. Unaware that Herbert was hiding below him, the dirty farmer squinted down the barrel of the 12-gauge at the uninvited guests approaching his home.

He yelled out, demanding to know what the hell was going on, and more importantly to offer a warning to the intruders to get off his land.

"I'll only ask once."

The attackers decided not to press their luck. They ran back to the Cadillac and took off, hoping that they hit Noble and that somewhere nearby, he was bleeding out. Little did they know that death doesn't come easy to Herbert Noble.

But they would soon learn.

Noble made it to the hospital, where he learned he had a bullet lodged in his lower spine. A little to the left and he would have been paralyzed, if not dead. The cops showed up and asked questions. Noble was at first quiet, but then did name two of his three assailants: Green and Grisaffi, who soon found the heat on them and their names splashed across newspaper headlines.

Noble had no intentions of naming the third man. His partner. The thorn in his side. No, Noble would handle him personally. It was time for him to send a message of his own.

Just two days later, driving through the streets of East Dallas, were two of Noble's men—an Airmen's Club pit boss named Slim Hays and a weasel of a man named Sonny Lefors, who would soon become a major player in the Benny/Herbert conflict. They waited with Hays's girlfriend outside Minyard's house, with strict orders. As soon as they saw Minyard's brand-new Oldsmobile pull into the driveway, the two were on the move, ambushing Minyard as he walked to his front door. They shot him numerous times. Minyard managed to get a few shots off but didn't hit anyone before his assailants took off.

As Minyard lay there dying, his hysterical wife called the police and Benny Binion, who showed up together. As Benny stared at the corpse of one of his top men, he knew he was in it now. He had taken a big shot and missed, for the first time ever. Now there was no denying it.

War had begun.

CHAPTER 8
WAR PART 2

Gunshots, car chases, bomb blasts, mutilated corpses. Chicago in the Roaring Twenties? Hell no, this is Dallas/Fort Worth in the Raging Forties as the seedy, gambling underground comes to the surface and provides a backdrop to a rivalry between two powerful men with high ambitions and no fear. The perfect setting for a dangerous game that would leave severe devastation in its wake as the players now maneuvered quickly and ruthlessly with no regard to the consequences.

Call it *Cowtown Noir*.

After Minyard was killed, Benny was furious! He battened down the hatches, surrounding himself with more hired muscle and adding more protection to his clubs. He knew better now than to underestimate Noble. Even with the failed assassination attempt, he thought that perhaps Herbert would have gotten the message. But when Minyard turned up dead, he soon realized Noble was unlike any competitor he had ever seen. He was a dangerous man. You don't wait for a dangerous man to the make the next move. *You* have to make it!

The timing still had to be just right. For Binion, that meant August of that year, enough time removed from the last attempt to avoid any heat and just possibly enough time for Noble to relax and not anticipate what was to come. Like a good poker player, it was about catching your opponent with his guard down and then striking hot and fast.

A Second Attempt

On August 19, 1946, Herbert got a message from a gambler and hired gun by the name of Jack Darby. He had been brought in by Binion loyalist and fixer Buddy Malone, as it was always good to have layers established between who was giving the orders. Darby was young and inexperienced, but had a temper and was trying to move his way up the syndicate. The kid was trying to fill out big muscle pants, and this could be the opportunity to do it, and even get a nod of approval from the boss himself.

Darby told Herbert he had some money that, ironically enough, the two had won together in a craps game off a delinquent named Eddie Gillihand. Eddie had finally paid up, and it was time for Noble to pick up his cash.

To get what was coming to him.

Hearing that Gillihand had his winnings was music to Herbert's ears. He arrived at the meeting point, a Dallas club, at around three AM. He walked to the front door and was met by Darby, who seemed a little agitated for a man who was about to celebrate a share in a victory.

"What's going on, kid?" Noble asked, eyeing him, cool as a cucumber.

He was met with silence.

"All right. Look. It's late. Let's get this over with. Where's the money?"

"Uhh . . . it's . . . uhh . . . upstairs, safe and sound. How about we . . . uhh . . . head on up and get it."

Herbert had to laugh. So this is how it was gonna go down, huh? There was no fear, though, not with this little shit who Noble wouldn't waste a squirt of piss on even if he was on fire. Noble had sized up the kid in seconds. He was no killer. He didn't have the stomach for it. This was just a boy playing grown-up.

Which is why Noble didn't even flinch when Darby drew his pistol and aimed it at him. Nor did he jump when Darby started firing, shooting twice at his feet to get him moving up the stairs. Herbert Noble didn't get nervous. He was just looking to see where and when he could turn this situation around, how he would get out of this one, and how much those involved would have to pay.

"All right, kid, I'm going."

Herbert trudged up the stairs. Rounding the top step he entered a dimly lit, dank, musty room that reeked of rat shit. Seated around a folding table were Eddie and another degenerate named Bill Holcomb. Noble just nodded at both of them.

Darby kept the gun pointed in Noble's direction. His nerves were overriding, getting the best of him. Once he was sure of his play, Noble met Darby's fear with his own eyes of cocksure confidence.

"Go ahead, do it, why don't ya? Let's see what you're made of."

Darby waved the pistol around, clearly unsure what to do with it. Noble knew if he was going to kill him, he would have done so already. Darby needed a reason, and Noble wasn't going to be baited.

Sure enough, as if on cue, Darby urged Noble to draw on him. Herbert had guessed right and he refused, hands comfortably stuffed in his pockets. Darby looked at his compatriots, unsure of what to do. They sat stoic; their job was clear.

The kid needed Herbert to draw so he could shoot him and claim self-defense. That's why the two spectators were seated at the table, to be witnesses. And extra firepower, but only if needed. Noble glared down Darby while Darby launched a verbal assault, calling Noble every name under the sun, even taking profane shots at his wife. If anything would get him, it would be that, but Noble stayed calm. This was going to be a piece of cake.

When the kid ran out of breath, Herbert began slow-talking Darby in a reassuring voice, like a hostage negotiator coaxing a lunatic to put the gun down. Herbert reassured Darby that it was

okay. He reminded him of their friendship—or at least their partnership—in the dice games and how they had wiped old Eddie here clean out of his cash. He also assured Darby that he knew someone else was behind this dastardly deed and that he didn't blame him.

"Come on now, how about you put the gun down?"

Eventually the meditative tone and congenial voice was convincing enough. Darby lowered his weapon, out of steam and realizing he was out of his element. The other two never stirred, even when Noble walked to the table, picked up his cash, and walked out the door, giving one last glance at Gillihand, who glared back at him with a scowl.

Yeah, he'll do.

Two months later, Gillihand's body was found on the side of the road, severely beaten and shot twice in the head.

Herbert Noble had survived another attempt on his life—albeit a soft effort—by Benny Binion, and that could not stand. It was time for more serious retribution, but now was not the time. There was another way to fight The Cowboy, to hit him both in his pocketbook and power status. That meant targeting his influence and winning an election.

The Times They Are A' Changin'

Millions of shards of tiny paper fall from the rooftops of crowded buildings. The stars and bars wave feverishly from the electrified crowd. All sizes of flags dance in the wind. Viewers line the street by the thousands. A voracious booming roar thunders from the crowd of frenzied patriotism. Cars and floats ease down the street one after another, traveling at a snail's pace while US service troops sit atop them greeting their admirers, waving and blowing kisses. They are modern-day superheroes!

Storefront signs read "Proud to be an American." Uncle Sam is the iconic vision. His portrait covers millions of posters littered throughout

the streets. The smells of hot dogs and popcorn fill the nostrils of this nostalgic setting. The ticker-tape parade celebrations unfold in cities across America. World War II has been over for a bit now and valiant troops are finally returning home after stomping the ass of the Evil Axis forces. Honored and proud, it was a tremendous time to be in the good ole USA!

Such was the scene in Texas as well. Citizens were dizzy with patriotic pride. The soldiers were kings, and the United States was on top with the rest of the world looking up. It was time to get home and make some babies.

And keep them safe.

With the problems abroad settled once and for all in the eyes of an optimistic and adoring public, it was time to look inward and settle the issues at home. Especially vice and violence. As reform measures swept across the country, the tide was also shifting in Dallas. Residents wanted to feel a sense of security. What they didn't want was the brazen violence that had been erupting in their fine city. Crime was escalating at an alarming rate. Violent crimes like homicides, robberies, and assaults were skyrocketing. The rackets were bringing in windfalls of cash, but they were also bringing constant mayhem.

Political leaders were looking to lay building blocks to a new future. Dallas was a thriving city. Civic and economic leaders looked to promote Dallas, and North Texas, as a prime destination. Not so much as a lawless gambling town full of bowlegged prostitutes, trigger-happy outlaws, and blood running through the gutters. Ambitious young veterans, presenting themselves as reform candidates for political office, preached a gospel of growth, prosperity, law, and order. Red light districts and gambling houses would fall on their onslaught. All would be well in the beautiful state of Texas. The end of the war brough ambitious dreams and everyone had visions of a better place to live, and they were willing to fight for it, especially at the polls.

Smoot Schmid was a tenured Dallas sheriff who had been in office since 1933. He was no ball buster. He wasn't even a penis prickler. He resembled more along the lines of a docile, gentle, easy-going lawman who enjoyed a nice swivel chair and a sturdy desk to prop his boots up on. He was the epitome of "If I can't see it, then I'm not worried about it."

In his earlier days, Schmid had a reputation—whether earned or not—for chasing outlaws up and down the blacktops of every farm-to-market road in North Texas. In those days, he liked to consider himself a young man in hot pursuit of lawbreakers, long before there was a Buford T. Justice.

Smoot gained notoriety by going to head-to-head with the demented killing couple, Clyde Barrow and Bonnie Parker. It was Smoot who deduced that the murderous gang would be returning to wreak havoc in Dallas. In 1934, Bonnie and Clyde sprung their accomplice Raymond Hamilton free from the Eastham Prison Unit. Schmid set up roadblocks with armed deputies on all roads leading into Dallas. He was certain the lead-footed speed demons would be careening back through his city within hours. There was no apprehension that day, but Smoot's mind was in the right spot.

On May 23, 1934, the lawman would get his revenge. In Arcadia, Louisiana, Smoot's deputies took part in an ambush the took down the infamous pair. Plenty of spent shell casings and cartridges covered the ground, but when the dust settled Smoot's men were left standing and Bonnie and Clyde's gang were pushing up daisies. Smoot wasn't there personally but since his deputies were, he had no problem sharing the credit.

By the 1940s, the Dallas Sheriff's Department was severely cash strapped. There was a short supply of able deputies with the war raging in Europe. Plus, the laissez-faire, fascist attitude that the city took to policing didn't help matters.

One man who wasn't cash strapped, nor lacking in fire power, was the illustrious Benny Binion. The Cowboy had a cozy, sympathetic

relationship with Sheriff Schmid. The two were known to share a cup of coffee. Smoot was one of "Benny's Boys," which meant Benny had Smoot under control. Not so much under his thumb; he didn't have to apply pressure as Smoot was simply indifferent to Benny and the gambling issue in Dallas. He didn't even seem to be that bothered by the killing, feeling like it was between the gangsters. As long as the locals weren't caught in the crossfire, let 'em at it.

Smoot had been calling the shots for years and wasn't about to hang up his poncho and gun belt no matter what types of sagebrush slashers or one-eyed monsters were laying low in the high grass waiting on him outside. The unencumbered sheriff was up for reelection, and he was a heavy favorite to keep his golden star. It was a crucial election for the city and even more critical for the likes of Binion. He needed his old buddy to win and hold down the fort, for all their sakes. But Smoot was a sure thing, right? So much so that he really couldn't be bothered with running an aggressive campaign. What was the point? Life was good, or at least, good enough.

The Underdog Barks

Steve Guthrie was a longshot candidate in the Dallas County Sheriff's race. Steve was like one of those yearling colts who had plenty of get up and go, lots of juice in the tank, but they might just crash into the railing or buck their rider off before they even make it past the first furlong.

Steve's odds were forty to one . . . *that he would even finish the race!*

What people didn't know was that he was a man of raw conviction. A man of divine courage. A man who believed in himself. Steve Guthrie was a thirty-three-year-old former army sergeant. He had a military mind and a black-and-white viewpoint on morality. He worked a series of odd jobs, and his biggest role within the police

force was as a traffic cop. Nobody gave him a chance in hell of defeating Smoot Schmid. He had better stick to what he knew best—writing parking tickets. However, Steve didn't see it that way. He was a man of the people. He was here to usher in a new era of reform.

With the proliferation of troops returning home, the wartime voices became loud and clear. The servicemen and women rallied around this new candidate. They were not required to pay a poll tax to vote, which meant there could be a turnout in droves to the polls of military- minded folks supporting Guthrie. His speeches resonated with those who had seen enough damn violence on the battlefields for ten lifetimes. Guthrie vowed "a crackdown on gangsterism." He promised to "wear out the Dallas County Jail." Making the round at civic functions, in between flipping pancakes at the Dallas Kiwanis Club, Guthrie announced, "I won't be able to halt these sinister things without public cooperation. If the people of Dallas County want gambling and continue to patronize the back rooms and clubs, our department will be at a disadvantage."

The stage was set for the 1946 election. On one side you had the seven-term lawman legend who was getting fat on the hog and quite settled in his ways. On the other, you had the huge underdog who was hungry, lean, mean, and ready to enact revolutionary war on crime.

As Guthrie put in the footwork by shaking hands and kissing babies, he found support from an unlikely source: Herbert Noble.

All politicians run on good faith, but what all politicians need more than anything is contributions. Elections are costly, and there is only so much a US Army solider or housewife can donate. With a man like Noble, the sky was the limit. He donated $15,000 to Guthrie's campaign, which was a significant infusion to the coffers for a local sheriff's race. It helped keep Guthrie visible in the public eye. The two men were seen as friendly and chatty. They became copasetic with a vision toward the future.

Herbert was concerned as much as anyone about the upcoming election. He knew it would be further devastation for him if Smoot won. But the landscape looked rosier with Guthrie as a new

connection. If Herbert could help him somehow get elected, it would be a major boost for his operations and a crushing blow to Binion's. He wasn't overconfident but slightly optimistic.

No matter what happened, he still felt the bottom could fall out at any time. That's why he focused on business with his gambling clubs outside the county lines. The clubs within the county were on their best behavior while he waited to see how it all shook out.

After a long and grueling campaign, the election came and went. The people had spoken. The die was cast. The winner was Mr. Longshot himself—Steve Guthrie! A miracle at the voting booth! The young colt proved he had the stamina. It was neck and neck, he had to stick his teeth across the line for a photo finish, but in the end, he won.

Not everyone was jumping for joy and singing "Hallelujah." Certainly not Benny. After the initial shock and despair dissipated, terror took its place. His main man Schmid was out, and Guthrie was in. Where did this leave him and his Southland Syndicate?

The sheriff-elect took to the podium and declared "the Dallas County Jails will soon be full." He was waging war against racketeers of all sizes. No one would escape his wrath, not if you were a lawbreaker. He would add additional ranks to the "Dallas Sheriff Posse" to bring it up to sixty members. It was patterned after the crusading El Paso Posse. Longtime Binion jock sniffer Dallas Police Captain Bill Decker was out as well, which led to more indigestion for The Cowboy. New Police Captain Carl Hansson took a page from Guthrie's playbook and announced he would follow suit and lock up the gamblers. All of these men were buddied up to Herbert Noble. This all spelled trouble for The Cowboy.

Chicago Comes to Dallas

With new blood in office and Benny looking weak, it also seemed like prime time for another player to try and enter the Dallas crime

scene, or at least test the waters. New leadership was taking hold in other areas besides law enforcement. In 1947, Tony Accardo, a.k.a. "The Big Tuna," was the new boss of the Chicago Syndicate or simply "The Outfit." Tony had earned his stripes as an enforcer under Al Capone. He also earned another nickname, "Joe Batters," for his love of the Louisville Slugger. The Chicago Syndicate was as dominant as any of the five Mafia families in New York. It was like a gigantic octopus with its massive tentacles twisting and turning, reaching into western portions of the United States. The Chicago Syndicate wrote the book on successful organized crime ventures. They were the gold standard. More importantly, they were on their way to Dallas, trying once again to gain a foothold after a failed attempt years earlier.

Paul Roland Jones was a small to midlevel associate connected with the big boys in Chicago. He had been kicked to the curb, shooed away from Dallas several years back for counterfeiting sugar coupons during World War II. His real intentions were to survey the landscape and report his findings back home. His consensus at the time was that it was too dangerous, too risky an endeavor. For one, Binion had the town locked down. Two, the authorities were already playing nice with The Cowboy and no one wanted to disrupt the apple cart.

Discussions centered around the idea of taking Benny out, but Jones put a quash on that talk, explaining it would bring unbearable heat to them all. The bosses agreed but still believed there was potential in Texas. They sent men down south to see if they get a foothold in the area without setting off a firestorm.

Decker, a deputy sheriff then, noticed a colorful crowd of seemingly out-of-place Italians making their way through his fine city. He went above and beyond his duties as a law officer, rounding up the tallywackers and hauling them out to the county line. He warned them of his boot making its way up their ass if they didn't hightail it on out of town and head north.

That was the end of it.

Good riddance, thought Decker. *Bye-bye, dagos.*

For now . . .

Directly after Guthrie's triumphant election win, the Windy City hoodlums made their return. A new sheriff meant a new dynamic. Guthrie had not been sworn in yet nor had his first cup of coffee when Jones made his acquaintance. Jones explained he was the man with the golden ticket. He would make Steve Guthrie rich beyond his wildest dreams. He boasted about his connections with the Chicago Syndicate. He claimed how lucky Guthrie was for making his acquaintance. The new sheriff took the conversation to heart. Dazzled by Jones's pontifications, he invited him to his home to discuss matters further. The dollar signs were aligning themselves within the universe and Jones could see success written on the wall, a chance to be the big man and make the play that would set up the mob in Dallas.

Jones accepted the invitation and arrived at the meeting with Romeo Nappi and Pat Manno, both Windy City wise guys. Vice detectives George Butler and Pat Gannaway were also in attendance. They didn't want to get left out of this gold mine. Because Butler was tied in with Noble, this gave way to the notion that Noble was in the background pulling the strings, setting up the players for the meeting.

The parties talked carefully but openly about opportunities and obstacles, most notably the structure of an operation like Chicago making its mark on Dallas. Guthrie wanted to know how this would all work, and Jones was more than eager to lay out the plan.

First, the outfit would be run by only one man from Chicago, assuaging any fears of too big of a Chicago Mafia presence in the county. "It'll be a man who looks like a preacher. He is not a dago, he is not a Jew. He protects the game."

Second, it could be done without violence. "We won't have to shoot nobody and you won't have to shoot nobody," Jones said.

Rather, Chicago, who by this point was a master at setting up and controlling vice operations in other cities, would rely on their experience and expertise and work to quickly and quietly push out the competition by simply presenting a smoother and more proficient gambling club.

Third, once they were in the city, they would spread even more money around to the higher-ups, flipping their loyalty and pushing Benny out. "And you should have forty thousand dollars a month," Jones told Guthrie. Plus, since they had their sights set on a long-term partnership, Guthrie's reelection campaign expenses would also always be covered.

During the meeting, Guthrie brought up the elephant in the room. "I don't have to tell you who Benny Binion is and you know who Ivy Miller is and you know who Dalton is and you know all the big boys in the racket here. And Binion picks off one million flat dollars." He gestured toward Butler. "And you know it yourself, George, one million in policy alone."

Guthrie kept the conversation going. "But suppose somebody comes and makes that offer to me, look who I'd be bucking. I would be bucking Will Wilson, the district attorney. I would be bucking (Texas Ranger Captain) Gonzalez. I would be bucking the judges down there."

Jones interjected, "Let me arrange that for you. I will show you how you can do that. Here is what I propose, and it's the only proposition I am interested in. It's the only proposition I am authorized to make or accept because it is the way we are operating all over the country . . . As I told Mr. Butler before seeing you, we are not interested in you for two years. If I thought you were going to be sheriff for two years only, I would have told Mr. Butler I was not even interested in meeting you because we have a lot on record. We control Binion. There will be no trouble. I'll show you. We won't have to shoot nobody."

The timing was perfect! Chicago was ready to shoot its shot. Guthrie and company were about to become richer than their

wildest dreams. It all sized up to be a great plan in the making. There was only one issue:

Steve Guthrie was playing coy.

It was a setup from the word go. The incoming sheriff had contacted the Texas Rangers and other local law agencies. They in turn had wired the house with bugs to record all conversations, which all were eventually transcribed and released. The house wasn't even Guthrie's, but a prop house. Rangers staked out across the street with binoculars and listening devices. Butler smiled and played along, but he was in on the charade as well.

The meeting lasted for half the day. Jones later told Guthrie, "If you don't make a deal with me, we'll still be friends. If we don't make a deal, you feel free to make a deal with anybody with the assurance we won't try to go ahead in defiance of you."

The meeting concluded with two more to follow at later dates. They were set up to continue navigating logistics, this time with other members from Chicago. The following meeting was of little consequence as the new representatives were a lot less loose-lipped than Jones. As for the second one, the mob sent a couple of nobodies, apparently wary of Guthrie's requests. It was time for the authorities to make their move.

On December 10, 1946, Jones and Nappi were arrested on bribery charges. Manno had returned to Chicago and was wanted by authorities in the same case. Guthrie held a press conference to share the results of the corruption plot. He proved to be the crime fighter as advertised. The "Eliot Ness of North Texas." In Jones's 1947 trial, the jury heard tapes totaling over ten hours of recorded conversation. The listening devices were concealed in radios and telephones inside the home. A secret recording device was also hidden in a pit dug underneath the house.

Jones was found guilty and served three years in a Texas penitentiary. He would later run into narcotics issues in Laredo, which sent him back to the hoosegow for another five years. Chicago's

experiment had failed. Guthrie proved to be the real deal, Dallas's newest crime-busting superstar.

The Writing on the Wall

Benny Binion went by the philosophy, "It's better to be pissed off than pissed on." He might not have been a mathematical genius, but he could summarize that two plus two equaled four. While Guthrie had essentially saved Benny's businesses from a hostile Chicago takeover, Benny saw the writing on the wall. He knew it hadn't been for his benefit. Guthrie was serious when he said he was coming for organized crime, and Benny knew that meant him. Whether it was a crusade of justice or Noble's influence didn't matter; Benny knew it was time to bounce. It was confirmed when, not long after, Benny got a message sent to him through various channels from Decker:

"If you don't get out of town, you're gonna be in prison or dead."

Within days, Benny informed his wife that it was time to head west. Vegas was calling his name. Benny let out squalls like a panther in heat. He recalled, "I just went to hollerin' and lit out runnin'!"

With his stud horse knocked out of the stable, his best friend, good ole intuition, paid him a visit and whispered in his ear, "Head west, young man, head west."

Benny packed two briefcases with $2 million and loaded them into a trunk in his Cadillac. Joining him in the car were his wife and kids, along with two bodyguards, R.D. Mathews and Al Meadows. They hit the road in the dead of the night. Benny understood the highways could be treacherous. Lawmen stopping and searching the car, desperados, heinous highwaymen looking to rob a bigshot like Binion. Mathews and Meadows were loaded with machine guns and kept their heads on a swivel for any potentially disastrous pitfalls.

The journey ended without incident. Benny immediately started taking advantage of connections he had in Vegas. His departure was a win for local authorities, but even more so for Noble, who saw his chief rival skip town with his tail between his legs.

However, The Cowboy wasn't the kind of man to be underestimated or to give up everything he worked for so easily. His operations would still run, even if he wasn't around to oversee them, and he wasn't going to forget about what Noble had done to him. No, not by a country mile. In fact, he was more determined than ever to see Herbert Noble in the ground. The Cowboy wasn't waving the white flag. He was only surviving so he could live to fight another day.

CHAPTER 9
WAR PART 3

Sonny Lefors shuffled from one row of one-arm bandits to another in a downtown casino. Sonny was a pathetic excuse of a foot soldier with the physical attributes of a starving hyena, especially the hollowed-out eyes that resembled two piss holes in the snow. He had the intellect of a dim-witted carnie, but he was dangerous. The man was morally inept and he loved crime.

He waffled outside the casino onto a sidewalk bathed in the neon Las Vegas lights. He had walked only a few feet when a Cadillac screeched to a halt beside him. Before Sonny could get his bearings, a neatly dressed hoodlum eased out the passenger side door. He quickly shouldered up to Lefors and jammed a snub nose revolver into his ribs. No words were needed, the message was clear.

Get in.

Sonny found himself in the back seat surrounded by goons. His face froze in place and his jaw locked in petrified fear. It wasn't the goons that worried him. It was the man perched next to him wearing a tilted Stetson and smug smirk.

The Cowboy signaled for the driver to take off.

Hours later, Lefors found himself gagged and tied to a chair, sweating bullets in the Binion ranch servants' quarters. He had been left there alone for hours. A torture of solitude. The tension was tearing his innards apart. His gonads swelled and his ass was chafing something fierce. He knew any moment the hit squad would burst into the room and take him to the woodshed one limb at a

time. Or worse yet, no one would come, and he would be left to rot away in his own filth. An arduous, agonizing death sentence, but perhaps fitting. Sonny was jammed up in a serious predicament. There was a damn good chance he would never walk out of this room alive. And for what? Herbert Noble?

Sonny's real name was Charles Lefors. He was also known as "The Groceryman" in underworld circles. He owned a grocery store on the west side of Dallas where he fenced stolen goods. He was connected to Noble and on occasion worked with his crew. Sonny was co-conspirator in the murder of Bob Minyard. He wasn't a total buffoon. He had been a criminal since he graduated preschool. His main problem was he let his bulldog mouth run over his hummingbird ass. His second problem was he had no loyalty. He had ninety-nine others, but you could stop with those two.

Sonny set foot in Vegas with $1,000 in cash and a revolver in his pocket, neither of them his. He schlepped around downtown in and out of the El Cortez Casino. He gambled and boisterously flapped his gums, babbling on about how he was "looking for business." The Groceryman couldn't keep a lid on his trap. It was clear he was a man from Texas and he was in town to do some harm. Benny soon got word of Lefors's arrival. Binion and company made their play to pick up their new guest and make him feel at home.

And now here he was.

Eventually, Benny and his men returned to interrogate Sonny.

Benny calmly asked, "Whatcha doing here?"

The squeamish Lefors let his mouth run nonstop. He explained that he had been sent by Noble on a reconnaissance mission to track Benny, spy on his operations, and if possible, put a bullet in Binion.

After a few hours at the ranch, Sonny was returned to the casino in one piece. He was given a new lease on life—backed by the fear of God—and a new mission. Sonny had always been a fool, a liar, a thief, and a scared little candy-ass who would sell out

his own mother. Now he would now be a mole working for Binion. He would be heading back to Texas to put the screws to his old boss.

The Long-Distance Leader

The Binions had settled into their new enclave in Nevada. They were safe and secure but had a case of the Lone Star State blues. They missed Texas. Benny was still pissed about how things ended there. Hellfire, the man had been driven out of his own damn town! He worked to pacify the group and test the waters on a possible return. This was a situation akin to handling dynamite. It needed timing and patience. He couldn't just storm back across state lines without careful consideration.

The Southland Syndicate continued to churn on even with its founder living 1,500 miles away. Benny remained the shot caller. He collected a share from all craps games and continued to control a lucrative policy racket in Dallas. The pressing issue was dismantling the fancy pants fruitcake that was causing him severe irritation in the bowels. Benny put the word on the street not only to his crew but to all hardcore killers: It was time to put Noble ten feet under. It didn't matter if the bullet went in the front or the back of the head. The initial bounty was set at $10,000, then it escalated to $25,000, and on to $50,000 with the added benefit of operation of a craps game.

The news of the sweetened pot blew from ear to ear of every hired gun in North Texas. Noble was in the crosshairs.

It's a hard road to travel when you know you have a pack of irreverent serial killers on your ass. If any man was up for the challenge, The Aristocratic Gambler was the ideal prospect. Some came to ply their trade and Herbert sent them to meet their Maker. The contract on Noble's head was proving to be no easy task. The "hits" just kept on rollin'.

Ambush at the Diamond M

May 20, 1948. A brisk night, wind whistling through pecan trees. The crickets chirped and whippoorwills sang. Herbert cruised down a dirt road with his windows down as he took in a deep inhalation of fresh country air. His life had been nonconfrontational for the last year. No attacks, just clean living. He was beginning to settle into the lull of civilian life. The ho-hum doldrums of a life without constant threat.

He eased off the gas as the Diamond M sign came into his headlights. Slowing to a roll, the gravel crunched under the tires as he made his way over the cattle guard. It was at the Diamond M where he felt the most relaxed, most at ease. He was calmer here. He felt safe.

A red flame burst from a shotgun and lit up the night.

Herbert was *throttled* sideways with buckshot torpedoing into his right arm and wrist. A cloud of smoke snaked out of the long barrel and the metallic smell of gunpowder spewed into the spring night air.

The vehicle raced toward the ranch house. Herbert made a mad dash inside. He was wounded but alive.

Noble couldn't see his attacker, but the method of the shooting—a home turf sniper attempt from the dark—led him to believe it was Lois Green. The vindictive coward had already tried and failed to get Noble once before, and Noble had ratted him out. Now he had come to finish the job.

"Not today," Noble said.

The next day Noble strolled into Methodist Hospital with a blood-soaked towel wrapped around his right arm. When asked by staff about the injuries, he claimed he had been messing around with his .38 and dropped it. The gun went off and hit him in the arm, he said. He promised to be safer around firearms in the future. They patched him up and blessed his heart.

The truth of what happened only came out when Denton County Sheriff Roy Moore paid a visit to Mildred, who spilled the beans. An investigation led detectives to learn that Green's partner Brazil had been shot just days before. He somehow survived, but had been talking up a storm about getting revenge. Brazil, who had also been a part of the first failed attempt on Noble's life, had a sturdy alibi for May 20, but his partner Green did not. Still, there wasn't enough evidence to point the finger and make an arrest.

A Valentine's Day Surprise

February 14, 1949. No doubt a day Herbert looked forward to. It was Valentine's Day, a day that Herbert celebrated with his one true love in this life, his wife Mildred. It takes a special type of woman to endure the lifestyle of a gangland boss who lives each day on the brink of disaster. She was that woman.

Herbert was rushing through The Airmen's Club to finish up some last-minute business. It was high time to get home to his sweetheart. A cigar-chomping associate stepped outside to survey the situation. He caught a glimpse of a body crawling beneath Noble's Mercury. The associate fled upstairs with his cigar still clenched firmly between his teeth. He alerted Herbert to his findings. Herbert first called law enforcement. Then he and a few of his personal burly bastards tore outside with pistols drawn. The mysterious man under the car was gone. Detectives arrived and conducted a comprehensive investigation. They located dynamite and a blasting cap planted on the undercarriage of the Mercury. The bomb had enough juice to wipe out Noble and decimate The Airmen's Club to rubble. There wouldn't have been a living soul left alive for two blocks. Disaster avoided yet again.

The Birth of "The Cat"

September 7, 1949. One of Noble's ranch hands loading hay at the Diamond M headquarters spied a peculiar black car traveling back and forth along the ranch's fence line. The vehicle continued to make the same pattern, slowing down at identical points each time. The ranch hand wiped the sweat from his brow, had a few bites of melon, and squinted to get a better look at the make and model. The driver in the black car saw the ranch hand watching him and sped away. The hand noticed the car was a black Ford. The same black Ford that had been scouting the same fence line a few days earlier.

The ranch hand went to his boss and relayed the bizarre state of events. Noble was bubbling over with red hot rage at the news. The kind of red hot you feel when a smoldering fireplace poker is shoved up your sphincter. The kind of rage that makes you see not only double but triple and quadruple mixed in with a kaleidoscope of blinding colors. There was a code among the streets and that code was a man's home was off-limits. Now Herbert was dealing with a threat near his hacienda for a second time.

He cocked his pistol and grabbed a .30 caliber carbine as well. Dusk was beginning to fall. The witching hour. Herbert slid into his Mercury and rocketed out into the sunset. He found the Ford traveling west on an intersecting dirt road. He flashed his high beams on and off. The Ford flashed his beams back on and off and sped away with a wall of dust trailing behind. Herbert's fury nearly ruptured a few of his blood vessels. His hands were ghostly white from gripping the steering wheel with such extreme pressure. He put the Mercury in high gear, the tires kicked up pebbles, and the race was on.

The chase weaved its way through the night for six or so miles. The two cars careening at breakneck speeds, swerving around corners and fishtailing from one side of the road to the other. Eventually, the Ford lost control and slammed into a ditch.

Herbert's feet hit the dirt with rifle in hand. He aimed toward the Ford and shouted obscenities of the most atrocious nature, ordering the perpetrators to get out of the car. Three despicable desperados obliged, piling out with their own brand of vengeance.

Guns started blazing in both directions.

Herbert felt a trifling pain in his right leg. He looked down and saw blood gushing just below the knee cap. No time for that. The adrenaline and the will to kill overrode the discomfort he was feeling. Herbert trudged forward and continued firing one round after another. The booming rifle blast sent the three sorry sumbitches scattering through the night, taking refuge in the pasture.

Denton County lawmen arrived after the dust had settled. They found Herbert suffering from severe blood loss. They ascertained that the attackers were still hiding somewhere in the brush. Herbert demanded that he ride alongside sheriff deputies as they tried to corral the assassins. He was madder than a wet hen on Sunday. The search was abandoned after the evildoers were nowhere to be found.

The deputies convinced Noble that to save his leg it was time for him to head to the hospital. Once again, Herbert made his way to Methodist Hospital, where he was greeted by doctors and nurses on a first-name basis. Hell, by this point, they should have just had a room reserved only for him!

Police investigated the incident and found that the Ford was linked to Jack Nesbit and Jim Thomas, two unsavory malcontents who worked for Binion. These six-shooter specialists had been burying bodies for years. Nesbit and Thomas were brought in for questioning. The bewildered hombres claimed it was *them* who were being attacked. Where were their rights, their civic protections? They were only returning fire in self-defense. They also understood the police had no evidence. Sure enough, once again, charges were never filed.

The news outlets and press jumped on this story. They clamored with stars in their eyes that Herbert Noble was no mere mortal

human. No run-of-the-mill gambling operator. No sir, no ma'am, this man Noble, who had survived the *fifth* attempt on his life, must have a golden horseshoe shoved up his ass. He must have nine lives. He must be . . . *THE CAT*!

Looking to Go Legit

Noble was also hit with the moniker "The Human Clay Pigeon" as well as "The Sieve" because his body was Swiss cheese with the amount of holes blown into it. Friends and family said he wore the names with pride, especially because he knew how much they would be eating away at his rival. Truth is, though, Herbert was also getting tired of it all.

Living life avoiding bombs and bullets on a regular basis can turn into an exhausting existence. The Cat's adrenal glands were maxed out from always being on high alert. Running the rat race, dodging the mouse traps, and avoiding the predators was becoming a strenuous and monotonous task. Like hiking up the side of a mountain in a blizzard, it will eventually wear you down.

Mildred shared in the spoils of being Mrs. Herbert Noble. She enjoyed the benefits of Herbert's freewheeling lifestyle. It allowed them many precious luxuries that neither had ever dreamed were possible growing up in the West Dallas slums. Country clubs, socialite gatherings, prestigious parties, multiple homes, minks, and pearls, they were all part of Mildred's regular routine. She was enamored with the sweet side of success. What she was *not* interested in was discussing her husband's illegal activities. Nor his notorious press clippings, which were becoming a frequent occurrence. She loved her husband and she stood by her man. But she also knew that all cats will eventually run out of lives.

Herbert felt the strain of the constant pressure in his business being placed on his marriage. He began to consider alternatives. His

passion (besides Mildred) had always been flying and planes. He had a runway with planes and hangars on the Diamond M. Following his heart, he started an airplane parts surplus business. Next, he set his sights on a decommissioned army airfield in North Fort Worth. Herbert negotiated with a group of partners from New York to buy the outdated airfield and turn it into a private airport. It would house storage, hangars, and maintenance facilities for aircraft repairs. The best part was that this new enterprise would be 100 percent legit.

Herbert had a pep in his step. He was spry and enthusiastic about this new prospect. It was all rolling in the right direction. Soon Noble would be the owner of the region's newest airport, a monumental achievement. The closing was only a few days away.

A Life-Changing Moment

Some days go down in infamy. In the lives of Herbert Noble and Benny Binion, the Dallas gang war, and the future of professional poker, November 29, 1949, was one of those days.

Herbert awoke and dressed in a snappy, suave blue suit with a subtle pattern, a designer scarf, and Italian silk tie. The Aristocratic Gambler looked mighty aristocratic. Why shouldn't he? It's not every day a man gets to close a deal on his own airport. He left his Oak Cliff home, kissing Mildred goodbye. A split-second decision was made to take her 1948 Cadillac instead of his Mercury. It's a life-changing day ahead, why not take the Caddy?

He drove southwest toward downtown Fort Worth. The air was cool and crisp. The leaves had turned an auburn brown. It was a picturesque time of tranquility. Herbert soaked it all in as he cruised in contentment. With this new deal, a passion project that would bring his family some financial security, he finally felt his life was coming around full circle.

Later that morning, Mildred left the house. She was headed north to the ranch to pick up one of their cooks and they would travel together to the grocery store. A feast was in the making! Party time for her and her benevolent husband later that evening. She was overjoyed at the prospects of a brighter, calmer future. Life is a crapshoot, and the Nobles seemed to be on the come-out roll, throwing nothing but sevens and elevens.

Mildred loaded herself into Herbert's Mercury, which was parked across the street. A full day of errands was upon her. She needed to get a move on. She jiggled the key into the ignition, turned it over, and . . .

BLAM!!

The Mercury erupted into a thunderous fireball blasting toward the heavens. The ground quaked violently. A fender catapulted over the Nobles' house and into their neighbor's yard. The explosion was so deafening it blew out the windows of houses up and down the block. Both car seats eventually came down from orbit, crashing into the middle of the street. The remains of the car doors and windows were reduced to tiny particles speared into neighborhood trees. The fire roared as plumes of black gasoline smoke crept into the sky, signaling a horrendous disaster.

Mildred's body was lit up like kindling in a bonfire. Her right leg was nowhere to be found. The rest of her body was shredded with thousands of lacerations, gashes, and holes, profound bleeding, and a face that was beyond recognition.

She died instantly.

A detonation device was connected behind the car's dashboard and triggered an exorbitant amount of nitroglycerin to ignite once the engine turned over.

A bomb meant for The Cat.

In Fort Worth, Herbert's head was in the clouds. His feet had yet to touch down from the anticipation and excitement. He was signing the last of the documents to finalize the transaction when US Attorney Frank Potter let him know that he had a phone call.

Herbert took the call, his partners and attorney all riding high as they watched him talk. The bright light of energy drained from his face. He was left anemic.

Noble whispered one word into the phone: "Dead?"

He nodded and hung up. Shell-shocked and devastated, he looked up at everyone in the room and uttered, "The bastard killed my wife."

CHAPTER 10

WAR PART 4

Herbert stood bent over, sullen, with his face pointed down. In front of him lay a body with a sheet draped over it, and he couldn't bring himself to look. Once he got the phone call, he had sped out of there with hell on his heels to get back to town. Now that he was here, he couldn't bring himself to look at the mangled body lying under that sheet. He knew it was her, but seeing her with his own two eyes would bring that reality crashing home . . . and The Cat was afraid.

The nervous funeral director at Lamar & Smith Funeral Home waited with trepidation next to the body for what seemed like ages. He had experienced this many times in his career with the bereaved. He softly and quietly cleared his throat, and it seemed to snap Noble out of his trance.

Herbert lifted his chin slightly and nodded, signaling for the undertaker to pull back the sheet. When he did, whatever seed of life that was in Noble's body oozed itself away and seeped into the underground, into the dark chambers of the earth. Where light does not penetrate, and nothing grows. Where souls go not to flourish but to linger in dormant hibernation. Where souls go when the excruciating trauma of life is no longer palatable.

Tears poured down his cheeks. He couldn't take his eyes from the remains of his beautiful Mildred. What was left of her charred and severed body. He couldn't look away from the carnage. He was glued to the travesty of misfortune that lay in front of him. The

silence ticked on like sand passing through an hourglass. The mortified undertaker, who had seen the worst of the worst, chose to cover his eyes. He reconciled that he may soon have to shake Mr. Noble free from his grief-stricken trance.

The waiting game suddenly ended. Like the flip of a switch, The Cat's life as he knew it was over. He broke into an unrelenting wailing and squalling fit. He let out a ferocious cry that came from deep within the belly. He grabbed Mildred and soon his hands were soaked in her blood. He wiped his face, and her blood mixed with a flood of his tears. His inexhaustible pain was nowhere near conquered. Herbert's framework of sanity was slipping away. The grief had him by the short hairs and was not letting go. The undertaker witnessed the metamorphosis from a strong warrior who walked through the doors into a feeble psychotic. Anyone nearby could hear Noble's wailing reverberating in the halls for what seemed like hours.

This was the moment The Cat snapped.

Herbert was eventually pried away and retreated home. Later that evening, a reporter stopped by to get a comment. He was taken back when a disheveled Noble greeted him with Mildred's blood still painted on his face. The reporter didn't know whether to run or hide. Herbert gave him a few quotes to chew on, declaring that he couldn't believe his wife was gone. He expressed the unwritten rule: that family was off-limits. He told the reporter that they had killed one of the best women that ever lived.

He put an exclamation point on it, pounding it home: "I wish it had been me."

Within days, Mildred Noble was laid to rest. Her solid-bronze casket was valued over $15,000 and weighed two tons. The casket was the most elaborate and expensive ever purchased in Dallas at the time. Several enormous leg breakers threw out their backs trying to lift it that day. The funeral was attended by over a thousand people with a car procession that stretched for miles.

Noble had an army of allies on both sides of the law. Mildred was a social butterfly whom ladies flocked to be around. They all turned out to pay their respects. Whether gangster, politician, lawman, or homemaking queen, one thing all could agree on was that the death was an atrocious calamity. A misstep of epic proportions.

The asphalt jungle never gives up the dead nor does it speak in riddles. If you listen closely the jungle is always talking, and it speaks the truth.

Everybody Knows . . .

The two suspects of the heinous bombing were front and center. Herbert knew, and the Dallas police knew the identity of the culprits. R.D. Mathews, a treacherous triggerman and one of the most the lethal enforcers to ever walk the mean streets of Big D. Wherever he traveled, death would follow. And Lois Green, Noble's *other* personal nemesis. The deviant who had his own star on the hit man walk of fame had tried multiple times to take Noble out. He was an unencumbered killing machine, who, like Billy the Kid, got off on watching bodies drop, floundering on the side of intense lunacy.

Both were connected to The Cowboy and his outfit. Both were eager to put The Cat in the ground.

R.D. was overheard discussing the Noble predicament a week before the explosion and announced he would be the one to collect on the bounty. There was no doubt he was involved. Police congregated around coffee pots and water coolers searching for any evidence that might stick. The harder they deliberated, the harder the truth continued to sink in: They had nothing. R.D. was arrested and brought in but released with the police having no leg to stand on. He was interrogated and given a sketchy polygraph. Mathews was way too slick for

any of these maneuvers. He knew the drill. He was in and out and back on the streets in no time. The charges against him were dropped. Time to keep flinging mud against the wall.

The swell of tension was escalating like a runaway wagon train with a team of blind mules headed for the edge of a cliff. The streets were set to ignite and blow sky-high at any moment. Law enforcement understood that Noble and his crew were capable of their own brand of diabolical destruction. They needed to get a handle on the turmoil before civilians were caught in the crosshairs.

Investigators corralled Noble and advised him to let them do their jobs. This was no time for rash actions and retributions. Relax, and justice will soon be served. This was the tune they sang, anyway. They pleaded with the audacity of a squabbling preacher man for Herbert to please, for God's sake, stand down. The more the detectives begged, the more evident it was to both parties that they wouldn't be able to deliver on any of their promises.

Herbert was quick to throw the press a few scraps of meat. He expressed his doubts about the boys in blue. "I don't think the police can do much about it. All those plans to kill me have been made by the same man, a kill-crazy man. The fellow who is behind this is 1,500 miles from Dallas right now."

Binion's name was never mentioned, nor did it need to be. The asphalt jungle speaks the truth, you just got to listen.

Reporters ravaged on like hungry wolves in a frenzy for more scraps. They pressed him for more sound bites. He wouldn't give in, only uttering, "He's a mad killer."

The press feasted on the story in Nevada by questioning Benny. He stated that he never met Mildred but had heard she was a fine woman. "I was sorry as hell to see her killed like that . . . terrible thing." He admitted that he knew Mr. Herbert Noble, but of course he wasn't trying to have him killed. Benny was in search of a steak dinner, so if you'll please step on out of his way . . .

The reporters made their notes, but they all knew what time it was. You don't need a weatherman to know which way the wind blows.

Lost in His House of Fear

Herbert followed these events with a spiraling plunge into the depths of mental mayhem. He retreated into the far recesses of his mind, where reality bids farewell and dismal paranoia takes control. Once there, any sane thoughts slowly digress and eventually slip away, overrun by haunting delusions and hallucinations. Like the clown who gets lost in his own house of mirrors, He becomes fixated on his face in the mirror staring back at himself while he howls with laughter, simultaneously wailing with tormenting pain as tears stream down his face. Unable to pull himself away, the clown is lost in his own delirium and can never return as a functioning member of society.

Herbert and the clown were becoming one and the same.

With Mildred's death, his one light in the fog was now snuffed out. Business took a back seat. Revenge and vengeance took the front. Herbert was driving the car, but he couldn't see the road as his eyes were blinded with rage.

If you wanted to speak with The Cat, you had to prepare yourself for a laboring pat down. It didn't matter if you were a friend or family. Everybody got the same treatment. If you didn't like it, that was too damn bad. Herbert became downright irritable for anyone to deal with. The Reaper was playing tricks with Noble. Everywhere he looked, death was lurking in the shadows.

He turned his home into a fortress, which became known as "The House of Fear." It was tighter than Fort Knox with a menagerie of locks and dials of all sizes. As the ranch was now his mainstay, he decided on surrounding the property with guard dogs.

However, not Dobermans or German Shepherds. Herbert chose a breed with much more aggression . . . the Chihuahua. He bought a pack of them to run roughshod over his premises and snap at the heels of any sodbuster that dare consider trespassing. Their high-pitched yelping was better than any alarm system Herbert could install. He could hear them yapping clear away in his barn. In case that wasn't enough, he also surrounded the place with peacocks and a special breed of vocal hens, all the best alarms nature could provide.

He turned the night into day with stadium-style floodlights that surrounded the ranch house. Herbert wasn't concerned with the glare interrupting his sleep. He had given up on that luxury of life. Instead, he caught a few brief winks here and there. He kept his rifle in one hand and his bible in the other. Like the walking dead, he meandered without purpose throughout the night with the rifle, the bible, and the guard dogs by his side.

His mornings were spent in prayer at the cemetery. Long-winded conversations with Mildred's headstone while Herbert cursed and ranted, vowing that hell would be paid for the abomination that was her demise. These rants were followed by uncontrollable bouts of crying. He would resume his feisty sermon, declaring that he would wait on no man to serve justice. He would seek it on his own, like he always had. Noble was one who took care of things, be it business or blood.

The Cat Sends a Message

R.D. Mathews would think long and hard about allowing another guest to stay overnight. R.D had laid low after his questioning and harassment by Dallas's finest. But an old acquaintance had contacted him looking for a place to stay. R.D. obliged and let him stay over.

The guest had ulterior motives.

Mathews slumbered peacefully in his bed, not with visions of sugar plums but burning bodies dancing in his head. He was startled by the creaking of a floorboard.

Before he became fully conscious a .22 bullet *shattered* his left eye.

Through his right eye he could barely make out a figure scurrying from his bedroom in the darkness. The gun residue hung in the air like a soupy haze. The bullet had blown out his orbital lobe, traveled through his skull, and exited out the temple.

Mathews wasn't going to take this lying down. He was no quitter. He propped himself up and stumbled toward the door. He used his one good eye (which was like looking through a peep hole) to locate his vehicle. It's not safe for a one-eyed man to be driving, especially late at night, but R.D. didn't let that stop him. He miraculously drove himself to the hospital, where doctors were able to tend to his condition. He survived, but was never the same, physically or mentally.

Revenge Long Overdue

Hollis DeLois Green, known simply as Lois Green.

A baby-faced executioner, a devil-spawn child, a killer's killer. Lois's name alone sent spine-tingling chills into the hearts of many in the Dallas underworld.

Lois was raised in whorehouse and his mama was a prostitute who never saw him as anything more than an accident and a burden. His daddy wasn't in the picture . . . but we already know who or what he was.

Lois spent his teen years stealing cars and raising exorbitant amounts of hell. After a short stint in jail, he traveled to New York City. Living life in the Big Apple, Lois continued his tradition of

living outside the law. He preferred the company of convicts over cops. He was suspected of killing a police officer but never convicted. His exploits earned him a reputation as a man to be avoided at all costs.

In Dallas he set up headquarters at a dive bar for degenerates known as "The Trap." No matter his character defects, Lois had executive-level attributes. He was a leader of a gang known as both "Lois Green's Boys" and "The Forty Thieves." The hooligans garnered that well-deserved reputation from their innate ability to steal everything from anything, whether bolted to the ground or not: banks, trains, trucks, houses, old lady's pocketbooks, etc.

They were also highly efficient in the murder-for-hire business. Lois believed from a business perspective that it was important to be diversified. Whether stealing or killing, no use having all your eggs in one basket. Green led by example, he was hands on, especially when it came to contract killings. He would never ask a man to do anything he wouldn't do.

Benny respected Lois's unique skill set of problem-solving techniques. He utilized him as a top enforcer. Green continued to outperform expectations year after year. Binion and Green leaned on each other. The Cowboy knew he would get the results he demanded when he dispatched Lois to flex his muscles. In return, Green received a big-time financial backer in his hip pocket.

Many criminals would have a longer life span if they could just shut the fuck up, or better yet, if they were mute. Green fit into that category. The homicidal killer couldn't help himself as he blabbered all over the city that he had blown up a woman in a car. Noble got wind of the news. He already figured that Green was a prime suspect, based on the previous attempts on his life, but this confirmed it. The new revelation sealed the deal for him.

Noble was burning the vengeance candle at both ends. It was time for somebody to go.

On December 23, 1949, Green and his gang were celebrating at the Sky Vu nightclub, a hangout for ill-reputed and onery degenerates.

Green and his crew were kings in this amoral den of sexcapades. The Sky Vu was legendary for its debauchery and triple-X throwdowns. It was a place where the sky was the limit for sexual proclivities. All ages were permitted and all orifices were available.

Herbert had a connection through a waitress that worked the club. She notified him when Green arrived that night. Green continued to pour libations down his throat and take in live music. Herbert casually waited as quiet as a church mouse hidden in the shadows next to Green's car, which was parked in an alley behind the club.

The air had a frosty bite to it. Green staggered out, liquored up to the brim, at around one AM. His dark gray topcoat danced as he stumbled along. His signature fedora covered his dirty blond locks. He reached his Oldsmobile and grasped the door handle. A noise blurted out from the darkness.

"Lois Green!"

Green swiveled around and caught a blast to the left side of his abdomen, partially missing and burying buckshot in Green's car door. Before the stunned Green had a chance to react, the second wave of projectiles donkey kicked him backward, burying deep within his chest and throat.

The third shot missed completely. It didn't matter, Green buckled and went down for the count. He lay dead on the cold pavement near the front right wheel.

Herbert grimaced a smile on the other end of a smoking shotgun.

A few days later, Noble received a copy of Green's morgue photo and exclaimed exuberantly, "There he is. There's the dirty son of a bitch."

Green's funeral was a cadre of Dallas's nastiest, most hard-assed criminals. The majority kept their mouths shut. Prying eyes and eager ears were everywhere.

Police went through the motions, but no one pressed too hard. There were three plausible theories. First, a rival within Green's

gang pulled the trigger. Second, Binion ordered the hit for punishment of the botched Noble bombing. Third, Noble was behind it. The prevailing theory was number three. No one seemed to care. The baby-faced executioner would no longer be disturbing the peace. Case closed. No arrests were made.

Fueling the Fire

If Noble relished in the small victory, his revelry was short-lived. On New Year's Eve, 1949, Herbert planned a peaceful night at home in Oak Cliff. A friend was scheduled to join him for a drink later in the evening. His daughter Freda Lou and her boyfriend were visiting from boarding school in Virginia. Someone needed to be home to chaperone and that someone was Herbert.

At around nine PM, he decided to make a quick trip to the nearby drugstore. After retrieving his keys, Herbert stepped out the front door and turned back to lock it. He twisted around and was immediately blinded by a sudden flash of high-beam headlights from a parked car across the street.

The hairs on his neck stood up. His internal radar went into high alert, but he was frozen by the flood of white lights.

BAM!

A gunshot echoed endlessly into the night. Nothing. First shot missed. So did the next couple.

Herbert's heart raced.

Then another shot erupted, and a rifle bullet pierced through his left arm, scattering bone fragments in all directions while continuously traveling through his left hip and lodging in his spine. The magic bullet wreaked havoc on Noble's body.

In throbbing agony, Herbert found the intestinal fortitude to turn back around and bang on the door with his good hand, yelling for help. A clicking of the rifle chamber and another shot was fired.

It missed. Freda opened the door and her dear old dad collapsed into her arms. The car sped away into the blackness.

Paramedics arrived on the scene. Noble's discombobulated mind could not make heads or tails of the situation. The overriding impending doom had taken control. Herbert was convinced the paramedics were in on the hit. He held them at gunpoint as his fragile mental state continued to disintegrate. Finally, he recognized an officer of the law who showed up on the scene, and the officer convinced him to allow treatment.

Noble had survived once again.

He returned to Methodist Hospital, which could now be considered his third home. The next morning, he allowed reporters to his bedside, lamenting on how he did not deserve this injustice, this gauntlet of horrors, this barrage of attacks. He downplayed his status in the crime world as that of a simple gambler, a man just trying to make his way against corrupt and evil forces hell-bent on destroying him.

"I can't go any longer like this. I am at the end of my road."

He left reporters with a sound bite that would leave headlines.

"I'm afraid I'm going to have to take the law into my own hands."

A shocking statement that suggested vigilante justice might be the only answer. The reporters smirked and wrote it down. The Cat was always good for a quote or two.

There is a "code" to this game, but sometimes the streets get to talking, and this time they were saying that in this most recent attempt, the shooter was none other than . . . Sonny "The Groceryman" Lefors.

No Place Is Safe

This shooting was no walk in the park. It exceeded expectations as far as recovery time. Five weeks after the attack, Noble was still in the hospital.

His mental, physical, and spiritual energy were all dwindling. His gas tank for living life was on empty. The three-headed soul-snatching serpent of depression, anger, and paranoia had reared its ugly head(s) and devoured the remnants of his trembling mind.

Perhaps Mr. Noble had sufficient reason to be nervous.

February 6, 1950, was yet another restless night in his hospital room. At around eleven PM, Herbert got out of bed and meandered around the room in his pajamas. He had always been a night owl, but now his mind couldn't shut off for even a moment's rest. He fought that depression, anger, and paranoia, along with a sense of dread that he was out of touch with a business he had worked so hard to build, but which now could be slipping away.

He flipped on the lights and ruminated on his situation. He also questioned the doctors' abilities to get him out of this place.

Suddenly, a booming sound cascaded over the entire room.

A bullet shattered the glass window, sailing through the room and blowing plaster off the ceiling before lodging itself above the bed. Noble's instincts took over. Herbert hit the ground and reinjured his arm. He crawled back into bed, unplugging his lamp, and yelped for help.

He would later describe the sound as a "cannon." Noble was in a secure private room on the fourth floor. An outdoor open courtyard was located below his room, which amped up his suspicions. The courtyard was surrounded by foliage and leafy trees, which provided ample coverage for a shooter. The assassin need only know what room number Noble resided in, and they could correlate the specific room window. Noble had run these assessments through the traps in his mind over a hundred times. He had expressed his concerns, and now his serendipitous nightmare had become a reality.

The gunman realized he had missed his target, shagged ass, and left the scene.

The Cat survived yet again.

The police remained consistent in their duties: They simply read the funny papers.

The press found themselves in a familiar position, coalescing around Herbert Noble's bedside like he was a sage shaman who spins yarns on how to live a long, healthy life. Herbert could counter with his own philosophies on how to stay alive during a bombastic gang war. Some reporters wondered if they would be rocked with shell casings, blasted to bits with a bomb, or have their throats smoothly slit with a straight edge for keeping company with the likes of The Aristocratic Gambler.

Herbert expressed outrage that "they" would try and get him at a hospital. He bemoaned the repeated blues that he was a victim and didn't deserve these unscrupulous attempts. He was fully aware that his enemies were watching his every move and even insinuated that one or two reporters might be working as spies. Then he cleared his throat and gave them his quote.

"I will not be run out of Dallas."

With the latest attempt, number eight, Noble's frantic state of mind shifted into a ferocious fury. He zeroed in on the bullseye. There was only one goal in mind:

Kill Benny Binion at any cost.

Lawmen on all levels knew that the dam was about to come crashing down. The wave of violence would exceed all levels of the wildest imagination. Enough was enough.

A sit-down was needed, for everyone's sake.

CHAPTER 11

WAR PART 5

In the spring of 1950, Americans were turned on to a new phenomenon. This newfangled contraption known as the "television" was taking the country by storm. One of the first people they got to see on the grainy black-and-white screen was US Senator Estes Kefauver and his traveling road show investigating organized crime in America, a national issue that both terrorized and fascinated the public.

Estes, a backwoods coon skinner from Tennessee, and his US Senate Subcommittee on Organized Crime was on a crusade to dig up dirt while investigating gambling in America. As the committee traveled from town to town, just like the circus, making its way through America's most violent hotbeds, a lineup of gold-star elite racketeers was paraded into the courtrooms. Such names as Willie Moretti, Joe Adonis, and Frank Costello would all be put to the test. Even high-ranking politicians such as Harold Hoffman of New Jersey and Mayor William O'Dwyer of New York were getting roasted in questioning by the committee. The intensified public scrutiny was creating a widespread ripple effect of concern within the underworld.

Two of the greatest areas of concern were Dallas and now, Las Vegas!

The bosses out West were concerned that their new counterpart, The Cowboy, was bringing hot grease to an already simmering skillet. The eyes of Texas were upon them. The slayings, the car bombings, the exploitation of human life, the collateral damage were all

taking a toll. The publicity from the gang wars seeped into media outlets across the country.

Action had to be taken.

Dave Berman was designated to deliver the message. Dave was manager and part owner of the Flamingo Hotel and Casino. He took control after the demise of the late great Bugsy Siegal, his former partner. Berman, a smooth operator with a sharp mind for numbers, was known affectionately by his moniker: "The Toughest Jew in Vegas." The man had no fear of violence. As a mouthpiece for some well-connected Italians in New York and Chicago, Berman had the right to lay down the law.

He took a seat with the brash Binion and explained that a change needed to take place. The heat that Benny was bringing was no good for business. He was creating a whirlwind of excitement that led to the shining of spotlights into the dark crevasses, the black holes that needed to remain black. Berman reiterated that serious people were becoming seriously concerned about The Cowboy's actions. It was high time to settle this beef with Noble. If not, there would be consequences.

Searching for Answers

Herbert Noble had no interest in peace offerings, or tribunal truces. He was on a deliberate, simple, straightforward mission: destroy Binion at any cost. However, he was interested in answers. He wanted to confirm his unyielding suspicions about who was ultimately responsible for his wife's death and the numerous attempts on his life. These questions seemed to have clear-cut answers, but Noble yearned for confirmation.

Those answers would be worth their weight in gold to put these debilitating repetitive thoughts to bed in his exhausted mind. The frying pan was heating up for Noble just like the rest of America's

most tantalizing hoodlums. Local authorities had twisted the knobs on the stove from medium to high in hopes of shutting down the killings and cutting down on the blood spilling, or at least trimming it down from a gallon to a pint. The pressure continued to mount.

The Cat had no inclinations of wanting to speak with this uncouth son of a bitch. On the flip side, an end to the feud could bring some much-needed harmony and peace, and perhaps settle those troubling thoughts. There was at least a consideration on Noble's part. A tiny sliver of hope that he might be open to a potential meeting. If the heavens were to align themselves.

There is only one reason to send a fox to a hen house, a pyromaniac to put out a house fire, or a con man to make a peace offering.

The answer: to make things worse.

Perhaps that was Benny's intention when he ordered the soft-bellied scoundrel Harold Shimley to travel from Nevada to Texas to settle scores.

The Wrong Kind of Middleman

Shimley was a despised gambler and notorious liar who claimed to run with the likes of the legend Titanic Thompson, even after Titanic claimed he barely knew the sad sack. Like so many others, Shimley was in awe of this superhero of the gambling world. Harold moved on to become a general flimflam man, a gratuitous grifter who had multiple aliases and committed several crimes as he roamed from state to state.

He had found himself kicking around Dallas during this time, having been booted from Houston for credit fraud. While in the Big D, he added to his rap sheet with theft, gambling, conspiracy, kidnapping, and more nihilistic behavior. Harold also occasionally

found solace in the scorching desert sun. Nevada became a safe landing spot for him.

Once in Vegas he somehow got wind of The Cowboy being directed from the powers that be to put his beef with The Cat to bed. Shimley interjected himself into the middle of this complex situation. He did have a past connection with both Binion and Noble, as the paths of criminals often tend to cross. He jumped at the opportunity and volunteered to be the middleman. A solution to this predicament might put him in the running for the underworld's version of the Nobel Peace Prize. A more reasonable expectation was to boost his sagging reputation while putting some greenbacks in his pocket.

Shimley got the go-ahead. On March 10, 1950, he reached out to Noble to set up a meeting. Noble initially did not feel the inspiration, but after deliberation, he reluctantly agreed. He had stipulations, though, mainly that the meeting would have to be somewhere far, far away from his ranch or home in town. The Love Field tourist court became the agreed-upon destination. Noble also required that his business partner from The Airmen's Club, Phillip Stein, be in attendance. As an extra precaution, Herbert solicited his friend George Butler, now a lieutenant of the Dallas Police Department, to witness the impending meeting. Butler arranged to have the affair recorded and transcribed.

The Possibility of Peace

As the sun rises in the east every morning, its rays bring a glimmer of hope. The possibility of a new day, new adventures, and a new life. The crime world was feeling this same posterity of hope. The agreed-upon meeting brought a sliver of optimism. That peace would prevail, and everyone could get back to doing what they do best: separating the general public from their dollars.

Shimley, Noble, and Stein all arrived on pins and needles at the designated location. Lieutenant Butler was close by, listening in on the conversation. After some back and forth about Stein's involvement, and his hesitancy to have anything to do with this matter, Shimley got to the heart of it right away.

> SHIMLEY: *Now the whole damn thing can be straightened out, and I know what I'm talking about.*

Noble was clearly uncomfortable early on and throughout this entire interaction, always on edge, hemming and hawing with everything Shimley said. Reading the transcripts, it's clear that he doesn't expect anything to come from this . . . but he's there for the slightest chance.

Because that's what a gambling man does.

Shimley did a little bullshitting, trying to earn Noble's trust and making it clear to all parties that he was there on behalf of Binion and Dave Berman.

> SHIMLEY: *I wouldn't harm a hair on your head, man. I'm your friend. You don't know what I've done. I never put you in any spot, have I, or did anything but talk to you like a friend would talk to a friend, have I?*
>
> NOBLE: *Yeh.*
>
> SHIMLEY: *I've been all over the country. Every——place out there, just like I told you. Now, I've made up with some people out there that own the big Flamingo Hotel, this eastern outfit that owns the joint. Your name and his name is the talk of the——country.*

Noble personified his Cat image by playing coy in the conversation. He listened closely, not giving an inch. He stayed steadfast in his main objective of determining who the dirty, mangy bastard was that ordered the hit on his wife. Sensing he needed to

get to it, Shimley professed that Binion was heartbroken beyond belief over Mildred's bombing, and that he claimed to have nothing to do with any of the attempts on Noble.

> SHIMLEY: *And the——himself claims he spent $10,000 on the investigation (of Mildred's death), and has it ironclad, and he hasn't had a thing, and swears and hopes his children will die if he's ever had one thing ever done to you in any way, shape or form. . . . I'm merely telling you what I've been told.*

Throughout this short conversation, Shimley repeated Benny's vow several times, telling Noble over and over that The Cowboy cried like there was no tomorrow over the unjustified event, while simultaneously raising five fingers and solemnly swearing on his children's lives that he emphatically had nothing to do with the hit. Later on, sensing that Noble wasn't buying it, Shimley once again reiterated Benny's vow with a little extra sauce.

> SHIMLEY: *He didn't only convince me, he convinced the biggest mob in the United States.*

Noble offered nothing in response, looking to Stein and grunting one-word affirmations. Herbert pondered the information while keeping his emotions to himself. He was more interested in what the jaybird was doing on the edge outside the window.

Shimley told him over and over how important it was for the people out West to bring an end to all this, for everyone's sake, claiming he had the solutions and that all could be forgiven. He, with the help of Stein, who had connections with Herbert and Benny, could bring an end to this entire misunderstanding. Stein stressed over and over that he wanted no part of any of this, sometimes pleading to Noble, who took his side.

It was time for Shimley to switch tactics, telling Noble carefully, in so many words, who he, the mob, and Benny believed was trying to kill him.

That got The Cat's attention.

Shimley pointed the finger at some associates of Delbert Bowers, Mildred's brother, who Shimley said had a vendetta against Noble for getting his sister involved in a life of crime that ultimately led to her death.

SHIMLEY: *He says, get that all stopped and kill those three down there in Texas. Not talking about you, talking about some other people, understand, connected with this Bowers, now I'm telling you . . .*
NOBLE: *Who? Who are they? Tell me.*
SHIMLEY: *I don't know who they are.*
NOBLE: *Oh, you do know.*
SHIMLEY: *No, I don't. I don't know who they are, but I will know and I think he (Stein) can help me find out.*
STEIN: *I don't want to be in on that.*

Playing both sides of the coin, Shimley suggested that if Noble would give the okay, Benny could and would immediately remedy the Bowers problem.

SHIMLEY: *Are you afraid of me, Herbert?*
NOBLE: *No, I'm not. If I was, I wouldn't even be talking to you.*
. . .
SHIMLEY: *By gosh, he can stop it.*
NOBLE: *That man out yonder?*
SHIMLEY: *You ain't kiddin'. He'll stop it or we'll kill all three of them—one or the other. And you won't have to have nothing to do with it either. You know that man, I mean loves them kids just like you do your daughter.*

But no matter what Shimley threw at him, Noble seemed unconvinced. Years of hatred for his rival had hardened his heart, and the loose lips of some sleazeball like Shimley wasn't going to soften it up, not when it came to Benny Fuckin' Binion. None of this was making any sense to The Cat, and he was getting tired of Harold's prattlin' and ramblin.'

Sensing he was losing the man, Shimley shifted to his last resort: getting Benny Binion on the phone so the two rivals could talk.

At first Noble wanted no part of a call.

NOBLE: Ask him what he wants to tell me.
SHIMLEY: Well, come on and talk to him.——it. Man's 1,500 miles away. Just talk to the——.

With a little push, Noble finally agreed to hop on. Perhaps a truce was shaping up after all . . .

Their talk lasted less than a minute.

After some initial forced pleasantries and chitchat about Noble having a cold and some bad write ups Mildred got in the local papers, Noble got to the heart of it.

NOBLE: Well, I just wondered, I just wondered, I didn't know what, what the score was.

Whatever Benny said on the other line didn't cut it.

Noble couldn't get off the phone fast enough and almost immediately handed it back to Shimley. He didn't do it out of anger. The Cat was too smart for that. He still wanted to see if anything could come out of this meeting. But he was certainly not convinced in any way, shape, or form that Benny Binion wasn't involved in his string of bad luck.

Shimley hung up the phone and continued to press Noble, thinking he had done his job, that progress had been made. He

continued to talk in circles about Benny not being involved, the boys out West being able to take care of those who were involved, whoever they were, and how he was Noble's friend and would be by his side for all of this. Then he offered up his final plea.

> *SHIMLEY: If we can get this thing straightened out and settle this thing for them, will you be friends enough with the man that we can all make money and open the town?*

Noble offered up a simple, "Yeh."

That was enough for Shimley.

Noble didn't argue, didn't push back, didn't fight. He didn't buy it either. None of it. The one opportunity for peace to happen between these two bitter rivals never really had a chance . . .

As the sun sets in the west, the close of the day is near. It provides a period of reflection. A time to take inventory of actions and the day's activities. A time to celebrate the wins and consider the losses. In terms of this meeting, one can only wonder, what could have been done differently? How could it have gone better? The day started with the ultimate gift of hope, the possibility of a positive shift. The possibility of peace. All those assertions soon became a distant memory. It all went by the wayside. What if a different character had been sent to negotiate? What if Benny had been more sincere? What if Herbert had been more open to the possibilities? What if Stein had played a bigger part? What if . . .

History could have been made in a progressive way on this day, if a set of different circumstances were put in play. Or maybe, just maybe . . .

Peace is overrated.

CHAPTER 12
WAR PART 6

Possessed.

Within days after the initial summit, Harold Shimley became a possessed man. The angelic spirit on his right shoulder had momentarily whipped the demonic spirit on his left. The result was a man destined to tell the truth. He could not tell another lie (not on this day, anyway). No, Shimley was not a man of conviction; it's more likely that on this day, the angelic spirit made him a better offer than the demon, y'know, the one working with the Big Man in the desert. There's a good chance that Shimley realized he wasn't going to get what he thought he deserved . . . or worse. More likely, the Big Man wasn't happy with how the "peace talks" went.

Whatever the case, Shimley had his come to Jesus moment and marched his ass right back down for another visit with Mr. Herbert Noble.

Now off the record, Shimley professed that everything he so gallantly spoke of during their original conference was a complete sham. A lie. Adamant and stone-faced, he pontificated as if he stood upon stacks of bibles. He would speak only the truth from this point forward, and the truth was that Binion still had a contract out on Noble's life.

Shimley swore that this was the whole truth, so help him God.

He did, however, have an answer. A simple solution to a nagging problem. It was time for Benny to take a dirt nap. He pleaded with Noble that he would be doing everyone a favor if he would just

get on with killing The Cowboy. His angelic spirit was inspired by some Old Testament vengeance, an eye for an eye. However, Harold was here to do more than just talk. He was a man of action and stick-figure artistry. He shared a hand-drawn map of the Binion compound on Bonanza Road in Las Vegas and gave it to Noble as a gift. He had high hopes that this information would allow Herbert to finally complete the perfect retribution.

Harold exhaled with giant relief. His new mantra: "The truth will set you free."

His honesty may have set him free, but that didn't mean his life could not be erased with a simple wink or nod. A short time later, Shimley was in Tulsa. He wasn't "living on Tulsa Time," more like borrowed time. As he entered a local five-and-dime, a barrage of bullets rang out for everyone in the vicinity to hear. The gunshots missed Harold's body, but the warning hit him right between the eyes. He took the message to heart and went directly into hiding, never to return to Dallas or Las Vegas again.

Noble parlayed his newfound treasure map into a solid-gold plan. First, he connected with a pair of colleagues located in Old Mexico in the aircraft salvage business. This group not only had access to an assortment of airplane parts but also big-time explosives. Noble put in an order for two miliary-grade bombs capable of mass destruction.

Second, Herbert utilized his aviation mastermind to its full potential. He was familiar with a wide array of airplane motors and mechanical engineering. He flew his planes on a regular basis. That was one love that had not been stripped of him in the tumultuous roller coaster of his life. Noble would mount the two bombs underneath one of his planes and fly west. He would do the deed himself.

Third, he needed a spot to refuel the plane between Texas and where he was headed. The chosen spot was Tucson, Arizona. For this leg of the plan, he reached out to Detroit kingpin Peter "Horse Face" Licavoli, a raucous rumrunner from the earliest days of

Prohibition. A fabled leader of the deadly Purple Gang, Pete once shot a man while reading the newspaper. Licavoli and Noble shared similar commonalities. Both had climbed to the upper echelon of their respected organizations. Both owned ranches. Both named their ranches after their beloved wives—Peter had his Tucson tract named "The Grace Ranch" for his wife Grace Bommarito. Most importantly, both men despised Benny Binion, making Licavoli a trusted ally. His ranch had an airstrip, and he obliged Noble to use it as a refueling station.

From there Noble could continue flying toward his ultimate destination, Casa Binion, to complete his ultimate mission:

Kill 'em all.

Meaning the entire Binion household. Benny, his wife, and their five kids.

With his plan set in motion, it wouldn't be long until Noble's palate would get to savor the cold, sweet taste of revenge.

Timing Is Everything

On April 12, 1950, Lieutenant Butler sipped his coffee and enjoyed the scenery as he traversed the back roads of Denton County. The peaceful interlude was a lullaby to the mind. He pulled into the entrance of the Diamond M. It was a customary friendly call to update Herbert on the investigation of Mildred's death and on general crime gossip floating around the streets.

George moseyed into the hangar and marveled at the assortment of planes Noble had accumulated. He located Herbert, shirtless and twisting wrenches underneath one of his most recent purchases, a cherry-red Stagger Wing Beech.

As George examined his surroundings, the feeling of serenity soon eclipsed. Through the corner of his eye, he spotted two cargo bombs, three feet in length, lying on the hangar floor. Butler

studied deeper and determined that Noble was in the process of welding bomb racks to the bottom of the plane.

Just what in tarnation was going on here?

Butler sucked in a deep breath and cleared his throat.

A startled Noble jolted upward and grabbed a reliable carbine rifle lying within arm's length. Within milliseconds he was on his feet and had the rifle aimed at Butler's noggin. George went for his gun, and a Mexican standoff was in effect.

Butler responded to the hostile situation with, "What the hell you think you're doing?!"

Noble was in no mood for visitors. His mind was working in overdrive as he yelled, "Get the hell out of here, George." Both guns were still poised, shouldered, and ready to fire. "Leave me to my business."

"Herbert, put the damn rifle down. Now." The lieutenant was no longer asking.

The tension ramped up, the seconds felt like hours. Butler never broke his steely gaze deep into Noble's eyes. He knew the man, knew he was quickly sliding off the deep end in the days since Mildred's passing. The boys at the station were taking bets on when he would snap completely. Would today be that day?

Or worse, would it be the day he would have to put his friend down for good?

He ordered Noble to drop his weapon once more, this time using a stern voice. Finally, Noble relented. He lowered the rifle and then dropped to his knees; tears flowed like a river from his eyes. In the throes of an emotional breakdown, Herbert couldn't contain the floodgates anymore. His friend and confidant looked on with puzzled but sympathetic eyes.

"I never had a chance," blubbered Noble. He wailed a woeful tune that Benny had caught all the breaks, and he couldn't compete with The Cowboy's trifecta of money, power, and influence.

In retrospect, Herbert had caught his share of breaks. His dark-horse sheriff winning the election proved to be a pivotal point in

shipping Binion out of town. His crew had snuffed out the life of multiple Binion operatives. Noble's wide-reaching iron fist clutched his tormentors' throat and squeezed the neck until their faces turned grapefruit red and eventually ended with no pulse. He had played his part in this war.

Butler sought to pacify instead of crucify. He provided comfort to Noble's mental despair. The two men went from pointing guns at each other to discussing harbored feelings of the heart. George induced Herbert into detailing the full extent of the bomb plot. He was even given the treasure map of the Binion Bonanza compound. Butler concluded that this was the inner workings of an evil genius hell-bent on blowing Binion's dick into the dirt at all costs. He consoled Herbert and explained all the possible reasons why his plan was flawed. It was only suited for the severely demented. Listening to the reasoning, Noble came around to Butler's way of thinking. Perhaps his cop friend did have his best interests in mind.

On one of the stranger days in his wild career, Butler managed to defuse the situation. He diverted a disaster. He felt secure enough to make his departure but made damn sure he confiscated the map before leaving the hangar . . . along with the bombs.

The Cat Survives Once More

Not long after the faltered bombing fiasco, Noble found himself soaking up the suds in a West Dallas Café. By his lonesome. A few cornbread clodhoppers trounced through the front door: Franklin Strong and Leroy Gross, remnants of Lois Green's Forty Thieves Gang.

The air breathed of violence to come.

Gross and Strong eyed Noble with disdain, but both left well enough alone.

Herbert refused to let sleeping dogs lie. He belted out a roar, "Where's the rest of you goddam thugs?" He followed up by slamming a half-empty beer can over Strong's temple.

The injustices of the world on full display.

All three men went for their guns. Holy frijoles! Another Mexican standoff!

This café was no ordinary café. It was a hangout for the city's finest off-duty brass. Surrounded by Johnny Law, the situation quickly de-escalated, and the guns were lowered.

On June 14, 1950, Strong, Gross, and another hapless goon, Fleming Van Derrick, decided to go on a hunting trip. They set their sights on Denton County. These fellers weren't on a snipe hunt, nor were they on the lookout for any jackalopes. They were hunting for only one kind of animal—a cat.

They set up their makeshift hunting blind across the road from the entrance of the Diamond M.

At nine AM, Herbert's black Ford rattled over the cattle guard at the entrance of the ranch. Strong and Gross popped up from their hiding spot across the county road and fired upon their prey.

The first buckshot punctured the Ford's left front tire.

Two more blasts tore open a side of the car as Herbert sped away.

He calmly drove to a neighbor's house, where he called the cops and changed his tire.

The Cat survived to purr another day.

Strong and Gross had signaled their intentions months in advance. Both had blabbed that they would be collecting on the bounty that was still being offered. Their impromptu meeting of Noble at the café prior was merely convenient timing.

All was not well, and it was only going to get worse. Herbert accepted that now, learning a new aspect of survival following each new attempt. In November 1950, a brush fire was started on the north side of his ranch. Noble sniffed out the ploy as an arsonist

hoping to lure him out of his home to take a pot shot at him. He didn't take the bait. Instead, he stayed inside and waited for the fire department to come put the blaze out.

Unraveling Like a Ball of Yarn

With the recent attacks, The Cat's paranoia started to run rampant. Everywhere he looked, he found faces in the shadows. His already fragile mental stability dwindled to even lower, unconceivable depths. He became a hermit, locked behind the prison walls of his own home, forgoing traveling outside except for emergencies. He stationed his armed men in shacks scattered around the vicinity of the Diamond M.

If he did happen to venture out, he took refuge in large crowds. Always making sure he sat with his back to the wall, his eyes peeled. His life was spent looking in the rearview mirror and never taking the same route twice.

Noble's distrust bled into those closest to him, as he refused to use his men for bodyguards, fearing someone would outbid him for his life. "I might pay some guy five hundred dollars to protect me and then some bastard pays him six hundred dollars to kill me!"

For added protection, Herbert bought more Chihuahuas and peacocks. A man can never have too many Chihuahuas and peacocks, especially when everyone's out to get you.

The midnight demon persistently plagued him. Sleep had all but vanished entirely. Herbert redacted to restless periods in bed with multiple firearms under the covers beside him. He lived like a jazz star, wired on uppers to keep his focus throughout the night. When he attempted to come down in the mornings, he ingested tranquilizers and washed them down with a gallon of vodka. Anything for a few moments of temporary relief.

He was just over forty years old, but all those close to him suggested he looked like a haggard septuagenarian. His face resembled lines on a roadmap. His body was frail, gaunt, sickly, and his hair had turned snow white. His opossum eyes were hollowed out and vacant. The once dashing and debonair Aristocratic Gambler was no more. In his place, a ragged zombie had emerged.

His infamy had become his downfall. Not only was Benny looking to face-plant him, but Herbert's mouth wasn't doing him any favors. Gunslingers were vying far and wide to collect on the ever-expanding bounty. They wanted to slay the beast the cat. Herbert was harvesting new enemies. The bloodsuckers were coming out of the woodwork.

Even Mildred's brother Delbert, whom Shimley presented as the main troublemaker who was causing Herbert so much grief. Times had changed, and now Delbert got in line as one of the many who sought to take Noble down. He was now convinced that Herbert was responsible for his sister's death. He bode his time behind bars hoping and praying that he would soon be released and have the opportunity handle Noble himself.

A Problem He Can't Shake

On the western front, Benny was feeling his own insecurities.

He had a nemesis that just wouldn't die. The lead cowpuncher was used to issuing orders and having them followed to the full degree. When he ordered a body to be dropped, the only question is should the body be found or should it disappear?

This was not the case with Noble. Just like Wile E. Coyote, he kept coming back for more. There didn't seem to be enough bullets, bombs, or brawn to put this man away.

The issue wasn't only that Noble seemed unkillable but now the squirrely sumbitch was trying to drop a bomb on his family. He was

trying to wipe them all out. Benny received a copy of Noble's map. He was updated with details of the entire plot. The Cowboy was put on high alert and the panic set in. He loaded his family into a Cadillac and sent them out to Los Angeles for their safety. He called it a "surprise family vacation," but his main objective was to get them away from the Nevada compound as fast as possible. Like any stable provider, the safety of his family came first and foremost. He had to determine that the coast was indeed clear before he could allow for their return.

Something else that concerned Benny was the fear that he was losing his grip. He now had experienced a couple situations where his people had flipped on him. The dissention in his ranks disrupted his mental clarity. Who would turn next? Who would he send out with a pistol, then later find they have it pointed back at him? This corrosive suspicion was gnawing away at him.

The internal shaky beast known as paranoia had set up shop in both Noble's and Binion's minds. If the beast is not dealt with, it will eventually work its way through the nervous system and devour the soul.

Benny headed the beast off at the pass. He took charge, as a leader always does. No more wasting time. It was skull-crushing time. He upped the bounty on Noble's head even more, ensuring that all the crack-shot mercenaries from around the country would pack their bags and head to Dallas. Enough was enough.

Noble's Revenge Tour Continues

The year 1950 was a savage one for gangland violence in Dallas. A wave of old and new hustlers upped the ante, seeking fortune in the vice trade. Some got tangled up in the Binion/Noble rivalry. They had dreams of cashing in on the bounty. But that's all they were, dreams. Many were living fast and dangerous. Their fate eroded just

as fast as they found themselves in body bags or worse. Some were simply never found.

A pair of soft-spoken Italians arrived on the scene and claimed to Noble they could take care of his "Binion problem." They, in fact, could not. Herbert openly expressed his distrust of them. They were soon discovered in a clump of ragweed on the side of a dirt road. Their bodies were beaten, ravaged, with their bones shattered. Their heads had also been blown off.

There were other crime factions battling one another for the city's underworld wealth. Some had no connections to Binion or Noble. They were going after one another like crazed pit bulls. Gangsters killing gangsters. It was a bloody time. The citizens, police, and politicians all questioned one another: Who exactly was to blame?

Gentleman Jack Todd had a criminal acumen that was off the chart. He excelled in all facets of hoodlum behavior. His high-caliber, crime-infested mind was at the top of its class. There were only a small number of racketeers in North Texas that functioned on his level.

Gentlemen Jack had a telekinetic ability to move stolen goods without a trace. His brethren—lethargic, simple-minded street thugs—operated on a first-grade level. Jack, on the other hand, had a master's in crime. He was a vice lord's wet dream. He could run all the rackets in his sleep.

When he was calm, Jack could be reserved, performing at an optimum level. Poised and confident, carefully considering his words before speaking. He was a cool customer. His quiet demeanor could lull a baby . . . but his violent nature knew no boundaries. He showed pure brutality with no room for mercy. A psychotic man-child periodically took over his senses and screamed to jump out of his skin. The beatings and lashings could last for hours or until Jack could retain composure.

Jack was a close friend of Lois Green and a pallbearer at his funeral. He was also the reputed successor to take over Green's gang.

Word spread throughout the streets that he was the perfect candidate.

He was also on Noble's radar.

On January 23, 1951, Noble spied Todd inside Sonny Lefor's store. He patiently waited in the chilly darkness.

As Todd emerged from the store, Noble rolled up on him. He collared Todd and demanded, "Get in the car, I want to talk to you."

Todd remained calm and collected. He obliged and got inside. As soon as Herbert started the car, Jack jumped out and fled across the parking lot to his parked car.

Jack stopped in his tracks when he heard the echoing of a bullet cycling into the chamber of a .30 rifle. He slowly turned to find Herbert with the rifle aimed in his direction.

"Get in the car, Jack, or I'll shoot your damn brains out right here."

Todd once again surrendered and followed orders. The car eased away with both men inside.

Noble chose to drive in the dark with the headlights off. Gentlemen Jack was considering that this could ultimately be his final ride. Noble had the rifle centered on his face.

At some point, while trying to drive and train a rifle, Noble lost control of the vehicle and slammed into a ditch. Todd grabbed the barrel of the gun. A tug of war ensued with Todd finally wrestling the rifle away. The two continued to struggle among each other for possession of the firearm.

A couple walked by and took one glance at the rough-and-tumble action happening between the two men in the front seat. "Go get a room!" one of them yelled. And then they saw the gun and the two wrestling for it. They quickly scampered away and called the sheriff's department. Two local deputies were a short distance away. They arrived and broke up the melee.

Noble had bitten off a chunk of Todd's shoulder. However, it was Todd who did the most damage by chewing off a large portion

of Noble's right ear. It would require over fifty stitches back at home sweet home: Methodist Hospital.

During the following interrogation, Noble pointed to a news story that had come out earlier in the week. Todd had been arrested at an airport with a jar of nitroglycerin gel and a safe-blowing kit, wire fuses, and blasting caps.

"That's the same stuff they used to kill my wife!" Noble shouted.

Both men were released with slaps on the wrists.

The Year of the Bombs

The year 1951 was the year of the bombs in Dallas!

In February, a bomb *blasted* outside the front doors of Sonny Lefor's store. Debris went flying in all directions. Sonny wasn't there at the time. Two men managing the store were in the back when the blast rocked the building. They were not injured.

There was a slew of suspects. The Cat and his crew were front and center. Noble was perturbed to find Jack Todd commiserating with Sonny. A bunch of low-down scum buckets, anyone associated with Lois Green was on Noble's hit parade. Lefor's betrayal by secretly switching sides to Binion was enough to sign his death warrant by Noble. The Cowboy was another possibility. Sonny's duplicity toward him created a burr under his saddle. Benny had given him a job to do, and he hadn't performed. He was a no call, no show. The Groceryman had issues with other gangs. There was no shortage of possible suitors for the job.

Then, on February 13, 1951, in the wee hours of morning, a jumbo pack of dynamite sticks was hurled through the sky and *shattered* the front glass doors of The Airmen's Club. The explosion obliterated the entire first floor. It was during off hours, and no one was at the club. A blunt message rather than an attempted slaughter. The

resemblance of the two eruptions was obvious: The explosives were the same used in both buildings.

Herbert's majestic gambling hall crumbled. His pride and joy cratered. The gut-wrenching devastation sent a heartbroken man into a shell-shocked coma. This club represented not just the start of his rise to power, but also the fruition of years of hard work and believing himself to be something more. It was what made him a player on the scene, a hotbed for his type of crowd that reflected both sides of the complicated man himself. It was elegant and rough, a peaceful refuge for gamblers and a headquarters for violence. It was sophisticated and dangerous, just like Noble himself.

Now it was gone.

There was no means to quantify the grief.

Life boiled down to one simple priority. Survival.

Fire in the Sky

Herbert confined himself to his ranch fortress for good. He played peek-a-boo with the sunlight, only taking to the skies as a refuge. On March 22, 1951, Herbert decided to exit his gloom, to soar above his problems, tune out the world. His last vestige of happiness: flying. His passion for flying planes had never wavered. It was a fine spring day to lift off and check on his ranch from the clouds.

He climbed on board his two-seater Staggerwing, checked the instruments and gauges, cranked the engine, and . . .

BLAM!

The entire nose of the plane ruptured. The front end was severed from the rest of the plane and fell to the ground. All that remained of the engine was a hunk of twisted metal.

The only reason Noble did not go up in smoke with the blast was that the craft's steel firewall separated the cockpit from the

front. Any other model would have shredded Herbert into a thousand pieces.

Investigators scurried to the ranch. They uncovered globs of nitroglycerin wired to the plane's generator. The identical substance used in Mildred's explosion. It was an obvious assassination attempt.

The authorities had no leads and no suspects. The Cat lamented and reiterated his original sentiment that a man 1,500 miles away was trying to kill him. Would any cotton-pickin' fool please listen?

Herbert set about repairing the front end of his plane. Within a week he decided it was time to give the friendly skies another try. He loaded himself in the captain's chair and prepared for takeoff. It wouldn't be long before he would have wheels up. He turned the ignition, and the trusty bird wouldn't start. He examined the engine and found that two cylinders were crammed full of nitroglycerin gel. Fortunately for him, the packing forced the engine to seize rather than ignite.

This Cat survived yet again.

Time for some canaries.

Noble was demoralized and downtrodden. A whipped pup who just didn't want any more of life's cruelties.

There was officially no place left that he was safe. The forces against him were closing in. In a last-ditch effort, he was persuaded to testify to state investigators about his connection to Benny Binion. The Texas authorities were advancing a case against organized crime, primarily spearheaded in Dallas. Herbert conceded his history in the gambling rackets, his interactions with Binion, the horrors and the bloodshed, and the numerous attempts on his life.

He broke the cardinal rule of crime: He named names. He sealed his own fate; Benny's wrath would rage. The bell could not be unrung.

BET

Money wagered during a hand to increase the action.

CHAPTER 13
DEATH

Death often rides a pale horse . . . but sometimes it drives a baby blue Chevy pickup.

The truck kicked up gravel as it drifted mysteriously like a spirit in the night. Plodding down the same county road, same route, same pattern. Inside the cab of the truck sat three diabolical desperados with nothing but pure meanness in their hearts. Multiple neighbors reported spotting the suspicious blue Chevy rolling down the county road that bordered the Diamond M Ranch.

The outlaws aboard the truck went to work during the moonlight hours. They approached the outskirts of the front entrance of the Diamond M with the silence and stealth of ninjas.

Noble's mailbox was located on the county road not far from the ranch entrance. A hole was dug directly under the mailbox, several jars of nitroglycerin gel along with multiple sticks of dynamite and blasting caps were buried. The blasting caps were connected to a thin, untraceable line that ran undetected across the county road and connected to the positive charge of a Delco car battery. Another insulated copper line was connected to the negative charge of the battery. The lines were routed together, the trap was set. The culprits hid in the scrub brush next to a barbed-wire fence within viewing distance of the mailbox. One of them held the other end of the insulated line connected to the negative charge of the battery.

August 7, 1951. The sun baked the crusty Texas soil. Another scorching summer day but through Herbert Noble's eyes, the

landscape continued to be cold and dreary. His day set in motion around eleven thirty AM as he hopped into his 1950 Ford sedan with a rifle, $500 in cash, and a deck of playing cards, which he never went anywhere without.

The sedan rambled out the front entrance and onto the adjoining county road. It came to a slow roll next to the mailbox. Herbert, with his window down, surveyed his surroundings. A man can only take so much pain. Trauma pummels the soul. What existence did he really have? He spent his life in a paranoid frenzy outrunning and outfoxing death at every turn. Now he was tired, too exhausted to care anymore. Whatever lay in the next realm, the next dimension, it had to be better than this one.

As he took a deep breath, his bleary eyes caught sight of movement in the brush. Definite danger. He could sense that the end was near. Why prolong the inevitable? He extended his arm across the open window toward the mailbox. A flash appeared; the outline a menacing figure, cigarette hanging from his lips, crouched and covered in the briars next to the fence.

Herbert held still. A moment of clarity.

A tear shook loose from his eye. He held his arm still for what seemed like an eternity. He blinked his watery eyes. He gingerly grasped the lid of the mailbox. He exhaled deeply and for the first time in a long time, a genuine smile crept over his face.

Peace at last.

As he pulled the mailbox lid open, simultaneously the figure in the brush touched the negative wire to the barbed-wire fence.

KABOOOOOOOOOOOM!

A cataclysmic explosion rocked the earth, creating a six-foot-wide divot. Oily black smoke ascended upward, miles into the clouds. The sedan was shredded into pieces, with parts scattered in all directions, leaving only a heap of smoldering, warped, contorted metal surrounding the blast.

The remains of the mailbox were located seventy-five feet away.

Herbert was finally able to leave this world. His body was annihilated. Only his head, shoulders, and arms were intact. The remaining body fragments disappeared. Parts of his flesh were found along a fluttering storm of cash and playing cards. Two distinct cards were lying face up near the heart of the wreckage: a Joker and an Ace of Diamonds.

A gambler until the end.

The Cat No More

It took two hours before anyone arrived at the scene. Neighbors exclaimed they heard the blast, but it was not uncommon to hear strange noises coming from Noble's ranch. A local farmer hauling hay on his way home passed the wreckage and called it in. He was so distraught he swallowed his tobacco.

Authorities from Denton County, the local sheriff, investigators, and the Texas Rangers arrived on the scene. Reporters soon followed. The only clue was the abandoned Delco battery and a few wires.

The list of possible suspects was long and lengthy. Extreme thugs with extreme prejudices. It could have been any one of the dozens that Noble had made enemies of, or that were seeking to claim that famed Benny Binion bounty, which, of course, Benny denied ever existed. In fact, in later investigations, authorities came up with a list of forty-two men and one woman who at some point or another had a hand in trying to kill Noble. The authorities did their work seemingly as best as they could, and there would be the occasional clue, rumor, witness account, etc. that would lead them a little further. But nothing ever came of it. There were too many possibilities and the killers covered their tracks pretty well. Plus, no one ever wanted to talk against Binion.

The news of Noble's death swept through bustling Fremont Street in downtown Las Vegas.

"I'm glad he's dead."

Benny Binion's response to his rival's utter demise. In private, that is.

The Cowboy was hounded by authorities and press for days, weeks, and months following the bombing. But no roads led back to Benny. With no concrete suspects, he was in the clear. He performed his usual song and tap dance in public, feigning concern, disbelief, and sadness at the unnecessary loss of life of such a great man. The denials were wearing him thin. The "shock and sadness" eventually gave way to a tingle of the truth in an interview with the *Dallas Morning News.*

"I didn't have a thing to do with it. That's the graveyard truth. But I don't care one way or the other. I just don't give a damn."

That tomcat of chicanery had finally run out of lives. Benny's Texas nightmare was now gone. With one less item to deal with, the future concerns were the building of his Vegas consortium, the ongoing legal issues that were dogging his survival and family, and the development of the Benny Binion brand.

THE TURN

The fourth of five cards flipped up on the board; a community card for all players to use for their final hand. Also called "Fourth Street."

CHAPTER 14

GO WEST

What if Paul Revere failed to make his alarming ride and shout, "The British are coming." What if Custer succeeded instead of facing his last stand? What if General Eisenhower failed to orchestrate D-Day? What if Kennedy had never traveled to Dallas in November 1963?

United States history is riddled with "what-ifs" of every kind. As is the history of poker.

What if Noble had not backed Steve Guthrie for Dallas sheriff? What if Guthrie had not won the election? What if Herbert Noble hadn't survived all those earlier attacks that escalated a dynamite-fueled feud? What if the two alpha dogs had learned how to coexist, accepting a truce as the violence escalated rather than turning a blind eye? These events coupled on top of one another would not have sent Benny, his family, and bodyguards packed in a Cadillac roaring over the asphalt through the dead of the night like a scalded dog, Nevada bound.

What if Herbert Noble was never blown to smithereens? What if he had survived? What if he killed Binion?

In our story, *that* is the greatest "what-if?" of them all.

The bombing of Noble was a pivotal point in the history of the World Series of Poker. This domino had to fall to keep the trajectory of the timeline on course. If the tables were reversed, if The Cat had defeated The Cowboy, then we would not have the World Series of Poker that we have today. Call it a blessing. Call it the way of the

world. Call it a series of unfortunate events. Call it a bloody battle of Texas gambling titans. Whatever you call it, Noble had to go for the next phase of our story to unfold.

The human mind is like a room stuffed with furniture. The room can only accommodate a certain amount. At some point the room becomes overrun with items and there is no more space. You must clear out the old to make space for the new. Or just scale back and enjoy some empty space. With Noble gone, Binion was able to declutter.

Herbert's ultimate demise opened the door for Benny to flourish. With no arch nemesis to duel, no war to keep his attention at high alert, it allowed the wheels to turn. His savvy business acumen was given free rein to consider all the next possibilities.

Viva Las Vegas!

The next chapter in Benny's life was firmly planted in the desert. He could see Texas in the rearview mirror. His casino, his money, his reputation . . . they were all in the Silver State.

Las Vegas in the late 1940s was a sleepy gambling town. It was like a newborn child who hadn't reached toddler stage yet. The Strip was just a wide patch of desolate highway with two main casinos, The El Rancho and The Last Frontier. The barren desert could bring chills to the heart or elicit provocative and wild imaginings of ideas and possibilities. It was all in the eye of the beholder.

Benny had been enamored with Las Vegas for years. The idea of a legal gambling destination, even if it was in the middle of a sand pit, enthralled him.

The conception of Las Vegas was born in 1931. The state legislature voted to legalize gambling once again (it had been banned a decade earlier), first to the Northern Club and quickly followed by others on Fremont Street. The legalization came because 1931 also

marked the beginning of construction of the tunnels on the nearby Hoover Dam, which brought workers and their families to town looking for something to do in their free time. City officials couldn't pass up the opportunity to help stabilize the struggling city's economy. The 1941 construction of the Las Vegas Army Airfield (later Nellis Air Force Base) brought even more people to the area.

The town became a hot spot with an array of bars, casinos, and world-renowned whorehouses. It also became a magnet for crime lords from all over the country who saw the opportunity to line their pockets. The blinking neon lights lured in gamblers and lost souls searching for unadulterated pleasure. The sinful escape gave downtown Vegas the illustrious nickname "the Glitter Gulch."

The fundamental business plan sounded foolproof. The sales pitch was a home run. How could a place like this not make money? Right? Wrong. It sputtered as the heat, the lack of a cohesive vision, and the inconvenience of traveling (trains, planes, and automobiles) kept the public away. Vegas needed pizzazz! A spectacular attraction that would elicit a stir and send throngs of tourists stampeding through the casinos' front doors. Most importantly, the mob needed a return on their investment.

The answer was a theatrical mobster named Bugsy Siegel. He had retreated from Brooklyn and reemerged on the West Coast. Working on behalf of Meyer Lansky, Siegel arrived in Vegas to oversee the syndicated horse racing wire. He was unimpressed with the dull, dusty gambling houses that existed there. These ancient relics had been the foundation of the town for eons. Bugsy understood that the sleeping toddler town needed more than a bottle and a nap. It needed a grand vision to wake up and mature into full adolescence.

This vision became the Flamingo, which opened with great fanfare on December 26, 1946. "Posh, Ritzy and Elegant." That's how reporters responded while gawking at the $5 million phenomenon. The casino was decked out in its Sunday finest. Visitors were shocked to see this level of luxury in a casino.

There was no torrential rainstorm in Vegas that night, but there was unexpected rain in Southern California and snow in the mountains, which limited flights into the area. Bugsy didn't sit alone despondently at the bar. On the contrary, he was on the balls of his feet, shaking hands, wearing a black tux and a pink carnation. His girlfriend Virginia Hill was on hand with her platinum blonde hair. Jimmy Durante and the Xavier Cugat Orchestra headlined the event. The three Georges were there—the actors George Raft, George Sanders, and George Jessel.

There was also one impressionable outlaw there for the opening night festivities—the one and only Benny Binion!

He was awestruck. "The biggest whoop-de-do I ever seen." He was equally impressed with Siegel, considering him the most charming, outgoing, and nicest man he'd ever met, despite rumors of his short, violent temper. Binion found him to be a kindred spirit.

The three-night opening extravaganza made an impression and drew people in, giving Bugsy hope that his plan would pay off. Unfortunately, once the opening buzz had died down, the crowds dwindled and Bugsy's baby failed to reap any serious profits. The casino, which was all backed by mob money, was in a nosedive, and so was Bugsy.

On June 20, 1947, he was shot and killed by a mob-appointed assassin at his girlfriend's home in Beverly Hills.

Still, the foundation for what Vegas would become had been set, and there were others who were eager to take the next steps.

The Cowboy Plays a Hand or Two

The horse trader from the North Texas prairie soon felt at home in his new surroundings. *Welcome to Sin City, Pardner!*

Benny may have been on the run but once he stopped to catch his breath, he aimed to firmly plant his flag in Vegas. He chuckled

to associates, "When I realized how good it could be up here, I said, 'Let 'em have Texas.'"

He saw a promising future. Like Bugsy, he also had a vision, if only a slightly different version.

Binion's first venture was a partnership with J. Kell Houssels and Meyer Lansky (the mob's financial mastermind) in the Las Vegas Club on Fremont Street. He described it as "an old run-down kind of place." Simple. A few table games, slots, and a bar. Dirt floors, ripped and worn furniture, flickering neon lights. It was nothing like the fancy joints he was used to running in Dallas.

But it was a start.

Benny had high hopes of constructing his Vegas legacy and building toward the future. However, his casino licensing procedure was at a standstill. Authorities were digging deep, looking to put the screws to Binion. They didn't have enough intel to close the book on him, but they kept delaying his license proceedings. This type of behavior made Benny's skin crawl and his short hairs twitch. Why couldn't they just leave him the hell alone?!

Less than a year after his initial stake in the Las Vegas Club, he relinquished his interest in the club.

Next stop, the Westerner Gambling House and Saloon. Benny wasn't there long enough to get a haircut. A disagreement between the partners left him with the sour taste of spoiled milk in his mouth. He soon left. Benny wasn't no warrior; he was a chief. He wasn't used to team dynamics. Where he came from, his word ruled supreme. Nobody was going to give him orders, not even the slick Italians from the Big Apple and the Windy City.

Stick with What Ya Know

The turning point came with the opportunity to purchase the El Dorado Club in May 1951. The decaying casino was on its last leg. It

needed resuscitation, and it needed it fast. The El Dorado Club was next to the Apache Hotel on Fremont Street and had two separate owners.

Benny purchased the El Dorado and the Apache for $160,000. For the first time in his Vegas ventures, he was the sole owner. Which meant he had free rein to lead his horse in any direction. He named the new establishment "The Horseshoe Club." It would encapsulate his brand, his blood, and his soul. Only one hurdle: the Nevada Gaming Commission.

The commission had issues with Benny's reputation and past "indiscretions." By this point, his feud with Noble was national news, and while Benny could deny involvement till he was blue in the face, everyone knew the score. Plus, there was a storm brewing with the authorities back in Texas. Bottom line: Benny Binion seemed like more of a headache than anything else.

Benny kept on trudging. He wouldn't be deterred. In the spring of 1951, a special licensing session was called. Benny took the stand. His silver tongue oohed and awed the crowd. His simple, down-home demeanor had committee members bent double in laughter. He greased the right palms and came off as a man of the people. Honest. Humorous. Hospitable.

His celebrated performance was enough to win over the most arduous of doubters. Benny received his gaming license.

The Lone Star Don Corleone Arrives

"ACTION, ACTION, ACTION!"

That was the tagline of the Horseshoe, which opened in August 1951, right around the time Noble finally got his. Benny proved to be an expert innovator.

This was no sawdust shithole or broken-down bronc rider's bunkhouse. It was akin to a southwestern land baron's sprawling

manor. The casino was the first in Las Vegas history to have wall-to-wall carpeting. The whole place was awash in the color red. Every barstool, carpet fiber, light fixture oozed with the Western aura of its owner. Scarlet velvet textures, sleek mahogany wood, plush furniture, polished brass, antebellum chandeliers—it was a portrait straight out of *Red River.* You could envision Gary Cooper, Humphrey Bogart, or John Wayne sauntering through the casino at any moment.

Benny's joint was not only a highfalutin cowboy country club. The restaurant featured beef from his own cattle back in Texas. The food was mouthwatering and inexpensive. He was the first to provide free drinks. He was also the first to send limos to pick up players at the airport. Benny's casino was an experience like no other. The Cowboy was an innovator. He knew how to take care of people. All types of gamblers felt at home at the Horseshoe. Benny welcomed them with open arms and looked after them like they were his own kids.

It also set the bar as having the highest betting limits in the country. The layout of the casino was designed to cater to the gambler, no matter the size of the bet. While Benny classed up the joint, there wasn't an emphasis on performing acts, but rather how he could make gamblers stay and play. The main floor had dozens of tables, all featuring dice games (namely craps). Benny didn't believe in separating gamblers, so there wasn't a high rollers area. Rich and looking to get rich mingled together. Benny gave everyone a chance, relying on a strategy that had worked for him since the beginning.

"Never turn down a bet."

He never forgot his mentor Warren Diamond's advice. Benny was here to teach these boys a lesson in the art of running a gambling house.

His brethren casino operators didn't share in his enthusiasm. Raising betting limits though the roof wasn't part of their playbook.

They soon learned that The Cowboy wrote his own rules. He took every kind of imaginable bet under the sun. Blondy Turner, a wealthy colleague, once called Benny on a direct line at the Horseshoe. He had an itchin' to wager, so he placed a $10,000 dice bet over the phone. Benny took the bet; he held the receiver close enough to let Blondy hear the stickman yell out that he had won his Pass Line bet. The next week, Blondy came to collect. He stuck around for a bit . . . and lost $200,000.

The Horseshoe became the premiere hot spot to bet on dice games. On one such occasion, a shooter approached the dice table and put down a $1 million bet. Benny never blinked an eye. The house won that bet. It went to show the heart and courage of Binion. He and the Horseshoe were one and the same. If one man ever embodied his own casino, it was Benny and the Horseshoe.

It was clear to onlookers that Binion was a "gambler's gambler." Every fiber of his body was filled with the raw emotion of a high-stakes gambling promoter.

Wanting to expand on this idea, Benny knew he needed to bring in card games. The wheels and gears turned. The light bulb went off, and he suddenly realized just how he could do it.

CHAPTER 15
THE MATCH

Benny had his casino, and he had his license. He was in an elite fraternity of lawful, legitimate casino owners.

His dice tables were generally hopping, but at times the action subsided. The dice players ran scorching desert hot or freezing sub-arctic cold. Like ocean waves cresting off the coastline, then screaming onto shore, only to slowly subside back out to sea. The players surged through the front doors of the Horseshoe, but the undertow of fickle odds and the luck of two red dice would eventually drag them back outside.

The rise and fall of those waves were just part of doing business in Vegas at the time, but Benny couldn't accept that. This was not a man who would stay happy with the status quo. He wanted to be the best and to have the consistency in the money flow that his rivals lacked.

He found it in the cards.

It wasn't long until card players started to flock to Vegas looking for some action. Binion, ever the pioneer and savvy businessman, saw the untapped potential. As such, he wanted to bring poker and other cards games into the fold, making the Horseshoe *the* place for any and all type of gamblers.

But he needed a way to spread the word, to let card players know they should come here to play, players not just in Vegas but from all over. He needed to become the P.T. Barnum of casino promotions. He needed a gimmick, a headline attraction. He wanted to stage an event that

would bring him and the Horseshoe some attention, hopefully from the public as a whole, but more importantly, from serious gamblers.

Then, like a donkey kick to the gut, the idea floored him. It was a shock to the nervous system. It was bold. It was grandiose. It was all Benny!

POKER!

Poker was the answer.

And not just any kind of poker. A heavyweight title bout between two of the toughest card-playing sluggers in the country. The Cowboy had just the two men in mind. The first was one of his poker idols. A world renown rounder, a continental sharp, a gambling icon—his excellency, Nick "The Greek" Dandolos. Over the years, Benny had connected several times with Dandolos. The Greek loved Vegas almost as much as he loved playing cards. Never one to turn down any action, or a chance to prove he was the best, he instantly agreed to play. Now Benny just needed to find him an opponent, and he had just the guy.

To meet him, let's backtrack for a moment to the mean streets of downtown Dallas in 1917 . . .

Small Boys, Big Dreams

Electricity was in the air. Movement all around. Some drove cars, some rode in horse-drawn carriages, and some strolled with distinct purpose. Businessmen in crisp high-dollar suits paraded up and down the sidewalks. Women in beautiful outfits strolled from one storefront to another.

Everyone was on the move. Everyone had somewhere to go.

Everyone except two raggedy boys in their early teens, who sat on the bustling corner watching the world unfold around them. The soles of their boots and shoes were worn flat. Their britches had gaping holes. Their shirts had been patched together and draped over their frames. Their faces were covered in grime.

Their partner in the trio was absent. They called him "Chill," a handsome and gleaming lad who had taken up performing. Singing, dancing, and acting. They knew Chill had the chops to be something special. He was going to make it out of here.

They eyeballed the hustle and bustle of the emerging city. The horse-drawn carriages clicking and clacking through the cobble streets, carrying the wealthy old-timers, the ones not affected by the changing times, content with what they had earned and how they had earned it.

The boys were fascinated by these new Model Ts with their piercing horns blaring in all directions, intersecting the horses and carriages.

Everyone seemed to have money. Everyone seemed to be blowing and going. Except these two boys, who were just trying to scrape together a few nickels and dimes. But what they did have was gold-plated ambition. One of these days they knew they would make their mark on society. They shared the fantasy of being as rich as their superhero gambling idols Titanic Thompson and Nick "The Greek." One of these days . . .

For now, the dream of escaping poverty was just that, a dream. They wavered under the sweltering Texas sun outside the Western Union Telegraph Company. Eagerly awaiting messages to arrive so they could deliver them around town for a few cents apiece. If it wasn't hustling messages, it would be selling newspapers, or another small-time errand service that amounted to nothing more than a few cents.

This penny ante endeavor was becoming tougher and tougher as more kids hit the streets and jockeyed for these positions. There were plenty of fights. The blood flew and teeth were knocked out. These two were in the middle of most of them. But they always had each other's back. They knew they could count on one another. They had a genuine respect for each other.

They were going to be somebody. The two boys were Benny Binion and someone who would not only remain a lifelong friend, but become a professional poker Hall of Famer, changing the game, and the story, forever. In fact, that young boy would eventually become the "Grand Old Man of Poker," a nine-time WSOP winner (including the first) who

would get a poker hand named after him (Ace-Ten) and would win and lose and win again a shit ton of money.

That boy was Johnny Moss.

A Brutal Beginning

John Hardie Moss Jr. was born in Marshall, Texas, in 1907. His father was the deputy sheriff, but with the incumbent sheriff losing his reelection bid, it sent John Sr. into a tailspin. He scrambled to find other employment opportunities to provide for his family. Times were tough and money was scarce.

With little to no prospects, he packed his wife, newborn son (John Jr.), and three older children into a covered wagon, hitched the mule team, and east they went. He stopped along the way at every town searching for any signs of work, but found nothing but rejection.

A month into the wagon drive, John Jr., who they called Johnny, watched as his mother Lena was stricken with unsurmountable pain in her stomach. She was on the receiving end of a burst appendix. This happened on a lone stretch of grassland with no town or people in sight. John Sr. understood his wife was in critical condition. He whipped the mules and raced to the nearest sign of civilization. The wagon wheels kicked up dust as they plowed forward at breakneck speed.

It was all for naught as Lena passed shortly after the family arrived in Fort Worth.

It was a devastating blow. Especially to young Johnny, who barely had a chance to know his mother.

John Sr. found a job with the telephone company in Dallas. He was a single father with four children to provide for. He was a determined man who rode a horse to and from work every day and eked out a meager living and lived in a one-bedroom shack. The sisters

shared the bedroom while Johnny and his brother slept outside on the porch.

Tragedy struck again, four years later, when a telephone pole crushed John Sr.'s right leg. His leg bones were snapped into fragments. A massive infection took a hold, which required amputation. The dreaded outcome meant that not only was the father afflicted with horrific and constant pain, he also was out of work.

The family was suffering, broke, and hungry. The tiny savings that John Sr. had accumulated evaporated in no time. The combination of the death of his wife and the debilitating injury left John Sr. suffocating in desperation. He was able to scrape enough credit together to buy a general store but with bills mounting and being incapacitated, the business went down the drain. He soon had to sell the store and his horse just to feed the family. John Sr. moved the family to an even smaller house, where Johnny and his brother were relegated to sleeping in a tent behind the house.

Tough times create tough people.

Johnny was exceptionally bright. His young mind was constantly churning. Still, he had to drop out of second grade to help support his struggling family. He took to walking six miles into downtown Dallas and working side hustles such as delivering telegraph messages and selling newspapers (where he met his buddy Benny) to scrounge up a few cents to buy a half-loaf of bread and bring it home to his father and siblings.

Despite the hardship, Johnny dreamed of a promising future. He looked to the action-adventure lifestyle of Titanic Thompson, the professional gambler extraordinaire, who traveled the country in luxury with plenty of cash and plenty of women. He and Benny could catch news reels of the legend at the local nickelodeon. Titanic and other gambling idols gave Johnny inspiration. If this once broke, countrified, shoeless kid who was now the beloved Titanic could make it out of the Ozarks, Johnny could make it too. But for the time being, his main objective was surviving and locating his next meal.

He fell into gambling, as did many other desperate men and boys of all ages, including his friend Benny.

One of his many stops while delivering telegraph messages was the domino parlor. It was here Johnny got his first taste of true gamblers plying their trade. He took notice as sums of money that would feed his family for a month slid across the table from the hands of one gambler to another. It all looked so easy; all it took was a single turn of a card or domino tile. Johnny watched and obsessed. Johnny felt the fever. The gambling fever.

Johnny became an ardent student; he took mental notes from the seasoned players in the domino room. He attempted to mimic all their moves and eventually got his shot to play. He lost a lot at first, but considered this his early education, his rite of passage. In his midteens, he also shot dice with several youths in a back-alley craps game. He consistently lost and did not understand why. He was a sharp kid. Why were the gods of luck and chance not shining down on him? Moss had self-confidence, he believed in himself. He knew he was sharper and more adept at the games than his opponents. Regardless, the losing sessions continued to mount, and Johnny began feeling demoralized.

Johnny and Blackie

One night, a deep, rich, confident voice came calling from his back shoulder.

"Hey, kid."

Johnny wheeled around to find a docile and dapper fellow dressed in a dark suit and a black, wide-brimmed fedora with a giant canary-yellow feather pinned to the top. The most impressive, devilish-looking character Johnny had ever encountered introduced himself as "Blackie."

Blackie flashed a wad of bills that would choke a mule. He noticed Johnny's style and admired it. He asked Johnny if he ever beat the game.

Johnny shrugged. "Sometimes."

Blackie retorted, "Well, how would ya like to beat it every time?"

Johnny watched stupefied as Blackie took control of the dice game and won one magnificent roll after another. Blackie winked and smiled at Johnny while continuing to roll them bones.

Johnny made it a point to connect with this strange but elusive character. Blackie recognized the scruffy kid and decided to mentor him. He was going to take him under his wing and teach him the ways of a savvy street hustler. Blackie took Johnny in as his protégé. He decided to school him in the ways of making money with cards and dice. Moss was enthused to have a man of Blackie's credentials to be taking an interest in him. It appeared his days on the bread and bean circuit would soon be ending. From here on out, he would be cruising on easy street.

Johnny's initial impression of Blackie was that he was a magician.

Truth is, Blackie was a bottom-feeder who swallowed up strait-laced chumps and suckers. Blackie *was* a magician of sorts—a master of deception. Highly skilled in the art of eye and hand deceit. His plan was to train Johhny to attack games as a team to take down larger payouts. He was grooming the impressionable kid to join him on the dark side. Blackie first trained Johnny in the art of dice manipulation. With Blackie's magic dice, Johnny found that he could throw a seven all day, every day, without skipping a beat.

He taught Johnny how to swap dice in the blink of an eye. The eloquence of sudden distraction. The mastery of oral enticement, chiding on players to place larger bets on the next roll. Johnny never saw Blackie have a losing session.

As Moss became more comfortable with cards, Blackie then schooled him with a cheater's cadre of tools: marking cards, pocketing cards, fake shuffling, dealing from the bottom of the deck, etc. Blackie had no shame; he took money in any way possible, and he expected Johnny to follow in his footsteps.

"There's a lot of people out there that like to gamble, Johnny," he said. "If you don't take their money, somebody else will. They're suckers, Johnny. They're all suckers."

Johnny was conflicted. On one hand, he was mesmerized by Blackie's cash, his new car, his fancy wardrobe, and his bombshell girlfriend. He was drawn into the realm of the quick buck. The philosophy that twisted gambling from a risk-taking situation into a solidified money-making transaction. This was huge for a young man who walked six miles to hopefully earn enough change to buy some bread.

On the other side, his father was a straight shooter. He instilled a decorum of moral values such as an honest day's work for an honest dollar. You reap what you sow. Only the righteous shall survive. His father may not have been financially wealthy, but he was definitely not morally bankrupt. Moss was uncomfortable with Blackie's methods. His tactics were out of bounds with the guidance of his father's teachings. This was an internal battle that Johnny was going to have to sort out for himself.

Fate intervened.

One afternoon Johnny witnessed Blackie emerge from a drug store in one of his best suits, with a deck of cards. He exclaimed he had a "fresh sucker" to play with that day and hopped in his car. Meanwhile, Johnny roamed the streets looking for action. Later that day, Blackie reappeared from the shadows. He was beaten all to hell. His face was bloody, his clothes were torn to shreds. His car was gone. He was in pitiful shape and propositioned Johnny to loan him a few bucks, as he was flat broke.

It was a sign from above. The answers to his questions came thundering in, loud and clear. It was time to move from the darkness to the light.

Johnny flipped him a few quarters, turned away, and never looked back. He vowed to play honest, straight, and fair. From here on out, he would be the best "sucker" that he could be. His connection with Blackie became the focal point that not only ushered him into the world of professional poker, but shaped the philosophy and approach that would help him be one of the best.

Playing Straight . . . and Winning

At first, Johnny was a pariah. He was not trusted due to his relationship with Blackie. However, those experiences soon proved to be the key factor in getting him a job inside the Otter's Club, a private poker club in Dallas. Mr. Wade, the delightful proprietor, knew Johnny over the years from his time at the domino parlor. He also understood that Johnny separated himself from the other youths fumbling their lives away on the streets. Johnny had a special eye for cards and a quick mindset to deduce situations.

Mr. Wade was initially not interested in having Moss around. No way could he consider allowing someone connected with the likes of that blackballed bastard into his poker club. But Johnny was convincing when he explained those days were well behind him.

Plus, he could provide a unique service, unlike anyone else: surveillance over players in the club, identifying any potential cheats. He didn't want any pay. All Johnny wanted in return from Mr. Wade was the ability to watch and learn how to play poker . . . *the right way.*

Mr. Wade accepted, and Johnny found himself immersed in the game.

Moss proved an immediate asset. His ability to spot foul play, card mechanics, and scammers was worth his weight in gold. His amenable personality proved to be the perfect blend of ruggedness and compassion. Johnny was no stranger to people. His time living on the streets helped fuel his skills of social interaction. He was clued in to all types of psychological traits. Those from the most depraved killers, the men and women of the clergy, and the pompous business elite. He had seen them all at their lowest levels. He knew what really made them tick.

The players at the club came to respect Johnny. He protected the straight players. Mr. Wade appreciated his junkyard dog mentality to weed out any crooked cream puffs. He was the ultimate table sheriff.

Mr. Wade was also considered to be one of the area's most accomplished poker players, even though, or perhaps because, he was quiet and reserved. He allowed Johhny to watch over his shoulder ("sweat him") while he played. In slower times, he would talk Johnny through strategies. They spent downtime in Mr. Wade's office discussing the nuances of various poker hands. He eventually allowed Johnny to step in and play with his chip stack. Mr. Wade would stand by him and evaluate. Later the pair would reconvene in the office to discuss particular hands during the playing session. Most games being played at the time were Draw poker and Five-Card Stud.

"You have to be ready to bet it all," Wade said. "If you're scared of losing what you have, then you can't play."

Johnny went from working long hours at the Otter's Club to also playing there on a regular basis. Mr. Wade grew fond of Johnny. He saw him transcend from a raw, skittish boy into a confident and strong young man. He was not only a club asset but also an investment. Mr. Wade bankrolled Johnny as he ascended to play in the bigger games at the nearby Elks Lodge.

Moss, the master student, was on his way to becoming an all-around master player, and raking in the profit. In less than two years

the kid who started working for Mr. Wade for nothing more than the opportunity to learn was now making upward of $500 a night playing cards.

Johnny Becomes a Legend

As his stardom increased, Moss ventured out. He toured the southern part of the country searching for the biggest games with the hottest action. He was following in the footsteps of his poker idols. His bankroll expanded, and he garnered the reputation of road-touring rounder.

Johnny circled back to Texas and found himself rolling from one oil field boomtown to another. Johnny found the wild and woolly West Texas oil field games to be the juiciest. He even signed on with Texaco Oil Company just so he would be eligible to attend their private corporate games. You had to be on their payroll at the time to play in these confidential games.

He spent significant amounts of time in Olney and Graham, Texas. Odessa also became a favorite landing spot for him. The spigot never turned off in the petroleum pantheon. New millionaires were being made every day in the oil business. It was not unheard of for Moss to make upward of a million dollars in a week, or even in a night, if the right amateur with the right head of steam stumbled into the game.

Johhny's signature strategy was patience and unwavering endurance. He waited for the right spot, the right cards, and the right player to make his move. Then he pounced like a mountain lion. Fearless. Before you knew it, Johnny was on top of you with his hands wrapped around your throat . . . and your breaths were numbered.

He was keen to slow-play opponents in the beginning while waiting until later in the session to set fire and come in with heavier

action-building pots. He would switch up the momentum on tired, weary players. Switching up or switching down, Johnny was always reaching for another gear. The pace kept players backpedaling. Eventually they would be running on fumes and wondering how the hell they ever got involved in a card game with the likes of Johhny Moss.

The road wasn't always paved in gold. One time in a game in Dallas, he won $250,000. He told his wife Vergie to go pick out her dream house. By the time she did, he had to tell her it was too late. He had given it all back at the track.

As Johnny's poker career evolved, so did his golf game. On one occasion, he played a heads-ups golf match against a wealthy business owner. Now, through his traveling rounder exploits, Johnny had become acquainted with elements of organized crime, and a couple of made men were there to witness the match. His criminal counterparts had wagered heavily on the outcome, and their money was all on Moss. The first nine holes, Johnny was getting crushed. The good fellas were furious and losing their minds. They devised a plan to bury the businessman in a hole rather than pay him the winnings.

Johnny caught wind of the execution plan. He thrust himself into the game. He played his heart out, sinking a birdie on the final hole to secure the win. Once the game was over, the frustrated business owner hollered at Johnny that he was the "luckiest man alive."

Johnny sighed and replied, "No sir, *you* are."

Johnny Meets His Idols

Sometime in the late 1930s, Johnny came face-to-face with Titanic Thompson. They met on a golf course in Lubbock, Texas. Johnny, like his contemporaries, was also a talented golfer. But he

wasn't in Thompson's league. The pair played a round on the links with Titanic getting the best of Johnny.

The conversation turned to cards, a heads-up No-Limit Draw poker game. Moss couldn't resist the opportunity to play against the legend. But the deck hit kept hitting in Thompson's favor. All his big draws came in, and he got paid off. Johnny lost $6,000 that day. While playing, the texture of the cards didn't feel exactly right to Johnny. They played again the next day. This time they played with a fresh deck. Moss came away with his original $6,000 plus another $10,000 and the keys to Titanic's Cadillac.

The session proved that Johnny could hold his own against a world-beater.

Soon he would get his chance to do it against another of his idols.

Benny and Johnny had remained in contact over the years. Each had come a long way from their days of running the streets in East Dallas trying to scrape together a few nickels and dimes. The third member of their group, Chill, had become a rising Hollywood star. His stage name was Chill Wills, and he had performed in over a dozen Westerns.

Moss was sitting deep in the saddle, riding the highs and lows of being a professional card player in Texas. There were more highs than lows, but there are always downswings, or "times you just run bad." It's part of the lifestyle of a professional poker player. One of those times was a detrimental loss of $80,000. Moss contacted Binion at the Horseshoe and explained his situation. Benny chuckled and said he was sending Johnny $100,000, and he could pay him back whenever he wanted.

Benny Binion was a man of the people, but there were very few of his acquaintances that he could call close friends. Johnny Moss was one of them. Friendships built on the dreams of young men last forever, and Benny knew Johnny was just the man he needed for this heavyweight poker fight.

The Match

Back to Las Vegas, 1951.

The continental card sharp Nick "The Greek" Dandolos strutted through the Horseshoe. He cornered Benny and expressed his objective. He was on a mission to play poker for the highest limits against the best in the world. Could Benny deliver?

Benny told Nick to hold tight, and he got on the phone with his old compadre, Moss. Johnny had just finished up a three-day marathon session game in Odessa, Texas. He had just returned to his home in Dallas when he got the call. Before he had a chance to catch his breath and recuperate, he told Benny that he would be on the next flight out to Vegas.

This was exactly what Benny needed. Further, it was a seed of an idea that would later in his life lead to a defining moment in the history of professional poker. In fact, most pros agree this event is where the World Series of Poker began. The Cowboy, Benny Binion, going all out to promote an event with the top players going at each other in a marathon session to not only win a bunch of money, but also to prove who was the best.

The game started between Nick and Johnny inside the Horseshoe. They played a combination of several different games: Five-Card Draw, Seven-Card Stud, Seven-Card Stud High-Low, Ace-5 Lowball, 2–7 Lowball. But Five-Card Stud was the primary favorite.

As the game kicked off, Benny noticed the energy that surrounded the table. Patrons were drawn from all corners of the casino to come take a gander. As rail birds, the onlookers jockeyed for position to catch the best possible view of the action taking place between the two heavyweights on the green felt. Even if they couldn't see the cards, they could see the men, and for most, that was enough. The crowd swelled; some speculated that it was six to seven people deep at times. Not just at peak hours, but late night

and early morning. The Vegas scene was fascinated with this match and with the men playing.

Binion took the initiative, realizing he couldn't pay for this type of publicity. He moved the game outside near the front entrance of the Horseshoe, setting up a table and maximizing both the viewing space and where and how he could keep promoting it.

The game became a death match of souls, a contest of stamina as well as mental capacity. It lasted days, and then weeks, and then months, sometimes for most of the day. Momentum kept shifting from man to man. These were two lions locked into a battle for life and death. Occasionally Moss would take a short catnap, during which time The Greek shot dice. Finally, he would call Moss's room asking if he intended to sleep his life away. Moss would head back down, and the duel would commence again.

The chips slid back and forth with each man nearly conquering the other several times. One of the potential turning points happened during a Five-Card Stud game. Nick's chip stack had dwindled to under $240,000. Moss had a nine for a hole card with a nine, six, and two showing. Nick had an eight, six, and four showing. Nick's last card was a Jack face up. Moss's last card was a three face up.

Nick bet $50,000.

Johnny thought he was bluffing and raised him all in with $140,000. He told Nick, "If you got a Jack, you win."

Nick went into the tank, thinking for several moments, then announced, "Okay, I have to call then."

He flipped over the Jack hole card to win a staggering amount. The win put The Greek in the driver's seat.

But it wasn't enough to propel him over the finish line.

Johnny retook the lead several weeks later. Unlike the key moment that put The Greek on top, Johnny's victory came via a slow bleed, hand after hand tilting in his favor, allowing him to bully his one-time idol into submission. The inevitable end to a hard-fought

war, The Greek finally waved the white flag with his conciliatory comment, a quote that lives on today in the hearts and souls of poker players everywhere. The most famous quote in poker history.

"Mr. Moss, I have to let you go."

And with that, it was over. The Greek got up, stretched, gave Johnny a nod, and strode out, still proud in defeat, into the desert sunset. Johnny left the table with the spoils, somewhere between $2 million and $4 million. Most notably, he cemented his reputation as the "King of Cards."

The match itself became the stuff of legend, as all important historic moments do. Over the years, people would debate whether it happened earlier than 1951, as well as where it took place, or if it even happened at all. But those who witnessed it know the truth, both what happened and its importance to the sport. That marathon match cemented Benny as a top promoter and casino owner in the bustling city, irking the other local proprietors. It also helped usher more professional card players into Vegas, with everyone coming to make a buck and prove their mettle.

Unfortunately, it also put Benny Binion directly in the crosshairs.

CHAPTER 16
THE FEDS

Benny's ascension through the crime-noir cities of Dallas and Las Vegas was no simple maneuver. It wasn't built on brute strength alone. He had the muscle and he had the firepower, but that was only part of the equation. The other key component that made him an all-star racketeer, a component in which Benny was a master, can be summed up in one word.

Corruption.

The Cowboy had a deep Rolodex. Friends in the right places. Friends in legal circles, cops, lawyers, judges, politicians. The civic-minded power players. Finding them and keeping them happy was a balancing act akin to juggling meat cleavers while riding a unicycle across a high wire with no net below. The secret was knowing who he could and could not finesse, and what exactly it would cost him.

He once stated, "I've bribed many a man in my day."

But it doesn't matter how many envelopes are delivered, how many briefcases are slid under the table, or how many palms are greased. There will always be the righteous few who claim to be unflappable. The straight-arrow crusaders who refuse to wallow in mud and mire with the indecent pigs of humanity. These folks, well, they have their own agendas.

The authorities in Dallas and other regions in Texas had their antennae up, their high beams on, and they were gunning for Binion, whether he was in state or not. They had been from the start. He was an elusive figure, like a drifter on horseback who blew into

an old Western town one day and disappeared the next. Benny didn't leave many hoofprints behind. He was cunning and strategic. He gave careful consideration to who he involved himself with in his varied business ventures.

His wide-ranging personal connections were constantly on the lookout for any irregularities or problems that might come his way. If they smelled smoke, they were eager to stomp out the fire or at least alert The Cowboy. If Benny ran into problems, they also knew they had a high probability of running into problems. It was only a matter of time.

Time was the key factor. Eventually, time catches up to us all, and Benny was no exception. One thing The Cowboy could bank on: If enough law dogs join the hunt, they will eventually sniff out their prey and send it scurrying up a tree.

The Raid

On a hot and sticky summer evening in 1949, more than forty Dallas police officers and sheriff's deputies swarmed dozens of locations linked to Benny Binion and his Southland Syndicate, led by Dallas Police Chief Carl Hansson, along with his sidekick Dallas District Attorney Will "Hop Along" Wilson. The pair rolled out a blitzkrieg of mass raids in search of any evidence to take down Binion.

One thing they had in common was that they were no friend to Benny Binion. Another thing that linked the two—Hansson and Wilson were allies of the enigmatic Cat.

Most of the raids amounted to nothing. But one, a horse stable in a muddy field about twelve miles north of Dallas, would prove to be the mother lode. On the outside it appeared to be nothing more than a nondescript cinder block building with pipe corrals surrounding it. A simple riding stable. What type of thievery could possibly be taking place here?

On the inside, the brains of the outfit were hard at work. When detectives burst their way through the front door, they found seven of Binion's head honchos. Detectives also located bundles of cash and policy game receipts. There were several vaults and file cabinets that unearthed the equivalent of *The Treasure of Sierra Madre.*

It was a paper trail a mile long that detailed Benny's numbers operations.

By this stage, Benny was safely tucked away at his Bonanza compound in Las Vegas. He swore up and down that he had left all his dirty Dallas dealings behind him. That business was in his rear-view mirror. Unfortunately, the evidence proved different. Investigators found an intricate paperwork trail that detailed a system of managers and districts, all leading back to Benny, who still reaped close to 70 percent of all the action. They also located Benny's tax records, which would prove to be a royal pain in Benny's rectum in the very near future.

Wilson attempted to build a case tying both policy games and a string of salacious murders to Binion. The fine folks of the Big D were both fascinated and mortified by the related homicide stories of the case. Names such as Frieden, Sam Murray, Laudermilk, Minyard, and Mildred Noble all linked to him.

They slapped the cuffs on Benny in Vegas, but he was soon released. The next plan was to have him extradited to Texas. Harry Claiborne, Benny's slick lawyer, would have none of it. He explained quite frankly that Benny was not in town for any of these crimes, so he couldn't be connected to them. That meant that he was not a fugitive and could not be extradited. The courts agreed and Benny was safe, for now. This news placed a speed bump in the road to arraignment. But Wilson was a determined crime fighter who believed in justice. He vowed to carry on the good fight.

Benny was the "King of the Ducks," a man well adept at ducking law enforcement inquisitions. Over the next several months, Dallas authorities would come calling, but Nevada judges blocked their

attempts at every turn. One Clark County judge, annoyed at the repeated attempts at one of their fine new citizens, even went as far to tell a Dallas interrogator to leave Las Vegas and never come back!

Benny could breathe easy for the time being, but the winds of change were headed in his direction.

The Bulls-eye Expands

Senator Estes Kefauver carried on his tirade to rid the United States of the evil empire known as "organized crime" with his US Special Committee to Investigate Crime in Interstate Commerce. The hearings of 1950 marched forward, and he was the one blowing the bugle and leading the charge.

The proceedings were televised, and Americans could not get enough of the sensational figures that were being shown front and center on their black-and-white grainy tubes. The sensationalism of the national event was causing a stir. Modern-day outlaws in silky suits sat behind a row of microphones being hammered by salty senators with deep-seated grudges.

Benny had no worries. Sure, he had some dealings here and there with some nefarious individuals who might find themselves in the committee's crosshairs, but they were minor and Benny was pretty fairly insulated. Plus, he had hightailed his ass out of Texas and was living "clean" in the city of perpetual sin.

Or so he thought.

Virgil Peterson, director of the Chicago Crime Commission, gave some compelling testimony that for the first time pointed fingers in Binion's direction. Peterson spent two days spewing details of every crime boss in America, including "the king of the rackets in Dallas." He elaborated on Binion's history and linked him to scores of highly decorated criminals and gangland bosses across the country.

Suddenly, Benny Binion became a target of the national government.

The committee eventually made their way to Vegas. With news of its arrival, gangsters and gun molls scattered like a covey of quail, including Benny. Nobody in the life sought out that type of publicity. Benny shagged ass to his ranch in Montana to lay low while the circus was in town.

Kefauver next led his committee to Los Angeles, and once again he subpoenaed Benny. Once again, Benny headed for the hills. He retreated to the Montana ranch where he spent time baling hay and palpating dry cows. The committee members' persecution pressed on. They called Lieutenant George Butler of the Dallas Police, who gave a full account of Binion's indiscretions, his tumultuous rivalry with Herbert Noble, and the blood-soaked carnage that was left in its wake.

The heat on Benny was growing.

A New Approach

In 1952, Henry Wade was now the Dallas district attorney. A devout crime fighter, Wade was hell-bent on prosecuting the unjust. He could be loud and boisterous, but he preferred quiet time and keeping his tone at low decibels. He chomped on cigars as if they were celery sticks. He was not into making friends, but he preferred not to make any new enemies. The list of haters was growing too long to count. He believed a man was only worth his weight in gold. Fairness and righteousness were Wade's two pillars of decorum. He was an extreme competitor who was out to beat any man whether the game was tiddlywinks or grab ass. You could bet Wade was in it to win it.

He struggled with acceptance and had issues with "just letting go." Such was the situation with the Binion case. For the love of God, how could justice not be served?

Nevada repeatedly refused extradition of Binion on gambling charges. Wade was livid. He decided to build a murder case instead. Who in their right mind would turn down extradition on a presumed murderer? He and his team combed the streets in search of anyone who would give reliable testimony against Benny. There were no takers; people understood it was harmful to your health to speak ill of The Cowboy.

The doors were shut, the case was going nowhere. It looked like it was time to pull the plug.

Until . . . those pesky tax returns!

It's the Little Things

As part of the 1949 raid at the riding stable, Benny's back-tax paperwork was sent to the Dallas office of the Internal Revenue Service. The case was kicked around from one department to another before eventually landing in front of Frank Potter, US attorney for the Northern District of Texas. He understood that he could not dismiss the case. He also understood the reality of building an actual case that would hold water was going to be against all odds, mainly due to the inflammatory character witnesses involved.

Nevertheless, the grand jury voted to indict Binion for tax evasion.

Potter deliberated and came to the decision that it would be best to try and settle the case. Benny could pay $20,000 in back taxes and a $15,000 fine. A simple cut-and-dried case. No big financial penalty, no jail, no forced return to Texas. The whole thing would be over. For Benny, it was too good to be true.

In July 1952, Wade got wind of the proposed settlement and went into a furious rampage. He called Potter everything but a white man and explained that this here plea deal would slam the door shut on Dallas convicting Binion of any major crime. Potter was blindsided

by the distraught district attorney, but he agreed. The plea deal held no weight in the halls of justice, so they started to dismantle it, with the full support of James McGranery, the US attorney general.

There was haggling between numerous parties, with Benny's camp complaining that the offer couldn't be rescinded. A state judge agreed, putting the plea deal back in place with the fine, a payment of the 1949 taxes, and five years' probation.

1949.

He didn't say anything about 1948.

The raid had also dug up Benny's 1948 returns, and there were even more discrepancies there. Wade and McGranery built their case, and once again Benny was indicted for tax evasion. This time, Benny Binion was asked to return to Dallas.

Concerned about his well-being, Benny expressed his fear, exclaiming to the judge, "If I fall into the hands of Texas authorities, I will be murdered."

The judge did not bite. He ordered the extradition.

Benny's lawyers appealed to the Supreme Court, claiming conspiracy, abuse of power, and a master-planned witch hunt. On April 13, 1953, the court announced that they refused to hear the appeal. Benny would be headed back to the Lone Star State to stand trial.

He was scheduled to return on June 8, 1953.

The Surrender

The FBI worried that Benny had plans to skip town. They countered by staging agents on surveillance and set up checkpoints along all highways leading out of Vegas. There were also agents posted at train stations and airports, hiding in bathroom stalls and at hot dog stands. The FBI was certain they had all their bases covered.

Never count The Cowboy out. On the evening of June 5, Benny, his son Jack, and trusted driver, the massive, hulking beast of a man

who went by the name "Gold Dollar," climbed into his 1952 Cadillac and hit the road with the pedal to the metal, reaching speeds over one hundred . . . and leaving agents in their dust.

The FBI had lost their man.

After several hours of searching high and low, headquarters was notified of the lost target. The top brass fumed.

Thirteen hours later, the blue Caddy was spotted on Route 66 in New Mexico, over five hundred miles southeast of Vegas . . . en route to Texas. FBI agents gave pursuit for several hours, but only stayed close, not actually approaching the car or apprehending Benny. Technically, he hadn't done anything wrong yet except exceed the speed limit. As they cruised into Lubbock, Texas, Benny made a stop. He got out of the car and approached the cars of his pursuers with a big grin.

"Aren't you boys getting tired?" he asked.

Benny knew they had been following him the whole time.

A day later, Binion was in Dallas wearing a new suit, white cowboy boots, and smoking a cigar as he moseyed into the Dallas County Jail. The press was out in full force, but the normally mouthy Binion had only one thing to say.

"I ain't talking."

Bill Decker served him with warrants on state gambling charges. He photographed and fingerprinted him. Benny posted his $15,000 bond and was released. Two days later, he was in a federal courthouse facing tax charges, to which he replied to all charges, "Not guilty."

The Sentencing

Federal prosecutors prepared for a battle, building a case and pulling together over a hundred witnesses, but Benny and his team surprised everyone by suddenly pleading guilty to four counts of tax

evasion. Benny's team thought a guilty plea might lead to some leniency in sentencing.

Benny was given a few months to get his affairs in order.

Part of that was how to handle the Horseshoe. He reached out to his old friend Joe W. Brown, a New Orleans businessman and avid gambler who was worth over $200 million. Brown agreed to buy a 97 percent interest in the casino and run the place. But that was just for show for the state authorities. The deal behind the deal was really for more like 25 percent and a promise to give managing ownership back to Benny when this all blew over.

Others stepped in to grab a piece of the Horseshoe to help provide him with the over $500,000 he needed to pay his tax liability in full. He once again thought taking care of this as quickly as possible would help with sentencing.

When asked later, Benny was coy about what he thought he would receive in terms of a punishment, but family members said everyone expected probation.

A humbled Benny Binion appeared in San Antonio for sentencing. He was given a chance to speak, and he pointed out how he had paid all the taxes in full. He implied that he would be willing to leave gambling behind him and focus on his family and his ranch in Montana. Benny Binion, for perhaps the first time in his life, tried to play dumb.

"I just didn't intend to cheat the government. I'm kinda ignorant and I got to gambling around, and well, you know . . ."

Judge Ben Rice didn't buy it. Shocking everyone, he rejected the plea and ordered a $20,000 fine and a sentence of five years in prison. Benny's mouth dropped and his family openly cried. He was allowed to hug them and say his goodbyes and then he was taken away. In the hallway, Benny found his strength once again, and as he emerged between two US marshals on the steps of the courthouse, in front of a throng of reporters, he exclaimed, "From now on, you're gonna have to find a new subject."

Benny Binion then reported to Leavenworth prison.

It was there that Benny had plenty of time to contemplate what would come next.

BET/RAISE

Increasing the size of the original bet.

CHAPTER 17
THUNDER ROAD

A straight and narrow seven-mile stretch of highway. That's how the casual observer might describe it. The ghosts of the ramblers that frequented the flophouses, gin joints, and gambling dens would call it a wicked, twisted, reckless road to self-annihilation.

Many a man traveled over this patch of asphalt. Many a man lost his soul in the process.

The 1950s should have been a time of tranquility in North Texas. Two of the biggest crime bosses in Dallas/Fort Worth were indisposed. Herbert Noble was dead. There was nothing left of him or his body. Benny Binion was locked up in the Leavenworth Federal Penitentiary. The citizens should thank their lucky stars, breathe a little deeper. The violence was over.

Right?

No.

Not. At. All.

We shift our focus back to the heart of the DFW metroplex. To a destination where violent crime, murder, mayhem, and chaos was an epidemic that had infiltrated the area and ran as rampant as scarlet fever or diphtheria. Let's take a stroll down one of the most vicious streets in America, a notorious stretch of highway that would serve as a breeding ground for the next pivotal point in the history of poker, how the game was played, and the Texas gambling pioneers that earned their stripes there. We owe a debt of gratitude to this infamous road that plunged many people straight through the fiery gates

of hell. A cast of colorful characters incubated in this area, busting their chops and placing their first bet here. Including one Texan who would later become the face of the World Series of Poker.

Welcome to Jacksboro Highway, y'all!

Hell's Half Acre

Jacksboro Highway wasn't always THE place to find trouble in Texas. First there was Exchange Avenue.

"One of the toughest streets in America."

That's how many poker players describe Exchange Avenue, and the residents there wore the reputation with pride. Located in the belly of "Cowtown," Exchange Avenue was literally in the stockyards of northside Fort Worth, about three miles due north from downtown.

"Where the West begins," that's Fort Worth's motto, and one need look no farther than Exchange Avenue to know why. The stockyards originated in the 1890s when meat packing giants Swift and Armor established packing plants along the Trinity River and the Union Pacific Railroad. It became a premiere cattle trading destination. Located on the Chisolm Trail, cattle barons from the big outfits—Waggoneers, XIT, Four Sixes, Pitchforks, and others—would have their cowboys drive the herds from the ranch onto the Chisolm Trail toward Fort Worth, where the cattle would be sent to market. After the exhausting trip, when the cattle were bought, the cowboys were paid. Then it was time to let loose and shoot out the lights. Bring on the dice, cards, whiskey, and dancing girls!

But Fort Worth was a thriving cattle kingdom even before the stockyards originated in 1890. It was one of the wildest Western towns of the 1870s, an outlaw's paradise. The rankest part of North Fort Worth was referred to as "Hell's Half Acre." It was a salacious sexpot with liquor, prostitution, and gambling, covering multiple square blocks. Saloons dominated and lawmen were encouraged to

stay away. These cowpokes had been in the saddle for way too long. It was time to kick their spurs up and possibly take a bath with the company of one, two, or possibly three ladies of the night. Gambling and libations followed. Perhaps more women and more booze. The last thing they needed was for some righteous lawman to be showing up with his tin badge shutting down the party.

This was part of the economic engine that kept Fort Worth financially afloat to the turn of the century and beyond. Bringing the cowboys to town was big business. Let them wet their whistle, blow their wad, and spread their hard-earned cash around. This philosophy kept many townsfolk employed. It was a rough-and-tumble world. Rabble-rousers roamed the dusty streets. Receiving a knife to the gut was as common as having a bowel movement. The Grim Reaper worked overtime here. The bodies piled up. It was no place for a candy ass. Only the merciless survived. Desperados, train robbers, and gunslingers—all these hell-raising hombres found refuge here. They had no regard for the law or the decent townsfolk. This place made Doc Holliday cringe.

The good times wouldn't last forever. Religious reformers and the temperance movement helped shape the new direction. After World War I, police tightened the belt on punishment. They aimed to curtail the vice trade of Hell's Half Acre.

But as we've learned, vice doesn't stop. Boozing, whoring, gambling, and the violence that comes with it just finds a new home. In Texas, the outlaws quickly found a new spot that would serve them just fine.

Welcome to Thunder Road

By the 1930s the action had shifted from the dirty, deadly streets of the stockyards, every hellion's favorite spot, to a new patch of asphalt called "the Northwest Highway."

It was originally opened in 1931 as State Highway 34. By 1935, the highway was redesignated as "State Highway 199" or "Jacksboro Highway." The Fort Worth side of the highway ran for seven miles before it turned into US Route 380/State Highway 59.

It first earned its reputation with booze. By this point, Prohibition was a thing of the past. However, the Texas legislature wasn't fully convinced. They limited the sale of hard liquor. Many of these counties became known as "dry counties," where no alcohol was permitted to be sold. This fueled the fire for the legendary highway to grow. With the underground sale of bootleg liquor, roughnecks, rednecks, ranchers, and rodeo hands flooded the highway in search of illicit spirits to quench their unholy thirst. After the alcohol, the gambling followed.

Moonshiners ran booze up and down this highway. Loaded down with liquor they drove the rubber off the tires of their souped-up rides, servicing the dry areas of Tarrant County. All this rumbling of exhaust pipes and piston-churning engines garnered the highway a new nickname: "Thunder Road."

In 1936, Fort Worth celebrated Texas's first hundred years with a celebration called the Frontier Centennial. This months-long bender allowed gamblers and moonshiners to operate with impunity. The money that flowed through the county was a huge economic boost to the region.

With war raging in 1942, a newly installed air force plant that built B-24 bombers and Fort Worth Army Airfield (later Carswell Air Force Base) brought thousands of men and women employees with government paychecks to blow on hooch at clubs sprouting up like spring daisies on the highway.

There were also the masses that worked at slaughterhouses and packing plants in the stockyards. You better believe those people had worked up a powerful thirst after sloshing around in knee-high blood all day. As well as the country club elite and the TCU students who weren't exempt from their urges of whiskey and gambling.

"Jax Beer Highway" had a fan base to appease.

The clubs on this highway to hell came and went, but some of the most notorious were the Four Deuces, 3939 Club, Black Cat, Black Sands, Hilarity Club, Coconut Grove, and many others.

The Four Deuces was a five thousand square-foot adult playground. It was a Spanish colonial casino that offered a semi-fine dining restaurant. Guests arrived by invitation only. The Four Deuces only catered to the highest of high rollers. Tens of thousands of dollars rolled through this hot spot nightly. The Four Deuces was in a league of its own. A majority of the others were dive bars and dance hall death traps.

By the 1950s, top-billed entertainers such as Bob Wills and his Texas Playboys, The Andrews Sisters, Tommy Dorsey, Benny Goodman, Harry James, and Fort Worth's hometown hero Bobby Peters could be found playing on the highway. Many like Willie Nelson played behind chicken wire for their own protection. The crowds were rowdy and unruly. Fists flew, knives slashed, and guns cocked. Bouncers worked harder than a one-legged man in an ass-kicking contest. The road goes on forever, but the party never ends.

Neither does the violence.

A New Capital for Crime

Extortion, prostitution, gambling, and hijacking. These were all hallmarks of criminal activities conducted on the Jacksboro Highway during the 1950s. The boys in the backrooms of the clubs were calling the shots. It helped that they had a select group of eager and willing law officers who turned a blind eye.

Until they no longer could.

The cops could ignore some greedy gamblers getting robbed and roughed up here and there over an unpaid tab or staring at the tip of a knife or down the barrel of a gun because they got caught cheating at

a game. No one was going to shed a tear for these degenerates as long as the crimes didn't step over the line. But as we've seen, the status quo rarely stays quiet. The competition on Jacksboro Highway was fierce, and the powder keg was about to be lit! It was only a matter of time . . .

Nelson Harris was raised on the highway. He knew of its treachery and hardships. During his teens he worked as a bouncer before the war. He graduated to work with the Green Dragon narcotics syndicate and was later convicted on drug charges and sentenced to Leavenworth prison.

On the morning of November 22, 1950, the day before Thanksgiving, Harris phoned his criminal lawyers in a panic exclaiming he was coming to see them about a matter of "life and death."

Around nine fifteen AM, Harris, who was just forty-one, grabbed his precious and very pregnant twenty-five-year-old bride Juanita and they climbed into his car outside their duplex off University Street on the west side. Juanita was due to give birth within the next week. Nelson leaned forward to twist the key into the ignition. Within a millisecond the car blew into a sky-high fireball, triggered by a bottle of nitroglycerin that had been wired to the engine starter. Harris, Juanita, and their unborn child were incinerated. They never made it to the lawyers' office.

Suddenly, the whispers about the deadly hoodlums on Jacksboro Highway were front and center. The citizens of Fort Worth couldn't help but read about the notorious activities taking place within their fine town, and Jacksboro Highway would never be the same.

The public was appalled at the grotesque tragedy. Many could stomach a gangster killing a gangster. But the news of the Harris family slaughter was a different sensation. A woman and an unborn child were murdered. The public demanded action. Police followed orders, even those on the take. A round up of gambling arrests were made within a few weeks following the blast. After a thorough investigation that expanded into "gaming, bribery and vice," a grand jury

issued indictments for thirty-two gamblers operating on the highway. It looked like progress, but the violence was just getting started.

Big Money with Big Enemies

Between 1943 and 1959, nineteen gangland killings took place on the Jacksboro Highway. After the brooms swept the asphalt clean following the Harris car bombing, the killing continued, and 1955 was one of the more dreadful years.

Clifton Edell Evans ran a rigged gambling house and a call-girl service. Police raided his home and discovered four thousand pairs of dice. In the spring of 1955, Evans disappeared. Police found blood smeared on the front seat of his Cadillac. Acting on a tip, a few months later, authorities located Evans's corpse in a shallow grave close to the Jacksboro Highway.

Tincy Eggleston had been honing his criminal craft for over a quarter century. He received an A-plus in his studies of being a genuine bad boy. In 1935, he served thirteen years for robbery then broke out of the Harlem state prison farm. Eggleston and his former partner Cecil Green were major players who controlled gambling and extortion activities along the highway. Tincy was also a key suspect in the Harris homicide. Within hours of their car bombing, Eggleston reported finding a similar device under the hood of his vehicle. It was believed that Tincy killed the Harrises then rigged a similar bomb on his car to divert suspicion.

On a brisk morning in 1955, Tincy left his modest home to collect an extortion payoff. Several days later, his body was found in a well east of the highway.

Cecil Green was another key suspect in the Harris bombing. Green was mowed down with bullets while he sat in his Cadillac at the By-Way Drive Inn tavern on the highway. He died the next day.

A trifecta of high-profile gangland murders to cap off 1955. All murders remained unsolved.

The body count continued to rise. In 1956, Charles Frank Cates, gambler and potential co-conspirator in the Harris car bombing, counted money in his small gambling house. The establishment was located behind Chenault's Dining Place on the highway. A phone rang, Frank answered, and the house went *KABOOM!*

The explosion rocked the neighborhood. Police discovered wires under the decimated house that ran 250 feet along the Jacksboro Highway. A suspect had been in a nearby car and subsequently detonated the bomb. Cates survived that attack, but police later found his shotgun-riddled body lying inside his car, within a mile of the well where Tincy Eggleston's body was discovered.

By 1957, Gene Paul Norris was listed at the top of the FBI's Ten Most Wanted List. Norris was considered a hitman in the Cecil Green slaying. He had larger aspirations than murder. His next cooked-up caper was the robbery of a bank. This was no ordinary bank. Norris planned to take down a branch of the Fort Worth National Bank located inside Carswell Air Force Base. This location held the base's payroll of $225,000 ($1.8 million in today's money). It was a staggering sum and a risky job for any hood to pull off. Police got wind of the plot. They closed in on Gene and his accomplice while they made a practice run. A high-speed chase ensued. Norris was cornered and shot over a dozen times before his bloody body finally hit the pavement. Police blocked off the road and covered the body with a tarp—located on everyone's favorite road, Jacksboro Highway.

From the Ashes

It's no surprise that the gambling history of Dallas/Fort Worth was bloody and bombastic. As we've seen, the Texas gambling pioneers endured many hardships to promote the games they loved. Many of

their cohorts died an unfriendly death while others languished, wasting away in a cell.

What makes this infamous seven-mile stretch of road so important to our story is not only the continuation of the murder and mayhem that escalated with the Binion/Noble war, but also two very important developments.

One of the factors was that the gambling go-to preference of this region was shifting from dice to cards. More specifically, poker, and with that the advent of a new form of poker called "Texas Hold 'Em."

This is where the legendary game took its roots. It was in the backrooms on the Highway to Hell and Exchange Avenue that the game began to be dealt on a regular basis. This was the breeding ground where the game initially grew in popularity. Hold 'Em's rise to fame was seeded in the town where the West begins. It was evident the game was destined for greatness on a nationwide scale. The game was on a trajectory to become the premiere game of poker.

The second important factor of this region was the history of a group of poker players who cut their teeth on the green felt in these backrooms. The ones that survived would eventually become the core founding members of the World Series of Poker. Jacksboro Highway, Fort Worth, and the surrounding towns would grow poker beyond anyone's wildest imagination. Cowtown is a major contributor to the progression of the story of poker.

Without the violence and blood-soaked body bags, the greatest poker players to evolve may not have found their destiny. They certainly would not have found the games in this area without the origins of the outlaws of the past.

Among these colorful players to soon emerge, one stands above the rest. He is cemented among the finest on poker's Mount Rushmore. In fact, he would become the future face of the World Series of Poker.

The one, the only, the Texas Dolly.

CHAPTER 18
THE TEXAS DOLLY

The plume of cigarette smoke chokes the life out of the room. The lights are fuzzy and dim. A lingering scent of rotten eggs and way too much perspiration saturates the nostrils. The atmosphere is tense and edgy. Muffled sounds from outside the door, in the bar, as pool balls kiss off one another. A rambunctious roughneck yells at his girlfriend over the jukebox that pours out solid country gold tunes.

Below the eye-watering haze are a couple of worn-down poker tables. Both are filled with cutthroats wearing faded Stetsons or sombreros. One has an eye patch. The games are kicking into high gear with one bright-eyed West Texas plow boy in the midst.

The one and only Doyle Brunson.

Now he's still a young man trying to make his way as a professional poker player, focused on the game, the cards, his opponents, and the pile of chips in the middle of the table, knowing that in a couple minutes they'll be a part of his stack. Just like all the rest.

A smiling waitress with several missing teeth sashays into the room carrying a loaded- down tray of Pabst Blue Ribbon beer.

Doyle plays the cards he is dealt and keeps to himself.

Around midnight, a stranger drifts in with pain in his eyes. He calmly walks to the table and whips out a six-shooter. He levels the pistol at the player sitting at a table right behind Doyle and squeezes the trigger.

BLAM! BLAM!

Players are sprayed with flecks of blood, brains, and skull fragments. The walls are painted crimson red. There's nothing left of the head, but the body remains intact, still sitting upright. The room goes quiet as all eyes turn to see what happens next, afraid to breathe. Doyle does the same, but his eyes also drift back to his hand, wondering what to bet to keep this pot going. For Doyle Brunson, the action on the table is always what's most important, gunmen be damned.

The stranger holsters his weapon and peacefully walks out. Nobody knows what the beef was he had with the victim, but the score has been settled.

Brunson looks at his hand—aces and sevens—which he will now forever call the "Next Dead Man's Hand," referring to the original Dead Man's Hand of aces and eights.

The experience shook some and they make for the exits. But the players, the real pros, keep the game rollin'. After all, there was still poker to be played and this was just another friendly night on Exchange Avenue!

The Godfather of Poker

Doyle didn't know it then, but that night was one of many in his early poker-playing years that would build a certain kind of toughness and resolve in the friendly, gentle, God-fearing man that he would use to destroy other professionals at the table with a smile, an "Aww-shucks" shrug of the shoulders, and a memorable quote (or piece of advice) for decades to come. That toughness, combined with passion, an affable charisma, and an intellect for all nuances of the game, would be the ingredients that would eventually make Doyle one of the most successful poker players of all time, and certainly the most respected. It's what would make him the Godfather of Poker.

When it comes to Doyle Brunson, the man is on a mountain of his own. He was the first player to surpass the $1 million mark in

poker tournament wins. A winner of an astounding ten World Series of Poker bracelets. He is tied for third all-time as a bracelet winner behind the two Phils—Phil Hellmuth with seventeen, and Phil Ivey with eleven.

He is one of only three players to win the WSOP Main Event multiple times (1976 and 1977), and one of only three players, along with Bill Boyd and Loren Klein, to have won WSOP tournaments in four consecutive years. He is the first of six players to win both the WSOP Main Event and a World Poker Tour title.

In January 2006, *Bluff* magazine voted Brunson the most influential force in the world of poker . . . and most would argue it's a title he still holds today!

Brunson and the WSOP are like two peas in a pod. He rarely missed the event since its inception in 1970 until his retirement in 2018 (though he would return for a ceremonial WSOP tourney in 2021, where he would place fifth). He made multiple WSOP championship event final tables before his back-to-back wins. However, since the event format changed to a winner-take-all, as a result these cashes were not counted on his stats.

World Series of Poker Bracelets (with $$$ Won)

1976 - $5,000 Deuce-to-Seven Draw ($80,250)
1976 - $10,000 No-Limit Hold 'Em World Championship ($230,000)
1977 - $1,000 Seven-Card Stud Split ($62,500)
1977 - $10,000 No-Limit Hold 'Em World Championship ($340,000)
1978 - $5,000 Seven-Card Stud ($68,000)
1979 - $600 Mixed Doubles Seven-Card Stud ($4,500)
1991 - $2,500 No-Limit Hold 'Em ($208,000)
1998 - $1,500 Seven-Card Razz ($93,000)

2003 - $2,000 H.O.R.S.E. ($84,080)
2005 - $5,000 No-Limit Short-Handed Texas Hold 'Em ($367,800)

His other WSOP cashes outside his Main Event wins in 1976 and 1977 are: 1972 (3rd), 1980 (runner-up to three-time Main Event winner Stu Unger), 1982 (4th), 1983 (3rd), 1997 (16th), 2004 (53rd), and 2013 (409th).

Beyond his accomplishments at the table, Doyle helped usher the sport to the masses, making poker success feel accessible to the average house game player. He's the author of multiple books on poker strategy, including his breakthrough book and the one considered the bible in the world of poker: *Super/System*. Originally self-published in 1978 (and updated in 2004), it takes poker players of all skill sets on a journey into the mindset of a world champion. The book is credited with transforming poker players' understanding of how the world's finest professionals played the game and accumulated tournament wins and vast amounts of cash. Brunson confessed that his book cost him money over the long haul as players were better prepared to deal with the game because of it.

As poker grew as a sport over the years, Doyle became a trusted and popular ambassador. He frequently played in the largest high-roller poker games around the world, though his home turf was "Bobby's Room" at the Bellagio. The regular game was the $4,000/$8,000 mix. While his focus was first and foremost on the game, Doyle never shied away from talking to fans, offering advice to young players and promoting the sport he loved.

Until the action started.

Doyle Brunson and professional poker became so synonymous that he even has Texas Hold 'Em hands named after him. The ten-deuce off suit is called "The Doyle" because he won the WSOP Main Event in both 1976 and 1977 with that hand, in both cases

coming from behind to complete a full house. His name also claims the ace-queen as he viewed it as a trap hand that he "tried" never to play.

With his attitude, approach to the game, and wild success, Doyle would eventually earn the beloved nickname "The Texas Dolly." With his signature Stetsons, animal-skinned boots, rancher shirts, and a warm drawl, he was Texas through and through. Unlike many of the others covered in this book, and several others he would play against, the game of poker itself was always most important to Doyle. While his colleagues were always looking for action anywhere and everywhere, no matter what it looked like, The Texas Dolly was different. As he once said in an interview:

"I'm a poker player who gambles."

Salt of the Earth

Born in the cotton fields of Roby, Texas (about three hours west of Dallas), on August 10, 1933, Doyle Frank Brunson was destined for greatness, though he might not have sensed it at an early age.

He grew up in a small farmhouse under the guidance of a hardworking West Texas family. They had no running water or electricity. One of Doyle's chores was to go outside to the well and fetch water for the bathtub. The family shared the same bathwater and since Doyle was the baby, he bathed last. The family had an outhouse with a door that didn't shut all the way.

Railroad tracks cut through the west side of the family's cotton field. When a train would roll through, the entire house shook like there was no tomorrow with pots and pans crashing to the ground. Hobos got off the trains and would often wander up to the Brunson house begging for food scraps. Sometimes they got 'em. At other times there was no food for anyone, including the Brunsons.

Tough times create tough people.

Roby (or as some refer to it, Longworth) had a population of around two hundred. They were two hundred of the saltiest and earthiest people you ever met. The town square had a general store, a one-room elementary school, and two churches . . . and that's all they needed, by golly! The nearest town of any size was Sweetwater fifteen miles to the south.

The Dust Bowl of 1933 swept the good earth clean. The skies turned brown, and the wind was the ultimate destroyer. The drought decimated crops. It made any common dry land farmer rethink their life's ambition. It was similar to the monkey who was fucking the skunk—the monkey hadn't had all he wanted but he had all he could stand. Many farmers stepped off their tractors, their boots hit the soil, they left the fields, and never looked back. Those who did stay were molded with a keen sense of hardness. The weather and market conditions beat them down like a sledgehammer. Every time they got up, that sledgehammer came swinging down on them again . . . only harder and faster. Their skin was reptilian, burned up and leathery from the scorching sun. If you could survive this life and come out the other side unscathed, you were built to withstand being run over by a Mack truck. Anything else in life was a walk in the park.

John Brunson was quiet, tight-lipped, and did not overly engage with his three children. His mind was on managing the family's cotton farm and feeding hungry mouths. Doyle, his brother, and sister all worked the fields picking cotton by hand.

Doyle's entertainment in those early years was traveling into town and playing with other kids. There were only three children his age who lived in town. A girl and two boys. The trio of boys would spend afternoons (when they weren't drenched in sweat from picking cotton) playing baseball with broom handles. One pitcher, one batter, one fielder—that's all you need. They swam in stock tanks on the farms and played Cowboys and Indians.

When Doyle was old enough, he headed to Sweetwater High School. His father was insistent on him helping with the farm, but his

mother Mealia also knew the boy needed an education. It was the only way he could both help the family and get the hell out of there.

Playing Days Before His Playin' Days

During high school, Doyle fell in love with sports. Sports enlightened his perspective. There was life away from the blinding red dirt fields. By the late 1940s his body sprouted into his trademark tall, lanky, athletic frame. He played every sport but football. While on the track team he ran a blistering 4:38 mile, which he would eventually get down to 4:18.

He was a natural phenom at basketball, playing guard at six three. Doyle had incredibly quick feet. He moved like a flash up and down the court. He helped take Sweetwater High to multiple state championships. He crafted his moves from alumni players, which gained him notoriety as a floor captain. Doyle was a deadeye dick shot. A sniper from the perimeter. The press considered him one of the elite long-range shooters in Texas.

He got his first taste of cards in 1949 on the eve of the semifinals at the state basketball tournament. The game was in Austin, and Doyle went to check in with a few classmates who were fans and made the trip to cheer on the team. They met up at a hotel room, and a game of Seven-Card Stud and Five-Card Draw broke out. Brunson had only seen the game played on TV Westerns. His friends offered him some free lessons and Doyle accepted. The stakes were for coins (nickels, dimes, and quarters), and he won a few dollars, and quickly. He collected his cash and bid adios. As he would say later, "Easy money." Whatever happened that night, the gambling bug had seeped into his bloodstream. He had a tiger in his tank, and it was about to come out.

The team lost the next day, but Doyle was awarded a scholarship on the University of Texas basketball and track teams. He procrastinated and by the time the paperwork was submitted, the scholarships

had already been claimed by other athletes. He promptly accepted another scholarship to play basketball at Hardin Simmons University in Abilene, Texas, about an hour from Roby. They played in the Border Conference (now extinct) against Arizona, Arizona State, Texas Tech, and others.

It was in the dorm rooms of this strict, straitlaced Baptist college that Doyle began to hone his craft of poker. Most nights there was a game to be played. He and his buddies couldn't get enough. He found he had an internal compass that pointed toward aces, kings, and queens. He didn't need teaching anymore. Doyle was learning from experience. He bankrolled himself by using the fifteen dollars allotted on his monthly scholarship stipend, which was set aside for "laundry." Doyle could fold his own damn clothes. The fifteen dollars was put to better use as an entry fee into the late-night dorm room poker sessions.

The university administrators were not on board with the flagrant gambling. In their eyes, Doyle should be doing more praying and reading the good book. They called him in on five separate incidents involving gambling issues. Brunson escaped any disciplinary action. He was a big man on campus. A bona fide basketball star. He was too great an asset to lose. Some light scolding would do. Any other student might have found themselves packing a suitcase and thumbing a ride back home.

Doyle would travel back to the farm for the holidays. Life was much more peaceful. He would never let on to his chosen profession. Then one year his father asked Doyle and his brother to gather around and play some poker. Doyle was shocked. He didn't know his father played cards. They played with matchsticks. Brunson's competitive nature took control, and he attempted some fancy bluffs. John Brunson could see straight through his son's maneuvering. Doyle exclaimed, "How in the world could you call that?" His dad replied, "I've been seeing plays like that for forty years." As it turned out, his father had helped put all the kids through college by playing Sweetwater poker games. Poker really was in Doyle's blood.

Tragedy Strikes

In 1953, his junior year, Doyle led the Cowboys to a conference championship victory over Arizona. The win put Hardin Simmons into the NCAA tournament and cemented Brunson as a top NBA prospect. The Minneapolis Lakers came calling. They had scouts arrive in Abilene and chase Doyle from one court to another. They were not shy about their intentions. They alerted the HSU basketball coach that they planned to draft Brunson in the first round the next year.

Doyle was exhilarated. How a simple farmhand was taking control of the basketball court and creating his own future was beyond his wildest comprehension. But it was no dream. It was all unfolding in real time.

However, just like in poker, when the good hands are rolling in, there is always a bad hand lurking around the corner.

Doyle had a summer job at a gypsum plant in Sweetwater. While loading a stack of the material into a truck, the stack began to sway and lost its balance. A two thousand-pound sheet of gypsum rock thundered down on top of him, shattering his leg. His tibia and fibula snapped like twigs. He was laid up in the hospital with ungodly pain. He had multiple surgeries. The results were all the same: There would be no return to the basketball court. A calamitous injury with disastrous results. In one breath, Doyle's basketball career was out the window. His dream of playing in the NBA was finished.

Doyle couldn't see it then, but the disaster would eventually set him on an upward trajectory toward immortality.

The Professional

In a quandary and not knowing which way to turn, Brunson returned to classes at HSU. He received a dual master's in

administrative and teaching education. Perhaps, being a school principal was his calling.

After receiving his master's, Doyle took a job as a traveling salesman for the Burroughs Corporation. The position required selling adding machines in Fort Worth, Texas. After only a few hours on the first day, Doyle soon realized he would rather have a root canal than to try to sell one more of these outdated machines that no one wanted. As heaven would miss the stars above, maybe he could find a square dance or hoedown revival to attend.

After seven months, Doyle had failed at every attempt to make a sale. He was starving to death. His situation had turned into dire straits. He prayed to God above, "Please don't send me back to the farm."

He gave it one more shot . . . and God (or the devil) answered.

He entered a pool hall thinking that if he didn't get a sale, at least he could get a cold brew. He reluctantly laid on his pitch to a disinterested manager. He was shot down once again, but the manager pitched him on the details of a juicy card game that was taking place in the back room.

Doyle had been polishing his poker skills throughout college. The main card games in the dorms were Lowball and Five-Card Stud. Doyle traveled to larger college towns on the weekends (Lubbock, College Station, Austin) to partake in livelier games with more affluent students. Kids who had more disposable cash. He made a few dollars and saved money for beer and other necessary expenses. Doyle was mentally prepared and subconsciously on the prowl for a card game to materialize. Anything to break up the monotony and misery of his sales job.

The manager was speaking Doyle's language. He proceeded back to the game, where he cleared over a month's salary in less than three hours. That was all the convincing he needed. Doyle had found the answer.

Poker.

He made the decision right then and there to play poker professionally full-time. And he just so happened to find himself playing in the hottest (and most dangerous) spot for poker action in America.

The Texas Dolly Is Born

Doyle chased the games between Exchange Avenue and Jacksboro Highway. It was during the hellacious heyday of the mid to late 1950s. A time when many rounders never made it home alive. As mentioned earlier, them beer joints, they were no joke. Doyle was right in the middle of the frying pan.

It was a thrilling time.

He played his longest-ever poker session in a bar on Jacksboro Highway. Five days and five nights without sleeping, very little food, and drinking tons of coffee. One of his opponents was a sweet feller named Virgil who worked at the local slaughterhouse. They were playing No-Limit Ace-to-Five Lowball and Virgil was popping pills, drinking like a fish, and chain-smoking like a chimney.

On day five, at the end of the hand, Virgil showed the winning hand. He stretched his arms out to rake in the pot (after taking one last shot of whiskey). Suddenly, Virgil clasped his chest, rolled his eyes, and dropped dead on the spot.

Virgil had been good friends with all the players at the table, Doyle included. But that didn't stop the group from playing for another twenty-four hours after paramedics cleared away his body.

It was one of several incidents where Doyle would see death at the poker table. It's all part of the adventure. Try to win at the game and then try and stay alive long enough to make it home with the dough.

Doyle was in another game playing Lowball with another friend whom he had just busted at the table. His friend keeled over from a

massive heart attack. He survived. Years later, Doyle was playing in Dallas with this same friend. They were playing Lowball, and Doyle busted him once again. Like clockwork the friend had another heart attack at the table. This time he died with his belly on the green felt. Doyle collected the chips. The body was removed. The cards were shuffled for the next deal.

He became accustomed to witnessing viciousness of the unnatural kind daily. One afternoon Doyle saw a shootout that left two of his buddies dead.

When the guns weren't blasting, and the knives weren't slashing, the fists were flying. Doyle got into his fair share of fights. Usually in support of friends who were running their mouths. Brunson was quiet and soft-spoken. He was more interested in cleaning up on the green felt than he was with mopping someone's ass across the floor.

These dreadful affairs, while exhilarating, made Doyle question his mortality. Why was he playing in these honky-tonk hellholes? These death chambers? The answer seemed to always come back the same: The money was just too damn good. It was worth the risk. For now, anyway.

One hair-raising night, Doyle was playing with deadly second-story men. They enjoyed robbing and stealing about as much as they enjoyed cards. Doyle and a few other pros were the best at the table. Doyle and company continually took all their chips. When the thieves would find themselves with their last chips slipping away, it was time for another bust out. They would go plunder more valuables and return with more cash. He said in his memoir, "We'd regularly relieve them of their ill-gotten gains. They'd go steal more money, come scurrying back, and we'd break them again."

This experience could have gone sideways in a hurry, but to everyone's good fortune nobody got shot, maimed, or killed.

Doyle played head-to-head on a regular basis with some of the most prolific killers in Texas history. It was all part of the landscape.

He had some close experiences with Gene Paul Norris and Tincy Eggleston. Doyle was prone to shakedowns just like the next man. Tincy wanted to stab his hooks into Brunson. He cornered him, demanding money. Doyle took a chance and told Eggleston to go to hell, uncertain of what trouble might head his way. Tincy didn't push the issue and backed off. The confrontation still kept Doyle's head on a swivel for the immediate future.

A man always had to be on his toes in Killer Cowtown.

A Taste of Texas Hold 'Em

Doyle's ears perked up when he heard the rumors circulating about this new game called "Hold 'Em." The players on the Jacksboro Highway told him the game was catching fire. He had to find out what the hell it was all about.

In 1958, Doyle traveled to Granbury, about forty miles south of Fort Worth. He sat down at the table and played his first hand of "Hold 'Em." He was instantly intrigued with the lightning pace of the game. The simplicity, each player being dealt two hole cards facedown, meshed with the complexities of five community cards dealt face up in the center of the table. The betting structure was enticing by allowing players with big bet mentalities to take advantage and push their edges. It was a game of setting traps one street at a time and engineering timely bluffs.

Doyle quickly developed a double-barrel strategy that would be a hallmark of his career: play big cards and position at the table.

Brunson had an epiphany after leaving Granbury. He and this new game of Hold 'Em would forever be linked together. The two fit like a smooth pair of leather gloves. Hold 'Em was his true destiny.

The game was spreading in popularity among Texas gamblers. If they hadn't played, everyone wanted to find out where they could

play. The game flowed like a raging river through the murky waters of the underground Texas poker scene.

As time marched on, Doyle garnered some unwanted attention. The eyes of law enforcement were upon him. The temperature was heating up. The gory murders and the amped- up violence on both Jacksboro Highway and Exchange Avenue were drawing in a heavier police presence. Doyle's running buddies couldn't stay out trouble, which didn't help matters.

Doyle wasn't looking for problems, but the problems found him. He was arrested on several occasions, a matter of being in the wrong place at the wrong time. If it wasn't the law watching Doyle's every move, it was the constant concern of brutal thuggery. The attacks were blatant and without regard for the human body. The percentages of being threatened, beaten, or robbed were increasing every day. The risk now outweighed the opportunity.

Doyle considered his possibilities.

He had heard the tale of the two colossal warriors, Nick "The Greek" and Johnny Moss, going head-to-head in Vegas, which added gasoline to his internal fire. He wanted to play the best. He had learned that there was a boatload of poker games being played in small towns all over Texas and neighboring states. There were excellent players in all these games. They were the boss players in their regions. Doyle had heard of some of these players, and he wanted to take his shot against them.

It was time to hit the road. Vaya con Dios, mother fudgers! Doyle Brunson was going to "the Circuit."

THE RIVER

The final card flipped over on the community board.
Triggers the final round of betting.
Where good hands die quickly.

CHAPTER 19

THE TEXAS CIRCUIT

They piled in their Cadillacs, Lincolns, broken-down farm trucks, or anything else with four good wheels and hit the dusty blacktops, cannonballing through the farm-to-market roads and onto the semicrowded new superhighways. They ate up the asphalt from the big cities to the small towns. From the dry, desolate western deserts to the wet, lush eastern piney woods. From the lapping shores of the southern Gulf Coast to the flatland feedlots of the northern Panhandle. They drove day and night with their bellies full of coffee and whites. The destination was never ending, from one country club, dive bar, dance hall, private residence, cattle barn, grain silo, penthouse suite, and so on, to the next.

This was the *road.*

This was the *life.*

This was . . . THE TEXAS CIRCUIT.

It was the preeminent journey that bridged the trail from Texas to Nevada. It was the incubator that hatched the first group of professional poker players that would be synonymous with the founding years of the World Series of Poker.

There was no glamour here. These were dark and dirty places with danger lurking around every corner. It didn't matter, though. All that mattered was you could play poker there, anywhere on this Circuit. These places were promoted through word of mouth only and opened, closed, and changed locations on the regular. They could be found in about thirty to forty towns across Texas as well as

Oklahoma, New Mexico, Arkansas, Louisiana, Mississippi, and Alabama. They were tough to find unless you knew someone who knew someone and even then, proprietors practiced extreme caution as both bandits and the law were always looking to bust up a game.

The Texas Circuit helped push the concept of the "road gambler," keeping its players on the move and bouncing from city to city like a professional tour, trying to stay one step ahead while also perfecting their craft and establishing their reputation among the game's elite. As Doyle Brunson said, they "traveled to wherever the action could be found."

The Texas Circuit is critical to this story for three big reasons.

First, it was *the* place where all these guys finally came together as one. It's where the legends got their start, refined their playing style, and where they forged relationships with one another. Some of these relationships connected while others collided. It's where the players first sunk their teeth into one another. Where the rivalries were born. Where prepubescent greenhorns got to play with their ancient poker idols. Without the Texas Circuit and its cast of renegade characters, not only would there be no WSOP, but there would have been no life in the concept of professional poker. The stories, the cards, the adventures are what fascinated the public and grew poker in these early years.

Second, it was *the* place where Texas Hold 'Em became the premiere poker game. It was on the Circuit where the game blew up like a hydrogen bomb. It became the pro's game of choice. The origins of Texas Hold 'Em are as murky as the headwaters of the Rio Grande. Wherever it came from, in the 1960s it took off as these eager and aggressive gamblers liked the multiple opportunities the game provided to both bet and beat your opponent. It was fast action, big pots, and legendary battles.

Third, it marked *the* inevitable end, the last gasp of the gambling road players. Like the siren who calls for wayward sailors to come visit her open arms, the Circuit whispered of untold riches and

adventure. Many young players hit the road to stake their reputation and bring home a shit ton of cash. Over time, the dangers, violence, and law enforcement's constant birddogging swayed the scales heavier on the risk side over return. It was good times while it lasted, but nothing lasts forever. They would need a new place to play, and they started to look west.

The Honor Roll

To really understand the Texas Circuit, you need to know the players, and there were quite a few, each of them with life stories worthy of a book of their own. Some have them. Together, they formed the personality of professional poker in its early days, outlaws in their own right who made up what they lacked in sophistication with intelligence and endurance. All that matted to them was playing poker and winning. These gambling pioneers who promulgated the game of Texas Hold 'Em and persisted in spreading its popularity are as clear as Rocky Mountain spring water.

Let's meet our honor roll of Texas Circuit hustlers, the true godfathers of the sport.

* * *

Felton "Corky" McCorquodale—the Circuit was gaining stature in the early 1960s. But Felton "Corky" McCorquodale had been traveling these roads for years. He was an elder statesman on the tour. He was like the great-uncle who wanted you to come sit on his knee so he could spin you a yarn about a hound, a house cat, and a barn. He was a relic from a Norman Rockwell painting.

Corky was born on August 23, 1904, in Fort Worth, Texas. He drove the roads like a wired-up, long-haul truck driver who had been up for days. He had been a regular in Vegas since the early thirties, but the Texas scene was his playground. This innovator did

not only play Texas Hold 'Em, but his key legacy was introducing the game at the California Club in Vegas in 1963. It was this introduction that eventually gained Corky worldwide prominence in the annals of poker history. His vision was simple: Spread the game he loved far and wide. He succeeded beyond belief.

Crandall "Dandy" Addington—The great Texas wildcatters, H.L. Hunt, Sid Richardson, Glen McCarthy, Clint Murchison. Add Crandall Addington to that list. Crandall played in life's biggest poker game: the Texas oil fields. Always searching for that next giant just like a one outer on a gut shot straight. Addington was a self-made oilman with plenty of money. He understood risk and played poker for the mindful challenge, which made him a treacherous player. He was also a patient player who was always ready to play the long game, which would eventually lead to him holding the record for the most final table appearances in the WSOP (seven).

Crandall resided in San Antonio. He was nicknamed "Dandy" for his chic cowboy cool Western attire—handmade ostrich skin boots, immaculate three-piece suits with silk ties, and a silver-belly Stetson. He had that movie star-esque quality about him. Addington was a regular on the Circuit throughout the sixties. He had a sophistication to his playing style that paralleled his classy clothing.

Jack "Treetop" Straus—The lanky six-six Texan dominated most opponents by his sheer physique alone. Most folks spent their time literally looking up at Jack. Famous for coining the phrase "All you need is a chip and a chair," Straus burned up the backroads chasing one game after another on the Circuit.

The guy was a legend; he would bet on anything with or without a pulse. He also had a knack for dodging payment when he lost on those bets. Players knew to be wary when the ever-entertaining Treetop proposed some action.

But he was a master at high-stakes Texas Hold 'Em. Straus was once in a game where he had taken down several large pots in a row. He was dealt seven-two off suit (the worst hand in Hold 'Em).

He raised and was called by one player. The flop came seven-three-three, damn good for his hole cards. Straus bet, and his opponent made a hefty raise. Jack contemplated and called. The turn was a deuce on a seven-three-three-two board. Straus offered his opponent a deal. For a mere twenty-five dollars, he would show the choice of one of his two hole cards. The opponent considered the proposition and tossed over a twenty-five-dollar chip. He chose a card, and Jack showed him the deuce. A long tank and the player concluded that Jack must have a pair of deuces in the hole, which would give him a full house with twos over threes. The player mucked his cards, and Jack took down a monster pot. A world-class bluffer, Treetop always added excitement to the game.

Bob Hooks—Bob was a true backwoods gambler. That's where he played in his first card game in 1945. Hooks was born in Edgewood, Texas, on August 18, 1929. His father was a renowned baseball coach at Southern Methodist University. He played first base for the Philadelphia Athletics and held the state record for the longest shot put. Hooks had his heart set on adventure, but there wasn't much happening in the dry county of Edgewood.

As a teen, Bob would see boys his age venture into the woods and play cards. "I had no car, no bike, no shows, no TV, no nothing," Hooks recalled. So, he took a trip into the woods with a friend. He watched as the adolescents played cards and got drunk. Bob came back, having won sixteen dollars in the game. That felt like life-changing money. It set the fire in Hooks's engine to leave that one-horse town in the rearview mirror. In his early twenties, he got some wheels and hit the highway as a permanent Texas road gambler. He developed a reputation on the Circuit as a solid, logical player.

Doc Ramsey—Doc was one of those players who sat up and took notice of Bob Hooks's playing ability. The two crossed paths in a game in Tyler, Texas. Doc was already a Texas mythic poker hero. He was a boss gambler and ran up and down the East Texas line. Ramsey asked Hooks his age. "Twenty-nine," Hooks replied. Ramsey, at

sixty-five, couldn't believe it. He exclaimed that he sure wished he was still twenty-nine. Hooks retorted in a deadpan manner, "I wish I had your money." From that point forward, Hooks and Ramsey became lifelong buddies. They traveled from Dallas to Houston and then back up to Longview. Then they'd start all over the next day.

After a decade of burning up the blacktop on the Texas Circuit, Hooks and a partner opened the wildly popular Am Vets Post in South Dallas in 1969. It was an illegal operation where they offered poker games and booze but hid under the charter of the Am Vets ruse. Bob would later sell the club to our next poker legend on this list to satisfy his wishes and head West.

Byron "Cowboy" Wolford—This Cowboy was someone who could get you laughing and laughing . . . all while draining your chip stack. He was charming, joyful, a bit flamboyant, and always cracking witty jokes that would get the table roaring. And he loved poker. More than that, he loved beating his opponents. As he would like to say, "I'd rather hear a sucker holler than a pretty gal sing."

Born September 14, 1930, in Barbers Hill, Texas, Byron didn't waste much time. He started playing poker at age six and won his first calf roping at age eleven. He was a mainstay on the pro rodeo tour during the mid-1940s to the 1960s. In his days of roping calves on the road, he hosted big-money card games out of his hotel rooms. He lost his prize calf roping horse Glass Eye in a card game. But he rebounded in another game in another town and won another roping horse with three aces. He named that horse "Ace" and won the Canadian calf roping championship on him.

Wolford was honored in the Pro Rodeo Hall of Fame in the early 1960s. By this time Byron was chasing cards full-time instead of calves. Known for his endurance at the table and his ability to pull off big bluffs, he roared from game to game searching for the ultimate high- stakes action.

* * *

This is just a fraction. The list is endless of the iconic players that were part of the Texas Circuit. Names such as Bill Smith, Aubrey Day, James Roy, Pat Renfro . . . and so many more.

It would be a travesty, however, not to focus on two of the biggest in their time. The traveling pair, with Doyle Brunson, who ravaged through the Circuit like a tsunami:

Brian "Sailor" Roberts and Thomas "Amarillo Slim" Preston.

The Partners

Doyle Brunson moved to the Permian Basin Pantheon known as Midland, Texas, in 1960. It's here that he meets up with his future Circuit-traveling compadres Slim and Sailor. This trio hit it off right away, forming a tight bond that they realized they could turn into fatter pockets. They were stronger together than they were on their own, and they were set to take the Circuit by storm.

Thomas "Amarillo Slim" Preston—Slim was extremely loyal to his friends, eager for any and all kinds of action, and a man who loved the attention, which he earned with his flashy Texas personality and dry wit. He was also a helluva poker player!

Slim was born on December 31, 1928, in Johnson, Arkansas. His family moved to Turkey, Texas, nine months later, landing in Amarillo a few years after that. Slim joked that he was so skinny as a child that he had to get out of the bathtub before he pulled the plug. Even as an adult, the six-four player averaged about 170 pounds.

Thomas got his start in the pool halls. He was a cue ball connoisseur and would have multiple legendary matches with Minnesota Fats, king of the sticks. That's where Thomas would eventually pick up his nickname "Amarillo Slim," staring down the eight ball.

He was a proposition man in the same realm as Titanic Thompson. In his memoir, Slim wrote, "If there's anything worth

arguing about, I'll either bet on it or shut up. And since it's not very becoming for a cowboy to be arguing, I've made a few wagers in my day."

He was a creative creator of proposition bets that included playing golf with gardening tools and pool with a broom stick. He once bet Bobby Riggs, Wimbledon champion in 1939, that he could beat him in a game of table tennis if Slim could pick the paddles. Riggs agreed and Slim chose cast-iron skillets. Slim had been practicing with the skillets for months prior to the match. Riggs didn't have a chance, and Preston took home a bag full of money.

On a separate occasion he leveled the same wager to a group of Tennessee gamblers. They had their best man practice night and day playing table tennis with a skillet. Once he arrived for the contest, Slim switched "paddles" and chose Coke bottles instead. Once again, the man with the deep Texas drawl took home the cash.

Celebrities were also fair game. Preston won $300,000 from Willie Nelson in dominoes and a whopping $2 million from *Hustler* publisher Larry Flynt in poker.

Slim got his feet wet in poker during his time in the navy in 1945. He played round the clock on war ships patrolling the Asian Pacific Rim. He transitioned into illegal bookmaking in the early 1950s. His Americana cowboy demeanor set most players at ease. His taco-creased cowpuncher hat and thousand-dollar boots added to his mystique.

Slim's name circulated fast in the pool world, and he was finding it harder to find suckers to take his bets. Poker was a different story. He could hit the road and find a slew of willing participants with cash burning a hole in their pockets. Slim was a notorious "reader," not of the cards or even the action on the table, but of his opponents' eyes. "They'll tell ya everything you need to know."

Brain "Sailor" Roberts—Sailor was one of the most colorful guys on the Circuit. He was a dominating player . . . when he had his

mind on the game. But, where his peers would like to play marathon sessions, Sailor loved to party and spend money on women with loose lips and wide hips. He also didn't care too much about holding onto his money, being more than willing to spend it on those women, knowing that his skills at the table would fill his pockets again soon enough.

He was born on March 7, 1931, in San Angelo, Texas. The Great Depression was taking its toll on this small West Texas town. A dollar was hard to come by, and the Roberts family felt the pinch. Brian took a job as a golf caddy at age twelve to help his family. The action on the links were a precursor to the craps games that followed. This is where Brian got his motor revved up for gambling. But what he really wanted was a new zip code. "Just to get the hell outta here, you know!"

That was Brain's main focus. After high school, he joined the navy. He traveled the world during the Korean War. This is where Brian got his nickname "Sailor." Cards and craps were a frequent pastime among the crew. Roberts received a tutorial in both. He came away from the seven seas with an A-plus in gambling.

A homecoming in San Angelo was not what he hoped. Brian was a world traveler. He had lived a life of adventure. The setting looked dusty and depressing. It was time to move on. He had built a decent size bankroll, and it was time to see just how good a player he really was. Sailor hit the Circuit and found his new home: the road.

He started small, but within weeks he found himself in the high-stakes matches, and winning. Poker was never about the money for Sailor; it was about the action. That's why he experienced so many ups and downs. He was a risk-taker who was more interested in having fun than strategically waiting out his opponents. He was also there on the Circuit, he admitted, for camaraderie and the friendships . . . which led him to Doyle and Slim.

The Trio

Slim, Sailor, and The Texas Dolly came together for their first meeting in Midland, Texas, in the early 1960s. The three realized that they all shared some commonalities. They all had similar backgrounds, and they were all diehard card hounds. They were intelligent and they studied the game with deep consideration. They were unique personalities, but they all shared their humble West Texas/ Panhandle beginnings. They came from the red dirt.

It was during this congregation in the Permian Basin that the trio embarked on a partnership. They would travel the Texas Circuit together, playing on the same bankroll. This plan would cut down on expenses and focus on getting from one game to the next. They would play individually and there would be no signaling, colluding, or cheating among them. It was straight poker.

The trio offered a unique perspective, especially as traveling partners. Slim was the people reader. He could spot tells a mile away. Sailor was a solid fundamental player. He understood the game to its core. Doyle would say, "Sailor was the best player I ever saw." Brunson had a little of both Slim and Sailor in him. He was strategic and understood psychology.

The trio would live in Odessa when they were off the road. The partnership was formed. Watch out Texas, here they come!

Doyle's Big Match

Doyle proved that he was not immune to the swings of professional poker. He experienced some intense low points. He would wonder if this was indeed the path that was meant for him. All that changed in 1963 after a cancer scare, a wife, and a new baby left him with a golden epiphany: Poker was his superpower. He became laser focused and won fifty-four straight poker sessions. Brunson

was on his way to cementing his legacy as one of the greatest of all time.

As the trio burned up the blacktop together, they replayed hands and discussed player tendencies. Doyle would write down hands and run calculations of what is considered "positive EV (Expected Value)" these days—the optimal playing strategy for a particular hand based on the game circumstances. It would dictate the percentage of the most favorable play based on thousands of handwritten recorded hands in a notebook. This was long before there were computers. They would figure these calculation odds after thousands of entries were logged in pen and paper while hauling down the highway. This intense prep work increased their knowledge exponentially. These were skills that would never have been acquired by traveling alone.

Along the way, each new game offered a new set of challenges, a new set of colorful characters to compete against. Every day was a new adventure.

All of our heroes in this story had a similar desire in life. They were searching for father figures. Sometimes they found one, but maybe he wasn't cut out as role model material. Titanic left home looking for his father. Unfortunately, he found him playing Stud and he later stole Titanic's winnings and slipped away without even saying goodbye. Benny found Warren Diamond, who brought him into his syndicate. Herbert found Sam Murray, who helped perfect his penchant for business. Johnny Moss found Mr. Wade, who taught him the fundamentals of poker.

If it wasn't a father figure, it was an idol. They may not have liked each other's personality, but they did idolize their playing ability. It's a rare opportunity to be able to play against your idol; it doesn't happen in many sports, but it does in poker. These men all orbited each other in the same universe. They knew of one another. No, they may not have liked one another, but the mutual respect was there.

For Doyle, his big match came against one such hero: Johnny Moss.

Every game, every stop, he heard the same story about the world-renowned homegrown phenom Johnny Moss. He hoped to meet and play against this master as he continued to chase the center white lines. The dream became a reality when he sauntered into a No-Limit Hold 'Em game in Houston. There he was, in all his glory, the wily card wizard Johnny Moss. Doyle was twenty-five and thrilled to take a seat at the same table with "The Man" he'd heard so much about. The other players were excited to watch the highly anticipated showdown.

Brunson was on fire and picked Moss apart. But what stuck with Doyle was a Moss laydown. Doyle had the king and nine of diamonds, and Moss had the king and two of clubs. The flop was king, nine, deuce. Doyle led out with a bet, Johnny raised, and Doyle reraised. The wise Moss sensed danger in the air and tossed his cards in the muck. The laydown showed Doyle that Moss was on the next level, as advertised.

The next one was even bigger as Doyle called it "the most important hand of my early poker career."

This was against Moss again, this time in the small Texas town of Brenham. On day three of a marathon session, he got into a hand with Moss and another opponent.

"I was holding (jack-ten) offsuit on a board of Kx7x8x2x3x," recalled Brunson ("x" meant offsuit). "I had none of that board, but when Moss bet $4,000, a monstrous wager in that game, I called him with just a jack high! I was sure he was drawing to a possible straight, and since I was drawing to the highest one possible, I felt I had to have him beat . . . There was a lot of money in the pot, but I had a read on Johnny."

Moss showed a busted straight draw with six-five and Brunson took down the pot in the "breakthrough" hand.

"That one hand defined the moment where I knew I was a top player, and from that point on, I was considered a world-class player by many of my peers," Brunson reflected.

With the Good, Comes the Bad

"One more time for the good times," sang Ray Price, the country singer.

While there were plenty of good times on the Circuit, danger lurked around every corner. It wasn't always the kind of danger that was present in plain sight. Sometimes, it hid in the caverns, the ravines, or the midnight sky, like the Boogey Man.

Bravado will only take you so far. Eventually, the evil can be overpowering.

The road gamblers were brave as they plundered through Texas like swashbuckling pirates in search of not only treasure, but a way of life, a sense of excitement. Adrenaline-pumping, heart-stopping, balls-to-the-wall, high-flying times. The games served the purpose. They allowed the players to get out, play against the best, and win big.

But the pitfalls of the road were about to catch up with them.

CHAPTER 20

COPS AND ROBBERS

The law dogs came barking!

Gambling had been illegal in Texas since Moses parted the Red Sea, but gamblers were adept at hiding games under the veil of disguise. Sometimes the poker games were "floating" (moved locally from place to place on a regular basis), other times their confidentiality was so low-key that no one came looking. The best prescription was to have these pesky patrolmen on the payroll. Unfortunately, that option was not always viable.

As the Texas Circuit was in its barnstorming heyday, new laws were being enacted. These laws tightened the belt on illegal gambling nationwide. The heat was getting even more intense with two *federal* laws passed in 1961.

The Interstate Wire Act, sometimes referred to as the Federal Wire Act, stated, "Whoever being engaged in the business of betting or wagering knowingly uses a wire communication facility for the transmission in interstate or foreign commerce of bets or wagers or information assisting in the placing of bets or wagers on any sporting event or contest, or for the transmission of a wire communication which entitles the recipient to receive money or credit as a result of bets or wagers, or for information assisting in the placing of bets or wagers, shall be fined under this title or imprisoned not more than two years, or both."

The Travel Act or International Travel Act of 1961 was another federal criminal statute used to wage war against globe-trotting

gamblers. It forbid "the use of the U.S. mail, or interstate or foreign travel, for the purpose of engaging in certain specific criminal acts." Illegal gambling was listed as one of the specific acts.

Basically, they were summed up as so: One, it was unlawful for a person to place bets or wagers over the phone or telegraph lines. Two, it was unlawful for a person to be involved in illegal gambling (poker) by using the mail system or traveling on interstates or internationally.

The Cops Come Callin'

These two federal laws passed and signed by President John F. Kennedy gave law enforcement a new set of tools to pursue would-be gamblers. More officers were hired through the city, county, state, and federal levels to crack down on gambling operations.

Agents were staking out airports, train stations, hotels, and most importantly highways . . . the home of the Texas road gamblers!

Johhny Moss once got caught with his pants down. Agents swarmed him and found $15,000 in his possession. He held his ground and refused to give up the money. A younger agent was persistent and desperately wanted to take the cash. An older, wiser agent knew Johnny and said, "If you take it from him, Johnny'll be in court on Monday with six eyewitnesses and will swear that you took $150,000 from him."

Moss was able to hold onto his money. Most weren't so lucky.

All the poker pros shared incidents of being harassed by authorities. It went with the territory. They all spent some amount of time singing the jailhouse blues, paying fines, being stripped of their pride, giving up their winnings, or simply enduring a cavity search. It was routine.

Treetop Straus devised a way to use this situation to his advantage. He owed a barbaric Texas bookie a nice sum of cash. Straus was avoiding him, and the bookie's patience was wearing thin. The ball breaker cornered Jack and explained it was nut cuttin' time. Jack promised that he would get the money within twenty-four and they agreed upon meeting downtown the next day.

The bookmaker and his crew showed up at the designated time and waited for Jack. A few minutes later, Straus was trotting around the corner with a bag full of cash. Suddenly, a car rolled up and screeched to a halt. Two undercover cops jumped out, grabbed the bag, put a beating on Treetop, and tossed him in the back seat. The event unfolded in front of the bookie.

The car roared away. Treetop escaped and laughed.

He had hired the cops!

A couple weeks later, Straus won enough at a poker game to pay off his debt. Everybody was happy.

There was a rhythm and flow to avoiding the authorities. The gamblers became adept at avoiding the long arm of the law, but that was only half the battle.

Bigger Problems

The law was a formidable opponent. They could shut you down and leave you with nothing.

But the bandits, the filthy animals, they were unhinged.

The games on the Circuit were relatively safe in the beginning. As time wore on, the level of danger increased. The bandits, hijackers, and gung-ho gun men had simple intentions: Stake out the poker house locations, bombard the players, take their cash. It was a simple transaction: your money for your life.

All the players carried guns, and they had secret stashes, and hidden pockets for their bankroll. Word of mouth circulated among

the players as to safe house locations. Many times, players would investigate a location in advance for their own safety.

The poker stakes were high, but the life stakes were higher. During any game, these road gamblers could face the hazards of hijackers, greedy game operators, card cheats, eager law men, jealous and emotionally wounded mistresses and wives, suicidal sore losers who had transformed into homicidal maniacs, and more.

Amarillo Slim lost count of how many times he found himself staring down the barrel of a shotgun, or how many times he had been hog-tied. After a while, players would say they got used to it and that it was just part of the business, but Slim said even after it became part of the road routine, he never got used to it. He said, "If you think it's easy to look down one of those double-barreled shotguns, you're wrong."

This was from a man who was later kidnapped in Colombia under the order of Pablo Escobar! Slim was down in Colombia for the grand opening of a casino when he was snatched up by the kingpin's men, bound with wires, tossed into a helicopter, and flown to a compound. The infamous (and paranoid) kingpin thought Slim may have been working for the US government. Once Slim was able to convince him that wasn't the case, the two hit it off and even played a little poker!

All the dangers these players were running into on a consistent basis took their toll. It's like a man who gets a whipping every day at two PM. Yeah, you get used it, but it doesn't mean you like it.

Crandall Addington understood the treachery that hid along those long, silent stretches of dark road. He adapted to the uncertain hazards. "We did have weapons," he proclaimed. "It was not really to use on each other. What we really wanted to be able to do was, if we won, we wanted to be able to get back to the car with the money. And so, not only did we have to beat a lot of really good players, but we had to dodge the hijackers and oftentimes sheriff of the county."

Doyle's Dustups

Doyle Brunson simplified it best, saying anytime there is a lot of money involved, somebody was going to try to get it, be it killers, con artists, cheats, or thieves. One sultry Sunday, Doyle, Sailor, and Slim were playing in a farmhouse outside of Austin.

BLAM! BLAM!

Suddenly, the windows shattered and the doors burst open followed by seven desperados in ski masks flooding into the room with shotguns aimed at the players. The players were ordered against the wall and forced to strip naked. Doyle's immediate concern was if this presumed robbery was going to turn into a donkey show!

The marauders searched everyone, and then asked if anyone was holding out on any cash they missed. They said they didn't have time to search everyone again. They were, however, going to select one man to put to the test. If the robbers found this person to have one stinking red cent on him then a punishment of a blown-off kneecap would be delivered.

The trio kept their mouths shut, while other players began squawking. One pointed to $800 in a shirt pocket. Others chimed in by forfeiting over their hiding spots. The leader of the squad was convinced there was more money . . . somewhere.

He asked Doyle who ran the game. Doyle said he didn't know. The leader pummeled him in the stomach with the barrel of his shotgun. He asked the question several more times and each time Doyle remained silent, receiving another blow. Brunson was beat to a bloody, pulpy, mess in his birthday suit. Running out of time and patience, the ringleader leveled the gun at Doyle's head and cocked the trigger.

Doyle's life was a blur, the gig was up, he gave up the guy.

The psychos left with the loot, including $6,700 from Doyle. All the players stayed alive.

On another occasion, Doyle was playing in a Lubbock game. It was a relatively small game, but there was a bookie playing there who had over $100,000 in a satchel. Hijackers crashed the game with guns drawn. They were stunned to see a well-known and highly respected leader of the underworld among the group. They took everyone's money but once they got to him, they treated him like royalty with the utmost kindness and respect. The hijackers took everyone's keys and wallets and dumped them in a field a few miles down the road. Their temperament shifted when it came to this local crime lord. They told him he could hang on to his belongings if he would please just not follow them, please and thank you, sir.

At least in this instance, Doyle was allowed to keep his clothes on.

Bad Timing

Sailor Roberts was playing in a game outside of Fort Worth. The law busted in and sent players trembling.

They demanded that everyone get up and step away from the tables. Sailor pleaded with them to wait until the hand was over. He needed to know if he won. He'd had a rough night and felt his luck was about to turn. The cops decided it was a reasonable request. Sure, they had a little time to kill. Go and run it out.

The hand was delt and Roberts was right: He won. His luck was turning.

"You guys pick *this* time to come barging in!" he shouted as he got up to hand over the cash. By this point he knew the routine . . . or so he thought.

These were no ordinary lawmen. These were thieves who masqueraded as cops. They proceeded to tie up the players and steal their money.

Hijack Proof, My Ass!

Then there was Beeville.

Moss had premonitions about playing in Beeville, but the action seemed too lucrative to pass up. The location was touted as "hijack proof." The building was a stone fortress with massive walls, heavy steel doors, and security guards patrolling the perimeter. Moss and fellow road gambler Pat Renfro arrived to join the game. Once inside, they found the man that sank everyone, Titanic Thompson, already in the game.

The game was hot and heavy. The road gamblers were beating the piss out of some local oilmen. Chips were being used in place of money, and the operators of the game kept running out and transferring the money off site.

The men staking out this game were not your average dirtbag hijackers; they were methodical with their planning and execution. They ambushed the money transporters at gun point, swiftly overpowering them and confiscating the cash. Next, they apprehended all the guards and muzzled them for silence. They followed up by disabling the players' vehicles. Nobody was going anywhere.

It was a masterfully orchestrated plan by sharp-minded criminals.

Ready to move in, the hijacking crew hoisted a member up by helping him stand on one bandit's shoulders to get access to an overlooking window. He broke the glass and tossed in two canisters of tear gas. The crew on the ground used bullhorns, shouting commands for the players to exit now or face more tear gas to come. The players followed orders and staggered out.

The hijackers, dressed in army fatigues and wearing gas masks, burst into the room with automatic weapons. They stripped all the players nude and took their possessions.

When the smoke cleared, the hijackers had cleared out, and the players had lost everything, including their dignity. Texas Rangers

and FBI arrived on the scene. They wanted to know why these men were there and more importantly why the victims weren't wearing clothes. The players got drilled from both ends—the hijackers and the law.

Moss was able to slip away from the fracas unnoticed. He found an old farmer and paid him fifty dollars to get him out of there. He said there were another fifty available for the old hayseed once he got him to safety. Titanic pulled his own magic trick and somehow also disappeared unscathed.

Even Pros Get Tired

This incident proved to be the final straw for Johnny Moss. He was tired of chasing the game, dealing with the fallout from the gangs and the police. He had enough of the turmoil, but he couldn't give up the action. His wife Virgie once offered him a grand a week to quit and he replied, "What good is money if you can't gamble with it?"

Still, he needed a better solution. He wasn't alone. It was getting harder for all the road gamblers to flourish in these perilous conditions. The adrenaline-pumping, high-flying lifestyle was wearing thin. All the players knew of at least one person who had been shot or stabbed for their money.

Doyle went through a period of regular threats, beatings, and robberies. He felt the cold steel of a knife blade against his throat. He worried about his wife. It was all getting to be an overload, but he knew he didn't want to give up playing cards.

None of them did.

So, like Benny before them, they started to look west.

CHAPTER 21
LAS VEGAS

They burned the tread off their tires. Always on to the next town, the next game. These juiced-up Texas road gamblers didn't have a chance to smell the roses; instead, they blew past them ninety to nothing. Time was wasting, the next game was calling. And as the challenges of life on the road started to pile up, a mystic energy in the distance whispered, "Come." A next-level vibration that was hard to resist. This power, this synth wave emanating from one place, and one place alone . . .

Las Vegas.

Many of the ramblers had dipped their toes into Sin City's dark waters. Moss, Treetop, Dandy, and Doc had all ventured there for periodic games then promptly returned to Texas. The destination was not completely foreign among them.

Doyle, Slim, and Sailor had tried their luck together in Vegas a few times in the sixties, pooling their money. First time they went, they somehow hit it big playing keno with the help of Corky McQuorcodale, winning around $50,000 that they grew a bit playing poker and then took back home. After running into some issues with some Texas bookies, the trio essentially broke up but hooked up to tackle Vegas again a couple years later. This time, focusing solely on poker . . .

. . . and they got killed! They lost over $100,000 in a few days and came back to Texas broke.

In the late sixties, Vegas called again and the trio pulled together another $100,000 and hit Sin City. Again, within a few days, they went broke. All of them got cleaned out, a combination of bad luck

and their fellow players simply outplaying them, as can happen to even the best of them. This time they left Vegas with nothing, not sure if they would ever return.

But one of them would. In fact, he'd become a regular. And when The Texas Dolly started to spend less time on the road and more in Vegas, he developed a feel for the action in the city and he started to make it his own. His presence there, along with his poker brethren, changed Vegas and professional poker forever.

Hold 'Em Takes Vegas

What flipped the script and made Vegas a prime destination and not just a stopover for the Lone Star legends was the growth there of the game.

Their game.

Texas Hold 'Em!

By 1967, the game had spread to the Golden Nugget, Stardust, and Dunes. The Golden Nugget was a true-blue downtown sawdust joint. It was home to crusty desert dwellers who scraped up nothing much more than lint in their pockets. While the game was being played there on a regular basis, it was not an enticing attraction. The Dunes became the launchpad.

"Big Sid" Wyman, part owner of the Dunes, was a creative innovator. He was a St. Louis bookie that operated a betting network worth over $5 million before coming to Vegas and going legit. Big Sid was a mammoth man with a big heart and healthy appetite for chorus girls. He also found Texas Hold 'Em to be exhilarating. He spread the game in the front portion of his casino. The Dunes was a high-society casino on the Strip in the late 1960s. Wyman had the ability to attract whales with money to burn, and he enjoyed big bet poker. Sid had connections with the Texas crew: Crandall, Doyle, Sailor, and Slim had all played at the same table with him.

Thanks to the Texas road gamblers, Texas Hold 'Em—or Hold 'Em as they called it—began to flourish. However, Vegas was not a poker town. In the late 1960s, there were fewer than fifty poker tables in the entire city. There were only seventy poker tables in the whole state of Nevada. Binion's Horseshoe did not even have a poker room at this time.

There was not a plethora of places to play Hold 'Em, but where there were, the action was ferocious. Nevada began to hold the trump cards. First, it was legal there. No need to worry about the law kicking in the doors. Second, there was a constant influx of tourists and cash. Vegas was now the healthier, safer option opposed to the grind of the Texas Circuit.

A World Away

Vegas grew into its adolescent years. No longer a toddler learning to ride a bike with training wheels, it was a now a fully developed teenager, smoking reefer and hauling ass on a screaming Harley.

Vegas was an isolated pleasure island. Rebellious in the fact that it just didn't give a damn what anyone anywhere had to say. While the rest of the country ruminated in flower power, the hippie movement, and protests over the Vietnam War, none of that mattered here. What did matter? Pleasure with a capital *P*. The everyday citizen needed a place to avoid real life and to wallow in ubiquitous ecstasy.

Let the good times roll, baby! Vegas awaits!

The Horseshoe dominated the Glitter Gulch alongside the Golden Nugget. However, the Strip attracted a string of newcomers. The Tropicana opened in 1961, Caesars Palace and Aladdin in 1966, Circus Circus in 1968, and the monstrous International Hotel Casino in 1969. They all had their own authentic appeal. Hey daddy-o, these are the swinging joints! Glitzy and dazzling with shimmering radiance, these places oozed with James Dean classic coolness.

Luck might be a lady, or she might be whore. Vegas said, "Let her be both!"

The Strip casinos understood the value of entertainment. They cashed in on such acts as the Rat Pack, Elvis, and Liberace. The entertainers wooed crowds on stage and left them in a lather. They could then cool off with a drink at a floating dice table in the pool. It doesn't get any hipper than that.

Celebrities, sports stars, and titans of industry such as Howard Hughes all flocked to the fabulous Strip. Hughes was eaten up by madness once he arrived. His mental state of psychosis tortured him daily. Vegas was his eventual landing spot for a reclusive hibernation.

The Mafia was also firmly entrenched in Las Vegas during the late 1960s. They all had their hidden points in the casinos. The Chicago Outfit had the Riviera and the Stardust. The Detroit family had the Last Frontier and a piece of the Aladdin. The Genovese family from New York had Caesars and the Tropicana.

With Bobby Kennedy out of the picture, organized crime made up for lost time.

Another of these key figures was also looking for a comeback. Home from behind bars with time served, he was ready to jump back in the saddle and spur on the snorting bronc. He was ready to take back what belonged to him.

We're talking of course about our old cow boss, the original outlaw . . .

Benny Binion.

Benny Is Back!

By all accounts Benny was a well-mannered inmate. He settled into his life behind the walls of Leavenworth and kept his head down. The days were long, and the nights were dark and frigid. He worked

on his diet, expressing to his wife Teddy Jane that prison would be the perfect place for him to shed a few pounds. He studied Catholicism and became devout. He took a variety of educational courses, upgrading his second-grade scholastic level. He also worked as a maintenance man for the prison fire department.

Binion was denied parole multiple times. It was not for a lack of effort. The Supreme Court became the white knight . . . in a sense. After a series of appeals, they swooped in and intervened, agreeing to consider whether his sentencing was excessive. Benny was not alone; the sentencing of Frank Costello, "The Prime Minister of Crime" out of New York, was also going under review. The best part is that while the Court took on the case, Benny could go free. On March 19, 1957, Benny posted bond, and the steel doors slid open. He returned home to Vegas, hugged and kissed his family, and immediately went back to work.

The gambling scene back in Dallas had changed quite a bit in the years Benny was in the clink. Truth be told, the criminal landscape was beginning to shift before he went away, but now his style of running a city was all but a memory. Business was still booming in the Big D, but it was different now. Gone was the laissez-faire era when Benny made his early fortune. The casinos inside hotels that had proliferated throughout downtown were in steep decline. High rollers spent less time playing games of chance and more time taking a chance on playing the markets. Politicians were more on the straight and narrow and tougher to influence as they pushed to make Dallas a center of commerce and even tourism for the country. The concept of the "cowboy" was less about culture now and more about a marketing gimmick.

Binion's bread and butter, the policy racket, once a mighty river of cash, had slowed to a mere trickle while being run by a conglomeration of ill-tempered no names. Benny had zero interest in dealing with any of them. Many of his colleagues had retired or were dead. The cold-blooded killer Ivy Miller was slowly dying from diabetes on a

ranch outside the city. R.D. Mathews, still with pieces of a bullet lodged in his skull courtesy of The Cat's people, had moved to Cuba to work in a Havana nightclub. Even Harry Urban, Benny's old partner with the slot machine company that often provided cover for The Cowboy's more illicit dealings, was out of the game, finding himself in a position Benny knew all too well: fighting the government over tax issues. The other smart ones that were still "in the life" had hit the trail for cities such as Reno and Vegas. Others set their sails toward the international scene—Cuba, Mexico City, Bolivia, and beyond.

Binion would always be a presence and a legacy in the city of Dallas and the state of Texas. But his time there was now truly done. He shoved all his chips to the center of the table: It was Nevada or bust!

As long as the government would get the hell out of his way!

Playing All Sides

The Supreme Court came back with their ruling. They denied Binion's appeal and ordered him back to prison. This decision perpetuated itself, triggering years of appeals, pleas, calling in favors, making deals, and legal wrangling on both sides. The courts wanted him to serve out the last 119 days of his term. Benny was hell-bent on not going back. As far he was concerned, he had done his time. He was a free man and that was all that mattered.

The ongoing legal maneuvering and logistics are entirely too lengthy to regurgitate. The Cowboy had friends, and he had enemies in such facets as big business, politics, and even less savory factions. His supporters lobbied on his behalf and wrote kind letters to the courts. His enemies lobbied in the other direction. They wanted his ass back in the slammer.

The government mounted extensive pressure by attacking his pocketbook. They claimed he now owed an additional $467,619 in

back taxes. Benny didn't have that kind of cash, but he knew who to turn to, and where to find it.

The Mob.

A developer by the name of Ed Levinson bought all of Joe W. Brown's remaining shares in the Horseshoe. This gave Levinson controlling interests. It all presented a perfectly legitimate paper trail. A nice developer with a clean record owning the casino, who could argue with those facts? Well, here's where it gets a little dicey. Ed was a front man for a consortium of mobsters including Meyer Lansky, Doc Stacher, Sidney Korshak, and others. Levinson was in the process of buying and building projects in all corners of Las Vegas. He represented the mob in all his affairs.

The money that was paid to Brown to buy his interests in the casino went to him on paper. In reality, the money went straight into Binion's hands. Benny was now firmly under the covers with the mob.

At the same time, Binion decided on playing second fiddle with the feds. Benny appeared as the model citizen, a man who had done hard time, learned his lesson, and was wiser for it. He was perceived as a man who just wanted to run his business on the straight and narrow with no shenanigans. Due to his history, his list of connections, and his new "Boy Scout attitude," someone in the FBI decided Binion could be a valuable informant.

Benny saw the upside to this proposition. He bit the fishing line like a largemouth bass. Only to spit the hook out at the last second while the FBI boys were looking in the other direction.

He gave up a few tips, low-level intel on low-rung gangsters. It was generally bullshit that amounted to nothing. Just enough excitement to allow the dog to chase its own tail. The tips were inconsequential. The only ones affected were the dregs of humanity. Always calculating, Benny never gave up any serious member of La Cosa Nostra. He did have fun with his FBI buddies and enjoyed

watching them squirm. It didn't hurt to have them on his side for once in his life.

He towed the line masterfully between both worlds: law and crime.

In 1963, the FBI executed a maximum assault on organized crime across the nation, including Las Vegas. Phones were tapped in major hotels and casinos. These wires allowed the Justice Department to take detailed notes outlining the mob's activities in Las Vegas. A full report was soon to hit the press with salivating details.

Mobsters were getting nervous. Whoever said there was no such thing as bad publicity was wrong.

One of the names in that report was Ed Levinson. Numerous pages were dedicated to him. The feds had plenty of spicy evidence on this so-called clean front man. Levinson's hidden superiors were growing more suspicious by the day. Just what in the hell would they find in that report?

Benny leveraged this news to his advantage. In 1964, he mortgaged his Montana ranch and borrowed more than $2 million from a bank. He came to Ed with an offer to buy back his casino. Seeing a golden parachute and a chunk of cash, Levinson and his underworld cohorts decided on the prudent decision. They sold.

Ten years after losing it, Benny had once again retained his beloved treasure, the Horseshoe. It was his, all his, and he was going to announce the news to the world. His first order of business? Change the neon signage to read "Binion's Horseshoe."

What to Do Next

With a felony conviction, Benny could never own a gambling license again, so his son Jack became the licensee and Benny served as director of public relations, but everyone knew who was in charge.

Once Benny had the money flowing back into his pockets, he became one of the city's biggest benefactors. He contributed to local and state politicians, continued payments to local law enforcers, gave to charities, and became involved in the local Catholic diocese.

But Benny still had other problems, namely how to take his business to the next level. The Strip was looking like it could be a problem for Benny. It had pizzazz, flashy shows, luxurious pools . . . and it was growing. Meanwhile, downtown Vegas was in essence, a fly trap with decrepit shops, trash- and mongrel-filled streets, and derelict bums on every corner. It couldn't compete with the glamour of the Strip.

Benny focused on the Horseshoe as the place for the *real* gambler. If you want a vacation, go to the Strip. If you want to gamble against the best and possibly win a fortune, come here. His high limits policy kept the gamblers rolling in, but Benny was worried he might need more. Benny was always ahead of his time when it came to gimmicks, things to draw a tourist and pro alike to his place. He had installed a nine-foot-tall golden horseshoe with plexiglass and behind it displayed a hundred $10,000 bills. A million bucks. Everyone who came to Vegas stopped to take a photo of the unimaginable sum, including, at one point, Charles Manson and his followers, and one can only imagine what *that* trip was like!

Still, Benny knew he needed something more. He needed an event like the match he had orchestrated between Moss and The Greek, something that would get people talking, putting him and his beloved casino front and center. He had been thinking about it for years, but didn't know how he could recapture the magic of that event.

The answer, surprisingly, would come from Reno.

ALL IN

The ultimate bet.

CHAPTER 22
TEXAS GAMBLERS REUNION

The mountain loomed massive, jagged, and steep. A glow of iridescent rays illuminated the mountaintop, and the treasure of prosperity that awaited there. At the base of the mountain, there was Big Brother, his name was Las Vegas, and Little Brother, who went by Reno, gazing upward at the impressive, majestic view.

Difficult terrain—Yes. Impossible—No.

The brothers eyed one another with disdain. They were not the best of friends . . . but they were family. They knew their destiny awaited at the summit. No more hesitation, it was time for acceleration. In the blink of an eye, they took off with fearless abandon, racing up the rocky slope. Big Brother was more athletic, stronger, and agile. He immediately took the lead. However, Little Brother was no slouch. What he lacked in physical size and strength, he made up for in courage and fortitude.

It soon became clear that the quest wouldn't be won overnight. It was a journey . . .

Like Atlantic City, Tahoe, and some of those overseas destinations, the city of Reno offers those looking to try their luck an opportunity to do so with less of the madness and chaos of Las Vegas. Reno promotes itself as being a bit more off-the-grid, while still offering luxury, excitement, and a chance to make it rich, which is why it has always caught the eye of tourists, experienced gamblers, and serious businessmen alike.

Reno has long been associated with the ideal image of an Old West gambling town. In 1902, Reno sported forty-eight saloons and sixteen licensed gambling halls. The action was located on the south side of the railroad tracks along Commercial Row, with top joints like the Palace, the Oberon, the Louvre, and the Wine House. The 1920s ushered in the reform movement known as Prohibition, but Mayor Edwin E. Roberts was no reformer; he was a progressive-thinking fellow. While the speakeasies and the flappers were the hit of the town, Mayor Roberts saw a promising future. In 1923, he dedicated himself to bolstering the economy by licensing all forms of poker games, advocating for overnight divorces, and allowing brothels to operate within the city limits. In 1931, unrestricted gambling went into full effect statewide, and within days clubs such as the Owl, the Bank, the Rex, and the Waldorf all applied for their gaming licenses.

Like Vegas, it was the thirties through the sixties when Reno hit the sweet spot and flourished.

Bill Graham and Bill Harrah, two of the most prominent free-wheeling casino owners in Reno history, led the charge.

Graham, along with his partner James McKay, owned and operated the Bank Club, which was at one point the biggest casino in the world and definitely the hottest joint in town. Graham was also no stranger to notorious figures like John Dillinger, Baby Face Nelson, and Pretty Boy Floyd, among others, who came to Reno to both hide from the feds and clean their money. After a brief six-year stint in prison for federal charges of mail fraud linked to a scam that bilked investors out of millions, Graham and McKay went back to work at their Bank Club, continuing to grow it as *the* place to play, not just in Reno, but in all of Nevada.

Bill Harrah was a visionary, a gaming legend that grew into an icon. During the early 1930s, he started small bingo ventures in downtown Reno like Harrah's Club Bingo, just two blocks from the Bank Club. He transformed his family operation into an empire in the following decades with more Reno spots like the Tango Club,

places in Lake Tahoe, and eventually the Holiday Casino on the Vegas Strip. But Harrah's heart was always in Reno. After meetings with Graham and McKay, he quickly became part of the local gaming fraternity and expanded from there. In fact, Harrah was responsible for creating the Nevada Gaming Control Board in 1955, which would eventually become the Nevada Gaming Commission. The organization represented casino owners and managers throughout the state, with a primary focus of regulating gaming and ridding casinos of corruption.

Thanks to trailblazers like Mayor Roberts, Graham, and Harrah, Little Brother Reno was able to stay within footsteps behind Big Brother Las Vegas on their upward race.

When a place is so full of rich opportunities, it's also going to draw in some big personalities . . .

Vegas Vic comes to Reno

Vic "Vegas Vic" Vickrey was born in Mississippi. He became a Texas road gambler and hit every poker room from Corpus Christi to Beaumont. He made the rounds and perfected the craft . . . not so much as a player but as a manager/promoter.

It was a dizzying journey as back then there was no dealer school or casino management degree. You just had to hit the road and figure it out. If you had the mental acuity to master the games, learn the spreads, decipher pot odds, and handle cards and dice, then you might survive.

Vic decided Vegas was the safer bet over Texas and soon relocated. He, like the other road gamblers, got tired of all the hiding, running, and trying to avoid the constant danger that came with illegal gambling on the road. He wanted to go somewhere it was legal so he could focus solely on building his reputation and his bankroll.

Once in Vegas, he talked his way into the dice pit at the Sahara Casino. He remarked to a young Sam Boyd, "I can deal these games as good as if not better than any of these guys out there dealing now."

He recalled, "He put me on a craps game, I was wheeling and dealing and really knocking 'em dead. Sam came up to me later and said, 'Well, I'll say one thing. You sure are fast. You just broke every rule of procedure we've ever had.'"

Vic replied to him, "We didn't have any rules back in Texas."

That was the start of a beautiful relationship. Vic kept the job and learned the protocols of being a Vegas casino dealer.

Vic dripped with class and oozed with self-confidence. His magnanimous personality would swallow you up like a bear hug. Before you knew it, Vic had you hypnotized in his mesmerizing grip. He was a marketing innovator and pie-in-the-sky casino promoter. One story is that he persuaded Dean Martin to meet and greet high rollers when he was working for the Riviera. He did so by building a small bar next to the showroom, which he called "Dino's Den." Vic would smoothly and casually take high rollers there and Dean would drop in for a few drinks, laughs, and photos. Sometimes friends would drop by with him, including the Chairman of the Board himself, Frank Sinatra.

Vic made the rounds; it's easier to list the casinos where he didn't work compared with the ones where he did. The Aladdin, Stardust, Dunes, Silver Slipper, Riviera, Sands, Tropicana . . . they were all part of his odyssey. There is the Vegas Vic neon cowboy that waves to gamblers on Fremont Street. Then there is the real Vegas Vic, renowned casino executive extraordinaire.

By the mid-1960s, Vic had journeyed to a higher elevation. It was time to see what Reno had in store for him. Once there, he would pick up right where he left off, finding that business leaders, gamblers, entertainers, and tourists alike wanted to be near him. So did aspiring entrepreneurs, like the man who would become his protégé and partner, Tom Moore.

The Student Becomes the Master

Tom was a San Antonio native. He and two hooligans ran an underground, illegal gambling operation on West Avenue in the early 1960s. They held table casino games and cash poker games six nights a week. It was a happening joint. Mounds of cash were changing hands. Pros and amateurs alike flocked to the club. One of those pros was Texas road gambler Crandall "Dandy" Addington.

Even though Tom owned a successful high-stakes club, he was still operating on the dark side. He knew the perils of dealing with Texas law enforcement and the hazards of federal agents who were hammering down on illegal gamblers across the country. The new anti-wagering legislation was making it harder for a straight gambler to make an honest living.

Tom knew of Reno, and he knew it could be a great place to rest his hat. In 1967, he decided to make the move. He even convinced his gambling compadre "Dandy" Addington to relocate with him. Tom saw promise in a diminishing fixture known as the Holiday Hotel and Casino. This place could be his oasis. It could make him a legitimate businessman. Tom brought in several partners to assist in the acquisition of the property, including John Monfrey, president of Falstaff Beer, and Austin Hemphill, a San Antonio car dealer. Addington even joined in for a piece of the action. The group purchased the property from Carl Hicks and David Burns, who had been running the hotel since the death of Newt Crumley in a plane crash two years earlier.

Addington reported on the situation, "I moved to Reno with Tom in 1967. In the process it was difficult for some reason for me to get a gambling license for the Holiday. I told Tom, 'There are seven of us introducing No-Limit Texas Hold 'Em in Nevada right now, so I'll just keep doing that.'"

Moore renamed the establishment "Tom Moore's Holiday-Hotel Casino," and it quickly garnered a reputation for high-limit wagering.

It was there that he found Vic and quickly formed a friendship that turned into a partnership. Tom wanted to grow the property even more and he knew Vic, the Vegas legend, could help. The duo worked on various promotions to drum up business and get the locals interested. But if Moore and the city of Reno were really going to make a splash, the key was to bring the big names that dropped thousands in Vegas to Reno and to get them gambling!

Bringing Texas to Reno

Tom may have been suffering from a special ailment known as the Texas Homesick Blues. He needed that spark, that rejuvenating shot in the arm, to climb back on the wild bronc of life and give it another ride.

Or maybe the man just needed another way to separate players from their cash. Whatever the case, Tom held the first Texas Gamblers Reunion, or as some called it, the "Texas Gamblers Convention," at his Holiday Hotel Casino in 1968. He invited the cream of the crop, the top Texas road gamblers, to attend his gambling summit in the High Sierras. The event was a culmination of different casino table games, which might have been part of the problem. The goal was to attract big spenders to splurge on craps, roulette, and blackjack games. It was an idea designed to drum up business during a slow period of the year. It also gave Tom a chance to commiserate with backslapping bosom buddies from Texas.

Unfortunately, the event came and went with little to no hoopla. The buzz was never generated. The fireworks never ignited. By all accounts it was a massive flop. There were only a handful of high rollers at the festivities, and they spread around a little cash, but it failed to attract the numbers Moore was searching for. The press either didn't know or didn't care to promote the event. It was such a dud that even finding accounts of the event itself is difficult!

Nobody thought much more of it, but sometimes a man just needs a strong woman by his side to stir the embers of creativity.

Poker Is the Key and the King

Tom Moore's wife LaFayne deserves the credit for changing the direction of the reunion from a discombobulated get-together into a promising extravaganza. The second reunion was established, but this time with a clear purpose in sight: a series of high-stakes poker games!

LaFayne pitched the idea to Tom that the following year's event should feature a series of poker tournaments. That's what these gamblers wanted to play, and that's what would draw them in. She also suggested that make it a true success, Tom should once again reach out to another Texas gambling dinosaur: Vic Vickrey.

Tom liked his wife's thinking. He contacted Vickrey. The two talked about who to invite and how to run the tournament itself. Vic even said he could scrape up $3,000 from the hotel to throw in for the winner, just to sweeten the pot. Not that these gamblers needed any more reason than competing against each other to see who was the best.

Tom got on the phone with his old friend Crandall Addington and exclaimed that they were going to have a second event.

"But let's make it an invitational poker tournament instead."

Addington perked up and replied, "That will probably work."

Moore had set his wheels in motion.

The (Real) Texas Gamblers Reunion

The word spread through the Lone Star State, and the players packed their dirty laundry and headed west. Like an epic cattle drive, except this was fueled by playing cards and poker chips.

Johnny Moss was semiretired, playing in small games around Odessa. After four months, he was growing bored and needed some action. Once the invitation arrived, he wasn't certain if he had the heart of the fight. His wife had to give him the nudge. "Go," she said. "Meet your old friends. Have some fun."

The A-list of top gamblers made the pilgrimage: Johnny Moss, Doyle Brunson, Amarillo "Slim" Preston, Puggy Pearson, Crandall Addington, Treetop Straus, Jimmy Casella, Sailor Roberts, Corky McCorquodale, Aubrey Day, James "Long Goody" Roy, Bill Davis, George Barnes, Jimmy "The Greek" Snyder, Johnny Joseph, Dusty Griswald, Billy Nichols, Bill Douglas, and more.

A couple of professional pool players who liked to try their hands at cards also made the trek: Marshall "Tuscaloosa Squirrel" Carpenter and the legendary Rudy "Minnesota Fats" Wanderone.

A gambling event wouldn't be complete without a couple notorious figures as well, and this one had them in both Titanic Thompson's old partner Nate Raymond (the man associated with Arnold Rothstein's final days) and Charles Harrelson, the father of famed actor Woody Harrelson, a professional hitman who would later get a life sentence for killing a federal judge.

The invitees also included Benny Binion and his son Jack.

For once in history all these great players could come together and play under one roof and not worry about anyone breaking out the handcuffs or the pistols. Some of the players were specialists in particular games, so in order not to give one person an advantage it was decided that a variety of poker games would be played, including Five-Card Draw, Seven-Card Stud and Seven-Card Stud High-Low, Kansas City Lowball, Razz, Ace-to-Five Lowball, Five-Card Stud (that was the only game Benny Binion still played), and of course . . . Texas Hold 'Em. Players would be allowed to rebuy as many times as possible. A system was set in place to loosely track who was perceived as winning and losing.

The competition to reign supreme was fierce. Gladiators clashed on the green felt. The games turned into mortal combat with poker chips used as battle-axes and spears.

Benny Binion recalled one battle between Johnny Moss and Puggy Pearson with over $130,000 in the pot. Betting went berserk, back and forth with neither backing down. In the end, Pearson took a long, hard gaze at his chip stack and then mucked his cards.

Moss revealed he only had an ace high!

The games went on for seven days. The players refused to back down and continued firing chips at one another.

Johnny Moss was selected as the winner . . . according to him. He was given a silver engraved platter, which he promptly lost soon after. Addington argued that it was he who actually won the event, as he took in the most money. He had no idea how on God's green earth Moss was named the winner. Addington did win the trophy for "Mr. Outsider," which referred to someone as the best gambler who was an "outsider to the scene."

No one saw a dime of Vic's $3,000.

There was no need with the heavy betting taking place.

The Birth of Something Bigger

The premise of the tournament was not about proving who was the best poker player. That was a byproduct. The intention was to attract the high rollers with the publicity of the event, get them into the casino and have them blow their fat wads on the blackjack and craps tables. That never transpired. The poker players were more interested in squaring off against each other and they left little room to splurge money on the traditional house table games.

Poker was not a moneymaker for casinos at this time. It was a courtesy for gamblers. Tom, LaFayne, and Vic all had visions, but

they didn't include making a profit at the poker table. It was supposed to be a publicity stunt.

As such, in Tom's eyes this event was still a "flop," but he had no idea what he had concocted. Like a mad scientist in the laboratory, his creation was coming to life. It just needed someone to add the final touches.

The Texas Gamblers Reunion was impactful for several reasons, but two stand out.

First, it was at this second gathering that Benny Binion and Doyle Brunson were first introduced to one another. This was the beginning of a lasting friendship, and a powerhouse business partnership that would grow the sport of poker beyond imagination.

Second, the promotion illuminated flashbulbs in Benny Binion's mind. He saw an untapped potential for the game of poker. He wasn't sure where he was going yet, but he knew, by God, this was *something*! Benny was busting at the seams with possibilities based on what he saw here. This could be the promotion he was looking for to compete with the ever-exploding talent (Elvis, Sinatra, the Rat Pack, Tony Bennett, etc.) taking over the Strip. Tom Moore confided that he had no intention of having a third reunion. This was music to Benny's ears. He would take over, but he would also make it his own, complete with a new name and branding, something that could become a tradition, event, and experience all its own.

THE WIN

Raking in the chips!

CHAPTER 23

THE WORLD SERIES OF POKER

Benny Binion's special friend, his secret ally, had made its inevitable return. Just like back in South Dallas some forty years ago when he and bootlegger Frank Bolding sat in the backyard discussing the finer points of thug life, *intuition* arrived on the scene and whispered in Benny's ear, moments before he blasted a cap in ole Frank's ass. Intuition had saved him that day, proving to be quick and reliable.

Now, once again, The Cowboy greeted his invisible fortuneteller as he would an old friend that had just returned home from war. The message may have been barely audible, but Benny absorbed every word.

Poker . . . Horseshoe . . . World Championship.

In 1970, Binion held the inaugural World Series of Poker at his Horseshoe Casino. The Horseshoe was not known as a poker paradise; its notoriety was given to its sky-high craps table stakes. In fact, the newly renovated Golden Nugget across the street was held in higher regard for the poker player. At least they had a functioning poker room with regular players. There was no poker boom at the time, barely even a poker bang. The poker business was virtually nonexistent.

Benny, always the pontificating gambling promoter, saw the initial event as a promotional tool. It would attract the right attention, like when he placed the million dollars in his horseshoe display. It was all an elaborate attempt to lure players inside his casino.

Benny was assisted by his sons Jack and Ted in organizing the event. It was a family operation, and by God, they were a family!

But How to Do It

Jimmy "The Greek" Snyder, publicist and notorious oddsmaker, had been relieved of his duties working for Howard Hughes's top man Bob Mayhew. Jimmy was sold on the idea of the World Series of Poker. He immediately made himself available to Binion and pitched a full-scale media marketing plan. Benny liked the oddsmaker and his ideas of grandeur. He figured if anybody could drum up publicity, it was Snyder.

Jimmy took off running and never let his foot off the gas pedal. He worked tirelessly to get coverage in many of the major newspapers across the country. Binion and Snyder both claimed it got written up in over seven thousand newspapers, which was remarkable as there were less than two thousand in the country at the time. But the reporting sparked interest and educated the casual gambler about this gambling joint out West called the Horseshoe.

It may not have brought the public in by the masses, but it did get America a little more acquainted with the casino. Joe and Jane Tourist from Des Moines might not book a redeye that night, but the next time they traveled to Vegas, they might just pop in the Horseshoe and see what all the hoopla is about.

Publicity was one thing; how to run the game would be another challenge altogether.

The Horseshoe didn't have a poker room as Benny didn't want to remove any of the profitable slot machines, blackjack, or craps tables. Instead, he emptied out the baccarat alcove and fitted it with three poker tables. This was where the tournament would be held.

Five different poker variations were chosen to be played: Five-Card Draw High, Deuce-to-Seven Draw, Seven-Card Stud, Razz,

and No-Limit Texas Hold 'Em. Each game would be rotated after an allotted amount of time. The players who benefited the most would be the ones who had the most discipline in all five of the variations. There was no tournament format; all games were to be played for cash.

Just like they had done on the Circuit!

The Kings of Poker

Benny invited the same cast of characters who attended Reno back for the WSOP, including many of the Texas road gamblers. In all, thirty-eight players were invited to make poker history. It was important to Benny to not only have the best of the best competing, but also the players most willing to help spread the word to their peers and draw in more gambling action to Benny's Horseshoe.

Titanic Thompson and Chill Wills, Benny and Moss's old childhood friend turned accomplished actor, served as co-hosts. Wills performed his "Francis the Talking Mule," a fan favorite, for the players and spectators. Chill was there to entertain. Titanic was there for legacy.

Thompson was no fan of Las Vegas. He despised the casino surveillance and did not adhere to the raking of the poker games (taking a percentage of chips from the pot). Benny made it worth his while and paid Titanic's trip expenses, as well as an appearance fee. The Cowboy begrudgingly did it out of sheer respect for his one-time hero. Thompson was not asked to play in the event; only his presence was required.

Once there, Titanic schmoozed with the players and busted out his old card and coin hat tricks. He did make time for playing a few side hands of Texas Hold 'Em and proved he was still (at times) a cutthroat card piranha by sucking away other players' chips. In no

time, he had amassed a nice mound of winnings. He successfully left the table with several full racks of poker chips.

Unfortunately, that's only half the story.

In the wee hours of the night, a sophisticated cat burglar snuck into the great Titanic's hotel room and relieved him of $10,000 in chips. It was a devastating déjà vu nightmare. Once again, the haunted spirits of posttraumatic stress reared their ugly heads. Thompson's sweet pappy robbed him in the same fashion back in Oil City, Louisiana, during the 1930s. He left with his son's loot and never even said goodbye. Even later in life, Titanic never did learn to sleep with both eyes open . . .

The play of the event went relatively smoothly. As the games went on, the players got more and more onlookers, including a few fellas that had a dangerous look about them. One such potential mugger spooked the players and Benny backed the onlookers away from the action. When they refused, he went up to the leader of the gang, and Brunson recalled that Benny said, "I know you're a young man who thinks he's tough. I'm an old man who knows he's tough. If you want to see who's tougher we can go to the garage and figure it out."

The kid stepped back.

A Successful Snoozefest

After ten grueling days of poker warfare, the remaining players were congregated around the final table. The players were then asked to cast a vote for the WSOP champion. The first round of ballots proved to be useless as each player uniformly voted for themselves. Well, of course they did! What did he expect?!

Whatever the case, Jack Binion took charge and instructed the players to vote for the "second-best" player, excluding themselves. The votes were tabulated, and the near unanimous winner was Johnny Moss.

Moss chimed in after the decision, "A lot of gamblers hate me, but they still vote on me being the best player in the world. It was pretty nice, you know, because there were a lot of good players in town. But most good players are only good at one game, and I was good at 'em all."

There were several award winners. Moss received a silver cup, not a WSOP bracelet, as the inaugural World Series of Poker Champion. Jack Straus was voted "Most Congenial Participant." Titanic Thompson received the "Legendary Player Award." He returned home with the award but unfortunately not with his winnings.

However, like its predecessor, the first WSOP was still slightly uneventful. Benny's primary goal was to get some deep-pocket gamblers together under the banner of a poker world championship and have those gamblers empty their deep pockets onto his tables and into his slots. His second objective was to use the event as a marketing tool to bring publicity to his beloved Horseshoe.

When the dust settled, the inaugural WSOP did little to achieve Binion's goals.

What it *did* do was bring our legendary poker personas together under one roof, for one event. Here they were, idols, predecessors, and protégées, all face-to-face. Some played against one another while others provided different roles. Titanic Thompson, Benny Binion, Johnny Moss, Doyle Brunson, and more had all come full circle. They did not realize at the time what they were on the verge of creating.

What was clear was that their paths had now converged, in one place, in one event. It was the start of something much bigger.

Creating the Modern Day WSOP

History may have been made, but the bottom line is that the 1970 WSOP was boring.

These sentiments were heard from reporters, such as Ted Thackrey with the *LA Times,* who covered the event. Thackrey made a few key suggestions to Binion, including being the first to recommend making it a tournament, rather than a series of games. He said the game and a tournament with such high stakes could attract some attention from media, other players, and tourists alike.

That was music to Benny's ears. Amarillo Slim, never at a loss for words, suggested to Benny the idea of a "winner take all freeze out tournament." That would get the juices flowing. Thackrey had one even better:

"Focus on Texas Hold 'Em. No-Limit Texas Hold 'Em."

Binion parlayed both ideas into one and came up with the current structure. A $5,000 entry fee, no rebuys, a No Limit Texas Hold 'Em, winner-take-all tournament. The brainchild was conceived.

The *real* World Series of Poker, the game we all know and love today, would officially launch in 1971.

Through the Looking Glass . . .

Let's wander through the front doors of the Horseshoe. We've crossed the threshold into a time warp, a replicated Wild West saloon circa 1880. The place is awash in red velvet with low- hanging ceilings and dark-paneled wood. A long mahogany bar stretches against the wall underneath wagon wheel chandeliers.

The aroma of crushed cigarettes, stale beer, and overcooked popcorn overtakes the nostrils.

Blue-haired ladies whoop it up as silver coins clink and clang from the slot machines in front of them.

In the café, Benny is seated at the end of a vinyl booth. He is chowing down on his favorite dish: homemade chili. A California crime syndicate associate with a shady disposition leaves the booth and in his place, two

bronc riders take a seat. Benny welcomes them with open arms. The riders discuss their sorry luck at the blackjack tables. "Well, we was wondering, Mr. Binion if there any way you could help—" Benny shuts them down. He calmly pulls out a wad of cash and forks over their losses, enough to get them home, anyway. Now he wants to discuss more pertinent business—how did they score in the last rodeo? Will they be headed to Cheyenne this summer?

Lynn Anderson's hit song "It Wasn't God Who Made Honky Tonk Angels" pours out from overhead speakers. On the mounted tube a new episode of All in the Family is playing. Archie Bunker would have enjoyed the scene at the Horseshoe; this was his kinda place.

Jimmy "The Greek" Snyder is setting up for press interviews. Jimmy wears a plaid suit with wide lapels. He already has odds posted for each player. The man has done his homework.

The first of the six entrants has arrived. A robust fellow with black horned-rimmed glasses gazes over the frenzied excitement. Doyle Brunson, a heavy favorite to take down the championship. Doyle's been perfecting No-Limit Hold 'Em since introducing it with the other Texas gamblers at the Dunes. He has a proven track record of winning in both Limit and No-Limit.

Johnny Moss follows in his cashmere sweater, derby hat, and khaki slacks. Johnny has the look of a tried-and-true champion. He's played them all and beaten them all. Moss exemplifies the stamina of a lion at the poker table. His calm, steady play and experience in pressure situations makes him the hands-down favorite for this year's event.

A real hell-raiser wobbles through the entryway. Sailor Roberts is a little woozy from last night's party with a few cocktail waitresses. Roberts, in his white pearl snap Western shirt and fire engine red ballcap, takes a moment to refocus his blurry vision. Sailor is not worried about his mind being slightly distorted with cobwebs; he plays his best poker fuzzy headed. The others are keenly aware of Roberts's lethal potential. He is deadly with or without a big chip stack.

A newcomer bounces in with a spring in his step. Jimmy Casella, all smiles in a black sharkskin suit. He is no newcomer to the poker scene but

is a newcomer to play in this magnitude of a poker championship. Casella is an East Coast prodigy, and his family connections lie deep within the bowels of organized crime. A decent enough player, though he is still considered the dark horse, and longshot in this field.

The man with the Panama hat, big cigar, and booming voice can be heard outside the casino. Puggy Pearson looks like he is headed for a tropical cruise in his Hawaiian shirt and white slacks. Pearson, the native from ole Rocky Top Tennessee is as jubilant as a pig in slop. His demeanor oozes with confidence. This man has already determined he is winning the championship . . . a week ago. Watch out, Puggy has the poise and the mouth to take out any player at any time.

The last of the crew shuffles in looking down on the rest. It's nothing personal but when you're Jack "Treetop" Straus, you're generally looking down at everyone. Literally. Jack has large, square-shaped bifocals covering his eyes, a shaggy beard, and a long-sleeve polyester shirt. Straus plays the highest limits in the country. He tends to play loose and aggressively. It's hard to determine how his style will perform in a freeze-out format. One thing is for sure, Jack is no stranger to big-bet poker. No one will be blowing him out of a pot.

These are the six entrants of the 1971 World Series of Poker. A tremendous field and all have magical aspirations of taking home the gold.

The game is fast and furious with chips flying from player to player. The action then settles down and the players gauge the tempo and energy of their opponents.

Casino patrons circulate around the tables, they become railbirds and watch the play unfold. For the first time in history, they can watch the highest-stakes players clash against one another within arm's reach.

Each player puts up a valiant fight to call themselves the best in the world. In the end it will be a heads-up duel between Johnny Moss and Puggy Pearson. Neither relenting, Puggy plays to the crowd and constantly jabbers. Moss is unencumbered by his noise.

Benny watches over his creation with satisfaction as the last two survivors leave it all on the green felt. For a moment, he reflects back on his

life, all the hell he's been through and the hell he's put others through. Or worse, like with his old rival The Cat. He wasn't perfect, but like another Vegas legend, he could say he did it "my way." It had already been quite a life and looking out over this batch of poker pioneers slugging it out, while more and more onlookers trickled in and dropped their hard-earned cash at HIS Horseshoe, Benny knew life wasn't over just yet. Everything had happened for a reason, and look where he was now . . .

In the end, Moss accumulates all the chips. He takes home the championship and $30,000 in prize money. The Grand Ole Master had won it again! Except this time with no voting or any debate. Johnny Moss is the 1971 World Series of Poker Champion!

After the game ends, Benny Binion saddles up next to Doyle Brunson and The Cowboy cooly states, "You know, Doyle, someday we may have a hundred people in this tournament."

THE NEXT HAND

It ain't over till it's over!

EPILOGUE
THE LEGACY

A hundred people.

That's what Benny Binion hoped for when he started to see a bit of momentum build in what he now called the World Series of Poker.

Little did he know.

In 1972, Benny added an extra $5,000 for each entrant and the buy-in was doubled to $10,000 per player. Amarillo Slim won the tourney, taking home the staggering $80,000 in prize money. This was a massive turning point for the sport, more specifically the World Series of Poker, as Slim was a salty, relatable, and captivating storyteller with a great sense of humor who didn't mind the spotlight. Benny was going to ride that tidal wave of attention cresting in his direction. After he won the WSOP, Slim made multiple appearances on *The Tomorrow Show* with Tom Snyder and *The Tonight Show* with Johnny Carson, as well as *60 Minutes*. He talked about his Texas roots, what Vegas was really like from a player's perspective, the ins and outs of tournament poker, and more, mostly to an audience that had never heard of the World Series of Poker, but were quickly gaining an interest and wondering if their card-playing hobbies could lead them to riches as well.

With each year, the jackpots grew, with Puggy Pearson taking home $130,000 in 1973. So did the number of players. Moss recaptured the title the following year, cementing his legacy as he won the tournament's first ever coveted gold bracelet, a symbol that still

resonates as powerfully in the WSOP today. The first real "star" of the sport made his presence felt in 1976 when Doyle Brunson defeated Jesse Alto with his signature ten-deuce hand . . . which he then used again to win the tourney the following year over Gary "Bones" Berland. The Texas Dolly's play is still talked about in poker rooms everywhere. He is also one of only three players to win poker's ultimate prize twice. The others are legends themselves in "The Kid" Stu Ungar (1980, 1981) and "The Orient Express" Johnny Chan (1987, 1988).

Doyle's book, the poker bible *Super/System*, grew the sport even more by giving hobby players and serious-minded gamblers alike tips and strategies on how to approach the challenging but highly addictive game of Texas Hold 'Em. Other books would soon follow, including *The Biggest Game in Town* by Al Alvarez, which chronicled in detail the events of the 1981 WSOP and gave fans a first-hand look at the excitement and drama of the event. These books opened the floodgates to poker literature with pros and amateurs alike sharing stories and offering advice on the tournament and its players, who now found themselves becoming celebrities.

Doyle would become the biggest of them all (still to this day!), eventually becoming known as the "Godfather of Poker," winning ten gold bracelets and making an astounding twenty-six final table appearances. He was also the first player to win more than $1 million playing poker.

One million dollars. Poker had come quite a long way since Titanic Thompson was learning the game on the road while in search of his father. Since Johnny Moss and Benny Binion were running on the streets of Dallas, one with ambitions of being the best card player and the other with owning an empire. Since Benny and Herbert Noble turned gambling into a war that led to endless violence and death . . . and to Vegas. These young men from Texas were all just trying to survive, to rise above their desperate backgrounds and find success and themselves in the world of professional

gambling. Their paths were rocky as hell, but each step, each event that unfolded, had led to the growth of the WSOP, and now it was growing beyond anyone's wildest dreams.

It would only take till 1982 before Benny's dream came to fruition and the tournament surpassed one hundred entrants. By 1991, it was double that. Today, it's in the thousands.

Throughout the '80s, '90s, and early 2000s, the sport absolutely exploded. Prize money rose into the millions, overtaking purses in Wimbledon, the Masters, the Kentucky Derby, and more. The size of the player fields grew exponentially, TV networks made contracts to cover the event, and the sport went international. The world met new professional players with unique personalities like Phil Hellmuth, Phil Ivey, and Daniel Negreanu, who started raking in the bracelets and the money, with even more coming from sponsorships.

The rise in popularity (and the playing field) skyrocketed again when an amateur player, Chris Moneymaker, won the main event in 2003, giving hope to weekend warriors everywhere. Though he wasn't the first amateur to win it all (Hal Fowler could make that claim to fame with his 1979 win), Moneymaker gained infamy with his win because of all the media coverage the event and its winner got.

His win also helped usher in the era of online poker, which also connected players worldwide to the WSOP, but not without its own roadblocks and controversies . . . but that's a series in itself.

In 2004, Harrah's Entertainment (now Caesars Entertainment) bought the Horseshoe and the WSOP, eventually moving it to the Rio Casino in 2005. In August 2024, Caesars sold the brand to GGPoker for $500 million. What will happen next for the event is uncertain, but it's safe to say the World Series of Poker isn't going anywhere anytime soon. The pots have grown to tens of millions and the number of entrants breaks records year after year. In 2024, that record was broken again when 10,112 players of all skill levels competed for the coveted crown with Jonathan Tamayo taking home $10 million!

The WSOP brand has expanded into over a hundred satellite tournaments as well, hosted all over the world, where players can compete in a variety of poker games for different bracelets. The sport has gotten multiple shows and expanded television and internet coverage, and bold and brave new players continue to make their name and their fortunes.

Nowadays, most current players don't think too often about their forefathers, the characters responsible for the tables they're playing at and the jackpots they're playing for today. After all, most of them are long gone. Titanic died broke and alone in a rest home in Fort Worth in 1974, having lost his money betting on the horses. Johnny Moss passed in Odessa in 1995 from natural causes. His friend Benny died on Christmas Day in 1989, having left a complex legacy.

Complex legacy is really perhaps the best way to sum up this period of history that laid the groundwork for this ever-growing business. Today, the World Series of Poker is part of our national fabric. It is a thriving corporate industry that provides not just entertainment, but opportunity to thousands of players worldwide. Like most things American, its past is made up of equal parts notoriety, ambition, and inspiration. Its past is made up of chance meetings, big risks, and extraordinary events. Its past is beautiful and dirty, and it took a lot of luck, intelligence, and hard work. None of it came easy. More than anything, poker's rise came from the players themselves, incredible characters that built their legends one hand at a time.

After all, as any pro gambler will tell you, poker ain't about the cards, but the players holding them. And that there's always the next hand.

ACKNOWLEDGMENTS

FROM PHILIP GUITAR:

I am grateful that, as a young boy, I was able to spend time with both sets of grandparents: Earl and Anita Guitar, and Dickie and Elmo Joy Ferguson. They have always been near and dear to my heart. Most of the greatest memories growing up were with them. They spent countless hours playing cards and board games with me. I really don't know how I got so lucky.

My parents have always been staunch supporters. They provided a stable home life with compassion and dedication. My dad, Phil Guitar, and I spent many days on the ranches together. My mom, Jane Guitar, is a creative force who was always around, and always taking excellent care of me. She is a massive creative inspiration to me with her music, love of the arts, and opera production. She showed me how to engage my inner muse, how to ignite my genuine authenticity. A classic, elegant woman who believes in manners and saving animals. Any event I participated in, my parents were there to cheer me on.

My sister, Catherine Guitar, and I have always shared a special bond. She was another game player with me. We love to play gin rummy and poker together. We would have a running total on our gin games, and I think one of us owes some money! She is also a voracious reader and some of the best books I have read are from her. I also appreciate her reading my scripts and stories.

My girlfriend, Ritz Voeun, is a constant supporter and the love of my life. Ritz reads my projects and gives me extraordinary notes.

She was vital in giving valuable feedback with this book. She is also a remarkable beta reader. That's one of the many reasons why we have such a special relationship. We both love books, we love the arts, we love spending time with one another and attending a variety of events! Ritz has continually cheered me on with this book. She is unbelievable and I am beyond blessed to have her in my life.

My cowriter Jim Martyka is a guy who always brings a smile to my face. I can hear Jim's voice and we both start laughing; it's infectious. Jim is kind and sympathetic. Writing this book with him has been an adventure . . . in a positive way. I thoroughly enjoyed the journey with him, and I learned a ton about writing.

I love and cherish this group! These are my people! They have helped shaped me into the man I am today. There are many others out there with whom I share a kindred love and respect for as well! Just too damn many to mention . . . *too damn many.*

FROM JIM MARTYKA:

I need to start by thanking my best friend and more, Mandy Muenzer. She is not only a truly inspirational and sweet soul who brings love and light to the world and my life, she is my constant supporter, gently pushing me to continue my writing adventures each and every day. Even though she is not really a poker player, she has always taken an active interest in this project and spent quite a bit of time listening to me ramble on about it. I love you tons, Tootsie!

I want to also thank my parents Cathy and Marty for their love and support. As early as high school I told them I wanted my career to revolve around writing (with a little acting and teaching on the side). Never once did they tell me to go find a *paying* job! They always encouraged the pursuit of my goals, consistently claiming that my happiness was all that mattered to them. They still do so today, and I am forever grateful.

My brother Chris is perhaps the biggest driver behind most things in my life, including this book. I am very fortunate to have a brother to whom I am so close. He and I share a strong bond built on many adventures, lots of both deep and ridiculous conversations, and many, many GREAT beers! He has been a wonderful sounding board for many of my various projects, always enthusiastic and honest in his support, regardless of what this "word wizard" is throwing at him. I love ya, bro!

I need to thank my friend, the extremely talented screenwriter and playwright Aaron Kozak, for connecting me with my cowriter and essentially helping to get this relationship and project going.

Speaking of my cowriter, there aren't enough words to describe the man, the myth, and the legend Philip Guitar. It has been an absolute pleasure working with him on this book. I can distinctly remember one of our first conversations when he told me about this project and how my jaw hit the floor. I knew he had something special here, and I am very lucky he brought me in to help him share the tale. Philip is a born storyteller, a talented and prolific writer, and just an all-around excellent human being. Happy to be your partner, bud!

Finally, thanks to all the friends and family through the years that played some nickel-and-dime poker with me, fueling my interest in the sport. I hope you all enjoy this wild ride!

RESOURCES

PRINT MEDIA

All In Magazine
American Heritage
Burlington County Times
Cigar Aficionado
Collier's
D Magazine
Forbes
Fort Worth Business Press
Fort Worth Weekly
Golf Digest
Las Vegas Business Press
Las Vegas Review-Journal
Las Vegas Sun
Martin County Messenger
Medium Magazine
Oak Cliff Advocate
Reno Gazette Journal
Sports Illustrated
Sulphur Springs News Telegram
Texas Monthly
Time Magazine
The Daily Inter Lake
The Dallas Morning News

The Desert Sun
The Fort Worth Star-Telegram
The Greek Reporter
The Guardian UK
The Joplin Globe
The New York Times
The Odessa News Times
The Washington Post
True Magazine

TELEVISION AND RADIO

Deadline
Gang Busters
NPR
PBS
The History Channel

WEB SOURCES

Angelfire.com
Binions.com
CardPlayer.com
Casino.org
CoolCat-Casino.com
DangerTV.com
GamblingSites.com
GutshotMagazine.com
HeadStuff.org
HistoricMysteries.com
MayhemInTheDesert.com

MentalFloss.com
One37pm.com
Online-Casinos.com
Over50Vegas.com
Parlettgames.uk
PokerKing.com
PokerListings.com
PokerNew.com
Ranker.com
SteveBadger.com
TheGoodGamblingGuide.co.uk
TheHendonMob.com
TXKToday.com

BOOKS

Bad Bet—Timothy O'Brien
Blood Aces: The Wild Ride of Benny Binion—Doug J. Swanson
Cowboys Full: The Story of Poker—James McManus
Cowboys, Gamblers, and Hustlers—Byron Wolford
Famous Gamblers, Poker History, and Texas Stories—Johnny Hughes
Gamblers & Gangsters—Ann Arnold
Gambling in America—William N. Thompson
I'll Do My Own Damn Killin'—Gary W. Sleeper
Johnny Moss: Champion of Champions—Don Jenkins
Nevada's Golden Age of Gambling—Al W. Moe
Positively Fifth Street—James McManus
Roll the Bones: The History of Gambling—David G. Schwartz
Super/System—Doyle Brunson
The Biggest Game in Town—Al Alvarez
The Godfather of Poker—Doyle Brunson
The Golfers—Peter Dobereiner

The Great American Pastime—Allen Dowling
The Green Felt Jungle—Ed Reid and Ovid Demaris
The Nine Lives of Herbert Noble—Comic Book by Antarctic Press
The Players: The Men Who Made Las Vegas—Jack Sheehan
The True Story of Titanic Thompson—Kevin Cook
The Unsinkable Titanic Thompson—Carlton Stowers
World Encyclopedia of Organized Crime—Jay Robert Nash

Also:
Legacies: A History Journal for Dallas and North Central Texas—A biannual publication published by Dallas Heritage Village, the Dallas Historical Society, the Old Red Museum, and the Sixth Floor Museum at Dealey Plaza

GOVERNMENT

Congress of the United States of America
Court for the District of Nevada
Dallas County Sheriff's Department
Historic Reno Preservation Society
Investigation of Organized Crime in Interstate Commerce
Texas Department of Health
University of Nevada, Reno
Warren Commission Report

ORGANIZATIONS

City Cast Las Vegas
Consumer Price Index
Denton County Junior Historians
GG Poker

Nevada Gaming History
PokerGo
World Casino Directory
The Mob Museum
The World Poker Tour
The World Series of Poker

POKER WARS